PENGUIN CLASSICS DELUXE EDITION

TITANIC, FIRST ACCOUNTS

TIM MALTIN has been studying the *Titanic* for twenty-five years and is the author of *101 Things You Thought You Knew About The Titanic . . . But Didn't!* He is currently working on a National Geographic film and book about his ground-breaking Titanic research, which will be released in 2012. Tim works in London and lives in Wiltshire, England.

MAX ELLIS, originally trained as a precision engineer, is a professional illustrator based in London. He is the winner of the British Illustration (AOI) award for humor, and his clients include *Advertising Age,* *Maxim,* and *Wired* magazines.

NICHOLAS WADE is the grandson of *Titanic* survivor Lawrence Beesley and is the author of *The Faith Instinct: How Religion Evolved and Why It Endures* and *Before the Dawn: Recovering the Lost History of Our Ancestors.*

Titanic,
First Accounts

Edited with an Introduction by
TIM MALTIN

Afterword by
NICHOLAS WADE

PENGUIN BOOKS

PENGUIN BOOKS
Published by the Penguin Group
Penguin Group (USA) Inc., 375 Hudson Street,
New York, New York 10014, U.S.A.
Penguin Group (Canada), 90 Eglinton Avenue East, Suite 700, Toronto,
Ontario, Canada M4P 2Y3 (a division of Pearson Penguin Canada Inc.)
Penguin Books Ltd, 80 Strand, London WC2R 0RL, England
Penguin Ireland, 25 St Stephen's Green, Dublin 2,
Ireland (a division of Penguin Books Ltd)
Penguin Group (Australia), 250 Camberwell Road,
Camberwell, Victoria 3124, Australia
(a division of Pearson Australia Group Pty Ltd)
Penguin Books India Pvt Ltd, 11 Community Centre,
Panchsheel Park, New Delhi - 110 017, India
Penguin Group (NZ), 67 Apollo Drive, Rosedale, Auckland 0632,
New Zealand (a division of Pearson New Zealand Ltd)
Penguin Books (South Africa) (Pty) Ltd, 24 Sturdee Avenue,
Rosebank, Johannesburg 2196, South Africa

Penguin Books Ltd, Registered Offices:
80 Strand, London WC2R 0RL, England

First published in Penguin Books 2012

3 5 7 9 10 8 6 4 2

Introduction and selection copyright © Tim Maltin, 2012
Afterword copyright © Nicholas Wade, 2012
All rights reserved

"The Sinking of the Titanic Seen from a Lifeboat" from *The Loss of the Titanic:
How I Survived the Sinking of the Titanic* by Lawrence Beesley, published by
Amberley Publishing, 2011. Reprinted by permission.

LIBRARY OF CONGRESS CATALOGING IN PUBLICATION DATA
Titanic, first accounts / edited with an introduction by Tim Maltin; afterword by Nicholas Wade.
p. cm. — (Penguin classics deluxe edition)
ISBN 978-0-14-310662-3
1. Titanic (Steamship) 2. Shipwrecks—North Atlantic Ocean. 3. Titanic (Steamship)—Pictorial
works. I. Maltin, Tim.
G530.T6T584 2012
910.9163'4—dc23
2011047511

Printed in the United States of America
Set in Sabon

Contents

Introduction

This book is as much for people who know a lot about the *Titanic* disaster as it is for those who know very little about it. This is because, for both experts and newcomers, if you want to know what really happened the incredible night the *Titanic* sank, you need to ask the people who were there. But the last *Titanic* survivor, Millvina Dean, died in 2009, aged ninety-seven, and she was only nine weeks old when the *Titanic* sank. In order to know what really happened on *Titanic*, all we have now is the recorded evidence of eyewitnesses.

Many of the most important of these eyewitness accounts were written or dictated by people who were there in 1912, immediately after their rescue. *Titanic*'s Assistant Saloon Steward Walter Nichols was even still wearing the pajamas in which he was saved, as he dictated his account to his sister. These first accounts provide the most accurate picture of what really happened that night and what it was like to be a passenger or crew member on the *Titanic* before, during, and after the sinking.

Titanic sank at 2:20 A.M. on April 15, 1912, on her maiden voyage. Under a perfect canopy of stars, more than 1,500 people drowned or froze to death that morning in the flat calm water of the North Atlantic. She was the latest in technology and contained within her steel walls a veritable Noah's Ark of nationalities, people from all different walks of life. But after *Titanic* had departed the scene that night, only the fundamentals remained:

The stars above and men, women, and children struggling and dying in the black water below.

Although there are a few full-length accounts, many are in the form of private letters written by survivors aboard the rescue ship *Carpathia* or interviews given by survivors to the newspapers after they arrived in New York. The evidence of 150 survivors is also recorded in the transcripts of the exhaustive American and British public inquiries into the *Titanic* disaster conducted in 1912.

This book draws on all of these sources. We begin with "The Sinking of the *Titanic* Seen from a Lifeboat," the fourth chapter from second-class passenger Lawrence Beesley's *The Loss of the* Titanic, written in 1912. Beesley gives us the most beautiful description of that terrible night, and his account immediately places his reader right on the spot, watching *Titanic* sinking. Beesley's is the most accessible full-length survivor account, written by a thirty-four-year-old man on his first voyage across the Atlantic. Beesley was a Cambridge scholar and later became the science master at Dulwich College in London. Indeed, at age seventy-nine, he taught my uncle—then twelve—at the Northwood School of Coaching in Middlesex, in 1956. It was Beesley's scientific account of the *Titanic* disaster that inspired me to look more deeply into its true causes, and his comment that the stars seemed to be flashing messages across the sky to each other was an important clue in explaining why the *Titanic* and the nearby *Californian* failed to communicate with each other by Morse lamp. Similarly, his description of the stars that night appearing to be cut in half by the horizon and throwing long beams of light along the sea to the survivors proved to be a useful description of the abnormal refraction or miraging present on the horizon that night, which had fatal consequences for the *Titanic*.

Beesley's account is followed by the complete text of *The Truth about the* Titanic, written by Colonel Archibald Gracie in 1912, before his death in December of that year from illnesses compounded by his traumatic experiences on the *Titanic*, which haunted him until the day he died. Gracie was swept off the deck by a wave caused by *Titanic*'s sinking and then sucked down by the giant ship, but his strength and physical fitness allowed him to escape onto the top of an upturned lifeboat, where he barely survived the freezing night, before being rescued by another of *Titanic*'s lifeboats and finally delivered to the welcoming decks of the *Carpathia*.

Archibald Gracie IV was the great-grandson of Archibald Gracie, a Scottish-born shipping magnate and early American businessman and merchant in New York City and Virginia whose spacious home, Gracie Mansion, now serves as the residence of the mayor of New York City. Coincidentally, one of Gracie IV's fellow travelers on the *Titanic* was John Jacob Astor IV, the richest man in the world and great-grandson of frequent Gracie Mansion visitor and personal friend of Gracie I, John Jacob Astor.

Fifty-four years old when the *Titanic* sank, first-class passenger Archibald Gracie IV was a real estate dealer, author, and military historian. Following completion of his book *The Truth About Chickamauga,* about one of the bloodiest battles of the American Civil War, Gracie decided he needed to relax and took a trip to Europe. Leaving his wife and daughter at home, he travelled eastbound on the *Oceanic,* where he made friends with one of the ship's officers, Herbert Pitman, who was later third officer on the *Titanic*.

Boarding at Southampton for his return passage on the *Titanic*, Gracie travelled as a first-class passenger in cabin C 51 on ticket number 113780, which cost him £28 10s. Several months before, he had undergone an operation in America but was in surprisingly good health. Before she knew her father had been saved, his daughter, Edith, was quoted as follows in the *New York Times:*

> "I hardly know what to say or think," said Miss Gracie this morning. "Why, only yesterday I received a letter from father, which he addressed to me from Southampton, England. He told me in the letter that he would be home in a few days, and I was awaiting word from mother as to whether we should both meet the *Titanic* or not. . . . My father, who was operated on several months ago, went to Europe to

recuperate. He had regained his health, and by the tenor of his letter anticipated surprising us by the wonders his trip had worked in building up his constitution."

Archibald Gracie IV died on December 4, 1912—officially from a diabetic coma—and was buried in Woodlawn Cemetery, New York. His obituary in the *New York Times* the following day stated:

> After the *Carpathia* had brought the *Titanic* survivors to New York Col. Gracie did nothing to banish the tragedy from his thoughts. On the contrary, he spent the succeeding months in correspondence with other survivors, gathering data for his book, *The Truth about the Titanic*. The events of the night of the wreck were constantly on his mind. The manuscript of his work on the subject had finally been completed and sent to the printers when his last illness came. In his last hours the memories of the disaster did not leave him. Rather they crowded thicker, and he was heard to say:
>
> "We must get them into the boats. We must get them all into the boats."

Early chapters of *The Truth about the* Titanic describe Colonel Gracie's personal experiences on board the ship, including his remarkable escape from death, from notes he made on board the *Carpathia* immediately after the disaster and before he arrived in New York. Chapter 3 is an attempt to deal with four points where the statements of survivors "were strangely at variance," in Gracie's words. The final two chapters present the record and story of each lifeboat on the port and starboard sides of the *Titanic*, respectively, giving the names of those aboard insofar as Colonel Gracie had been able to ascertain them at the time, including conditions aboard each lifeboat and incidents that occurred in the transfer of the passengers of each to the rescue ship *Carpathia*. These final chapters also include firsthand accounts by survivors in each of the lifeboats, where these were available to Gracie. Colonel Gracie was eventually transferred to lifeboat No. 12, the last one to reach the *Carpathia*.

Within the first few paragraphs, Gracie's account gives us important information about the navigation of the ship:

> The Captain had each day improved upon the previous day's speed, and prophesied that, with continued fair weather, we should make an early arrival record for this maiden trip. . . . In the twenty-four hours' run ending the 14th, according to the posted reckoning, the ship had covered 546 miles, and we were told that the next twenty-four hours would see even a better record made.

In fact we now know that the captain was attempting to beat the maiden voyage time of *Titanic*'s slightly older sister ship, *Olympic,* a record set the year before, in June 1911. He hoped to arrive on Tuesday evening instead of on Wednesday, as scheduled, in order to generate publicity for the second of the Olympic Class liners. As Titanic's owner, Joseph Bruce Ismay explained at the U.S. Inquiry into the *Titanic* disaster: "It was our intention, if we had fine weather on Monday afternoon or Tuesday, to drive the ship at full speed. That, owing to the unfortunate catastrophe, never eventuated."

Gracie speaks for the majority of *Titanic* passengers when he then memorably informs us that during the four days of the voyage preceding the disaster, "I enjoyed myself as if I were in a summer palace on the seashore. . . ." Gracie had undertaken vigorous physical exercise in the ship's squash court, gymnasium, and swimming pool on the morning of the collision and had retired early on the night of the wreck, with the intention of continuing his fitness regimen the following day. He had therefore enjoyed three hours of invigorating sleep before the collision occurred at 11:40 P.M. and explained, "I was thus strengthened for the terrible ordeal, better even than had I been forewarned of it."

At first glance, it might appear to the modern reader that Gracie's account is overly formal or stuffy, and certainly Colonel Archibald Gracie was a man of tradition and formality, even by the standards of 1912. He came from a strict and privileged background, and his book is partly aimed at those in his own social circle. But when read closely, Gracie's account is surprisingly full of how he *felt*, rather than simply what he *did*. That emotion is of great interest to the modern reader, and the lack of it is the eternal frustration of most of the eyewitness evidence given at the courts of inquiry into the *Titanic* disaster.

In the following paragraph, Gracie attempts to describe in some detail a particular sensation he felt at an important moment during that terrible night:

> When I first saw and realized that every lifeboat had left the ship, the sensation felt was not an agreeable one. No thought of fear entered my head, but I experienced a feeling which others may recall when holding the breath in the face of some frightful emergency and when "vox faucibus haesit," as frequently happened to the old Trojan hero of our school days.

The full quote that Gracie is referring to is *"Obstupui, steteruntque comae, et vox faucibus haesit,"* meaning, "I was stupefied, and my hair stood on end, and my voice stuck to my throat." This is a description of the physical effects of fear, from Virgil's *Aeneid*, and gives us a real insight into how he and others on *Titanic* felt at that awful moment of realization.

Gracie's account also gives us important glimpses of how others may have felt, as in the following passage, where he describes seeing the *Titanic*'s owner, Bruce Ismay, shortly after the collision:

> Entering the companionway, I passed Mr. Ismay with a member of the crew hurrying up the stairway. He wore a day suit, and, as usual, was hatless. He seemed too much preoccupied to notice anyone. Therefore I did not speak to him, but regarded his face very closely, perchance to learn from his manner how serious the accident might be. It occurred to me then that he was putting on as brave a face as possible so as to cause no alarm among the passengers.

The chief value of Gracie's account is that it is a highly detailed one from a very observant witness who was on board the

Titanic until she sank. He therefore also gives us many very important facts, as in this shocking and heartrending passage, where he describes the final minute before *Titanic*'s plunge:

> We had taken but a few steps in the direction indicated when there arose before us from the decks below, a mass of humanity several lines deep, covering the Boat Deck, facing us, and completely blocking our passage toward the stern.
>
> There were women in the crowd, as well as men, and they seemed to be steerage passengers who had just come up from the decks below. Instantly, when they saw us and the water on the deck chasing us from behind, they turned in the opposite direction towards the stern. This brought them at that point plumb against the iron fence and railing which divide the first and second cabin passengers. Even among these people there was no hysterical cry, or evidence of panic, but oh, the agony of it!

These were probably third-class men who were not allowed up to the boat deck under the order of women and children first, and women who had elected to wait with them. As well as Gracie's own experiences and observations, *The Truth about the* Titanic also includes several shorter accounts by other survivors, including a wonderful one written by Miss Elizabeth W. Shutes. Gracie introduces this account as "one which I freely confess moves me to tears whenever re-read," and it is a haunting account of that night, very accurately remembered and well described.

Gracie's book also gives us a very good idea of the relative calm aboard the *Titanic*, even as every lifeboat was being launched. His attempt to explain the history of each lifeboat is a useful one, especially his piecing together the extraordinary story of the lifeboat identified as Collapsible A, which he called a "boat of mystery" at the outset of his research. Most significantly though, he documents how on the port side of *Titanic*, the order was apparently women and children only, whereas on the starboard side of the ship, men were freely admitted into the lifeboats once all the women who were immediately available had been loaded.

Titanic did not have enough trained deck crew to adequately man and launch her sixteen lifeboats within the time available. The loading and lowering of each of her boats therefore had to be rushed as quickly as possible. In addition, the lifeboats could not very practicably hold the sixty-five persons that each of them was certified to carry; moreover, no general alarm was given, and the passengers truly believed that the *Titanic* was unsinkable. As a result, many of *Titanic*'s lifeboats went away grossly underfilled, at least on paper. Nevertheless, women and children accounted for only about 10 percent of the 1,500 people who died in the *Titanic* disaster, even though more men were saved than women.

Gracie's account is followed by four thrilling accounts that came out as a result of the U.S. Inquiry into the *Titanic* disaster. Third-class passenger Daniel Buckley tells us there was water on the floor of his cabin as soon as he jumped out of bed, and his story about a woman throwing a shawl over his head so that he could remain in the lifeboat in which he escaped is almost certainly the genesis of the myth that several men escaped disguised as women. It's important to note that his testimony that the third-class passengers had as much chance of escape as the first- and second-class passengers is not inconsistent with his earlier testimony that steerage passengers were prevented from accessing the first- and second-class deck area immediately after the collision; this was normal practice before the order to abandon ship had been given, and this was not given until 12:30 A.M., fifty minutes after the collision.

John Collins, *Titanic*'s assistant cook for the first-class galley, gives an amazing and moving account, including how he was washed off *Titanic*'s deck with a whole crowd of people and the tragic fate of a child passenger.

Titanic's baker, Charles Joughin shares his unusual account, which begins in the A deck pantry when he heard *Titanic* begin to break up and rushed toward the stern with hundreds of other passengers. He describes how these passengers were then thrown together as the ship gave a great list over to port and how he escaped over the outside of the starboard rail and then stepped off the back of the sinking ship, without even getting his head wet!

Last in this section of testimonies from the U.S. Inquiry is Junior Marconi Operator Harold Bride's statement to his employers, which he submitted to the inquiry and which details important wireless information, as well as his final moments aboard ship and his scramble to get onto an overturned collapsible lifeboat.

Bride's long account of his experiences on the sinking liner, published in the New York Times on April 19, 1912, then opens a selection of survivor accounts published in newspapers at the time. These all give unexpected details about the sinking, such as when Bride explains that even Captain Smith laughed at his joke that they should send the new SOS distress signal, because it might be their last chance to send it.

Third-class passenger Laura Cribb casually notes the violence she witnesses by an officer, and first-class passenger Hugh Woolner graphically describes the terrific roar as Titanic took her final plunge as being "like thousands of tons of rocks rumbling down a metal chute."

An account given by Margaret "Molly" Brown to the Newport Herald and serialized by that newspaper on May 28–30, 1912, is also included. Contrary to her portrayal in various films about the Titanic, Molly was a highly sophisticated and very well-educated champion of women's rights; she had been holidaying with the Astors in Egypt. Her account of the atmosphere in the corridor outside her room immediately after the collision is revealing and tragic:

On emerging from my stateroom, I found many men in the gangway in their pajamas, whom I had overheard a few moments before entering their staterooms saying that they were nearly frozen and had to leave the smoking-rooms. They, while standing, were chaffing each other, one of them remarked, "Are you prepared to swim in those things?" referring to the pajamas. Women were standing along the corridors in their kimonos. All seemed to be quietly listening, thinking nothing serious had occurred. . . . This gallows humor immediately after the collision is also borne witness to in many other survivor accounts. Colonel Archibald Gracie immortalized his friend James Clinch Smith, who did not survive the disaster, when he recalled in

The Truth about the Titanic how it was from him that he first learned
that they had struck an iceberg:

He opened his hand and showed me some ice, flat like my watch,
coolly suggesting that I might take it home for a souvenir. All of us
will remember the way he had of cracking a joke without a smile.

All of these jokes were one way of coping with the terrible situation in which *Titanic*'s passengers suddenly found themselves.
By this time most of them had less than three hours to live.

First-class passenger William Sloper remembers the over-
politeness of passengers and the difficulty in filling the first lifeboats owing to the faith the passengers had in the unsinkability
of the *Titanic*. On the contrary, newlywed Vera Dick casually
describes the band playing jolly, happy tunes "when the guards
shot the jaw off an immigrant who tried to crowd into one of the
boats, brushing the women aside."

Finally in this section of survivor accounts published in newspapers, Assistant Saloon Steward Walter Nichols describes the
horrible shriek that went up after the sinking, the cries for help
and weird shouts that sounded like the noise "if you've ever been
around when they were feeding a kennel of dogs." All of these
accounts are unique and bear the hallmark of authenticity in the
surprising facts they reveal.

The final section comes from Logan Marshall's *The Sinking
of the* Titanic *and Great Sea Disasters*, published in 1912. We
have included seventeen-year-old Jack Thayer's description of
becoming separated from his parents, jumping from the *Titanic,*
and watching her break up while swimming in the water nearby,
before drifting all night on an upturned collapsible lifeboat, as
well as James McGough's account, which is interesting when
compared with Molly Brown's, whom he was responsible for
placing in a lifeboat, especially where he says that he was forced
to enter a lifeboat "though I admit that the ship looked a great
deal safer to me than any small boat."

Besides survivor narratives, this edition includes a contemporary report about the preparations on land to receive the survi-

vors, as well as one on the arrival in New York of the rescue ship *Carpathia* and the work of collecting bodies from *Titanic*'s wreck site.

Although not written by survivors, these chapters really bring home the contemporary impact of the disaster, which still reverberates to this day. In 1912, the *Titanic* created one of the first global media storms, with the *New York Times* devoting its first twelve pages to the disaster. This impact is rarely put into context today. The sinking of the *Titanic* on April 15, 1912, was as shocking to the world as the destruction of the Twin Towers on September 11, 2001. The only difference between the following details written in 1912 and a contemporary disaster is that now helicopters would be thumping the air, and there would be an international press camp broadcasting live to the world via satellite:

> In anticipation of the enormous number that would . . . surge about the Cunard pier at the coming of the *Carpathia,* Mayor Gaynor and the police commissioner had seen to it that the streets should be rigidly sentineled by continuous lines of policemen. . . . there were 200 men, including twelve mounted men and a number in citizens' clothes. . . . twenty ambulances [were] ready for instant movement on the city's pier at the foot of East Twenty-sixth Street. . . . hospitals in the city stood ready to take the *Titanic*'s people and those that had ambulances promised to send them. The Charities ferryboat, *Thomas S. Brennan,* equipped as a hospital craft, lay off the department pier with nurses and physicians ready to be called to the Cunard pier on the other side of the city. St Vincent's Hospital had 120 beds ready, New York Hospital twelve, Bellevue and the reception hospital 120 and Flower Hospital twelve."

These chapters from Logan Marshall's 1912 edition also include a poignant, early list of survivors, details of the mission to recover bodies from *Titanic*'s wreck site, a list of the identified dead and a firsthand observation of scores of bodies being seen from the rail of the steamship *Bremen* as she steamed near the awful scene:

We saw one woman in her night dress, with a baby clasped closely to her breast. . . . The bodies of three men in a group, all clinging to one steamship chair, floated near by, and just beyond them were a dozen bodies of men, all of them encased in life-preservers, clinging together as though in a last desperate struggle for life.

The final section of this edition includes a letter to the *New York Times* by Lawrence Beesley, published on April 29, 1912. This highly intelligent survivor reviews the disaster, its probable causes, and the means of preventing such an accident in the future, then asks—and answers—many of the questions that are still being asked today. Nicholas Wade, a grandson of Lawrence Beesley, contributes an afterword to this edition, reflecting on the centennial of the *Titanic*'s sinking as a family member of one of the ship's most noted survivors.

One hundred years on, the world is still gripped by the *Titanic* disaster. This is because *Titanic*—the floating city—is a metaphor for the whole of civilization, and her untimely death at the hand of God or nature is a metaphor for the human condition. The story of the *Titanic* shows us our utter helplessness, our best achievement confounded by a lump of ice, and leaves us asking the eternal question: Why? The *Titanic* forces us to confront this question, which generations of experts and newcomers have grappled with, turning for more information to the first accounts of those who were there.

TIM MALTIN

A Note on the Texts

Text selections for this edition have been drawn from the following archival sources and books: Brooklyn Public Library; Cleveland Public Library (*Cleveland Plain Dealer*); Library of Congress (*New York Evening Journal, Hartford Times, New York Sun*); Missouri Historical Society Archives (*St. Louis Post-Dispatch*); *Newport Herald*; *New York Times*; *Washington Post*; *The Truth about the* Titanic, by Archibald Gracie; and *Sinking of the* Titanic *and Great Sea Disasters,* edited by Logan Marshall.

Lawrence Beesley, "Chapter IV. The Sinking of the *Titanic* Seen from a Lifeboat," from *The Loss of the* Titanic: *How I Survived the Sinking of the* Titanic, ISBN 9781445604435, published by Amberley Publishing 2011, is reprinted with permission.

U.S. Senate and British Inquiries are drawn from the following: Evidence Before Senate, 62d Congress, 2d Session, *Titanic* Disaster. Report No. 806. Report of the Committee on Commerce United States Senate pursuant to S. RES. 283 directing the Committee on Commerce to investigate the causes leading to the wreck of the White Star Liner *Titanic*. Washington Government Printing Office.

In the Wreck Commissioner's Court: Proceedings before the Right Hon. Lord Mersey, on the Formal Investigation Ordered by the Board of Trade Into the Loss of the SS *Titanic*. Printed for His Majesty's Stationary Office by Jas. Truscott and Son, Ltd. (959 pages + 18 pages of appendices).

Titanic,
First Accounts

Titanic Classics

Lawrence Beesley's
The Loss of the Titanic

CHAPTER IV

The Sinking of the *Titanic*
Seen from a Lifeboat

Looking back now on the descent of our boat down the ship's side, it is a matter of surprise, I think, to all the occupants to remember how little they thought of it at the time. It was a great adventure, certainly: it was exciting to feel the boat sink by jerks, foot by foot, as the ropes were paid out from above and shrieked as they passed through the pulley blocks, the new ropes and gear creaking under the strain of a boat laden with people, and the crew calling to the sailors above as the boat tilted slightly, now at one end, now at the other, "Lower aft!" "Lower stern!" and "Lower together!" as she came level again—but I do not think we felt much apprehension about reaching the water safely. It certainly was thrilling to see the black hull of the ship on one side and the sea, 70 feet [*c.* 21 metres] below, on the other, or to pass down by cabins and saloons brilliantly lighted; but we knew nothing of the apprehension felt in the minds of some of the officers whether the boats and lowering-gear would stand the strain of the weight of our sixty people. The ropes, however, were new and strong, and the boat did not buckle in the middle as an older boat might have done. Whether it was right or not to lower boats full of people to the water—and it seems likely it was not—I think there can be nothing but the highest praise given to the officers and crew above for the way in which they lowered the boats one after the other safely to the water; it may seem a simple matter, to read about such a thing, but any sailor knows, apparently, that it is not so. An experienced officer has told me that he has seen a boat lowered in practise from a ship's deck, with a trained crew and no passengers in the boat, with practised sailors paying out the ropes, in daylight, in calm weather, with the ship lying in dock—and has seen the boat tilt over and pitch the crew headlong into the sea. Contrast these conditions with those obtaining that Monday morning at 12.45 a.m., and it is impossible not to feel that, whether the lowering crew were trained or not, whether they had or had not drilled since coming on board, they did their duty in a way that argues the greatest efficiency. I cannot help feeling the deepest gratitude to the two sailors who stood at the ropes above and lowered us to the sea: I do not suppose they were saved.

Perhaps one explanation of our feeling little sense of the unusual in leaving the *Titanic* in this way was that it seemed the climax to a series of extraordinary occurrences: the magnitude of the whole thing dwarfed events that in the ordinary way would seem to be full of imminent peril. It is easy to imagine it—a voyage of four days on a calm sea, without a single untoward incident; the presumption, perhaps already mentally half realized, that we should be ashore in forty-eight hours and so complete a splendid voyage—and then to feel the engine stop, to be summoned on deck with little time to dress, to tie on a lifebelt, to see rockets shooting aloft in call for help, to be told to get into a lifeboat—after all these things, it did not seem much to feel the boat sinking down to the sea: it was the natural sequence of previous events, and we had learned in the last hour to take things just as they came. At the same time, if any one should wonder what the sensation is like, it is quite easy to measure 75 feet [*c.* 23 metres] from the windows of a tall house or a block of flats, look down to the ground and fancy himself with some sixty other people crowded into a boat so tightly that he could not sit down or move about, and then picture the boat sinking down in a continuous series of jerks, as the sailors pay out the ropes through cleats above. There are more pleasant sensations than this! How thankful we were that the sea was calm and the *Titanic* lay so steadily and quietly as we dropped down her side. We were spared the bumping and grinding against the side which so often accompanies the launching of boats: I do not remember that we even had to fend off our boat while we were trying to get free.

As we went down, one of the crew shouted, "We are just over the condenser exhaust: we don't want to stay in that long or we shall be swamped; feel down on the floor and be ready to pull up the pin which lets the ropes free as soon as we are afloat." I had often looked over the side and noticed this stream of water coming out of the side of the *Titanic* just above the waterline: in fact so large was the volume of water that as we ploughed along and met the waves coming towards us, this stream would cause a splash that sent spray flying. We felt, as well as we could in the crowd of people, on the floor, along the sides, with no idea where the pin could be found—and none of the crew knew where it was, only of its existence somewhere—but we never found it. And all the time we got closer to the sea and the exhaust roared nearer and nearer—until finally we floated with the ropes still holding us from above, the exhaust washing us away and the force of the tide driving us back against the side—the latter not of much account in influencing the direction, however. Thinking over what followed, I imagine we must have touched the water with the condenser stream at our bows, and not in the middle as I thought at one time: at any rate, the resultant of these three forces was that we were carried parallel to the ship, directly under the place where boat 15 would drop from her davits into the sea. Looking up we saw her already coming down rapidly from B deck: she must have filled almost immediately after ours. We shouted up, "Stop lowering 14," (in an account which appeared in the newspapers of 19 April I have described this boat as 14, not knowing they were numbered alternately) and the crew and passengers in the boat above, hearing us shout and seeing our position immediately below them, shouted the same to the sailors on the boat deck; but apparently they did not hear, for she dropped down foot by foot—twenty feet, fifteen, ten—and a stoker and I in the bows reached up and touched her bottom swinging above our heads, trying to push away our boat from under her. It seemed now as if nothing could prevent her dropping on us, but at this moment another stoker sprang with his knife to the ropes that still held us and I heard him shout, "One! Two!" as he cut them through. The next moment we had swung away from underneath 15, and were clear of her as she dropped into the water in the space we had just before occupied. I do not know how the bow ropes were freed, but imagine that they were cut in the same way, for we were washed clear of the *Titanic* at once by the force of the stream and floated away as the oars were got out.

I think we all felt that that was quite the most exciting thing we had yet been through, and a great sigh of relief and gratitude went up as we swung away from the boat above our heads; but I heard no one cry aloud during the experience—not a woman's voice was raised in fear or hysteria. I think we all learnt many things that night about the bogey called "fear", and how the facing of it is much less than the dread of it.

The crew was made up of cooks and stewards, mostly the former, I think; their white jackets showing up in the darkness as they pulled away, two to an oar: I do not think they can have had any practise in rowing, for all night long their oars crossed and clashed; if our safety had depended on speed or accuracy in keeping time it would have gone hard with us. Shouting began from one end of the boat to the other as to what we should do, where we should go, and no one seemed to have any knowledge how to act. At last we asked, "Who is in charge of this boat?" but there was no reply. We then agreed by general consent that the stoker who stood in the stern with the tiller should act as captain, and from that time he directed the course, shouting to other boats and keeping in touch with them. Not that there was anywhere to go or anything we could do. Our plan of action was simple: to keep all the boats together as far as possible and wait until we were picked up by other liners. The crew had apparently heard of the wireless communications before they left the *Titanic*, but I never heard them say that we were in touch with any boat but the *Olympic*: it was always the *Olympic* that was coming to our rescue. They thought they knew even her distance, and making a calculation, we came to the conclusion that we ought to be picked up by her about two o'clock in the afternoon. But this was not our only hope of rescue: we watched all the time the darkness lasted for steamers' lights, thinking there might be a chance of other steamers coming near enough to see the lights which some of our boats carried. I am sure there was no feeling in the minds of anyone that we should not be picked up next day: we knew that wireless messages would go out from ship to ship, and as one of the stokers said: "The sea will be covered with ships to-morrow afternoon: they will race up from all over the sea to find us." Some even thought that fast torpedo boats might run up ahead of the *Olympic*. And yet the *Olympic* was, after all, the farthest away of them all; eight other ships lay within three hundred miles of us.

How thankful we should have been to know how near help was, and how many ships had heard our message and were rushing to the *Titanic*'s aid. I think nothing has surprised us more than to learn so many ships were near enough to rescue us in a few hours.

Almost immediately after leaving the *Titanic* we saw what we all said was a ship's lights down on the horizon on the *Titanic*'s port side: two lights, one above the other, and plainly not one of our boats; we even rowed in that direction for some time, but the lights drew away and disappeared below the horizon.

But this is rather anticipating: we did none of these things first. We had no eyes for anything but the ship we had just left. As the oarsmen pulled slowly away we all turned and took a long look at the mighty vessel towering high above our midget boat, and I know it must have been the most extraordinary sight I shall ever be called upon to witness; I realize now how totally inadequate language is to convey to some other person who was not there any real impression of what we saw.

But the task must be attempted: the whole picture is so intensely dramatic that, while it is not possible to place on paper for eyes to see the actual likeness of the ship as she lay there, some sketch of the scene will be possible. First of all, the climatic conditions were extraordinary. The night was one of the most beautiful I have ever seen: the sky without a single cloud to

mar the perfect brilliance of the stars, clustered so thickly together that in places there seemed almost more dazzling points
of light set in the black sky than background of sky itself; and
each star seemed, in the keen atmosphere, free from any haze, to
have increased its brilliance tenfold and to twinkle and glitter
with a staccato flash that made the sky seem nothing but a set-
ting made for them in which to display their wonder. They
seemed so near, and their light so much more intense than ever
before, that fancy suggested they saw this beautiful ship in dire
distress below and all their energies had awakened to flash messages across the black dome of the sky to each other; telling and
warning of the calamity happening in the world beneath. Later,
when the *Titanic* had gone down and we lay still on the sea
waiting for the day to dawn or a ship to come, I remember looking up at the perfect sky and realizing why Shakespeare wrote
the beautiful words he puts in the mouth of Lorenzo:

> Jessica, look how the floor of heaven
> Is thick inlaid with patines of bright gold.
> There's not the smallest orb which thou behold'st
> But in his motion like an angel sings,
> Still quiring to the young-eyed cherubims;
> Such harmony is in immortal souls;
> But whilst this muddy vesture of decay
> Doth grossly close it in, we cannot hear it.

But it seemed almost as if we could—that night: the stars
seemed really to be alive and to talk. The complete absence of
haze produced a phenomenon I had never seen before: where the
sky met the sea the line was as clear and definite as the edge of a
knife, so that the water and the air never merged gradually into
each other and blended to a softened rounded horizon, but each
element was so exclusively separate that where a star came low
down in the sky near the clear-cut edge of the water-line, it still
lost none of its brilliance. As the earth revolved and the water
edge came up and covered partially the star, as it were, it simply
cut the star in two, the upper half continuing to sparkle as long

as it was not entirely hidden, and throwing a long beam of light along the sea to us.

In the evidence before the United States Senate Committee the captain of one of the ships near us that night said the stars were so extraordinarily bright near the horizon that he was deceived into thinking that they were ships' lights: he did not remember seeing such a night before. Those who were afloat will all agree with that statement: *we* were often deceived into thinking they were lights of a ship.

And next the cold air! Here again was something quite new to us: there was not a breath of wind to blow keenly round us as we stood in the boat, and because of its continued persistence to make us feel cold; it was just a keen, bitter, icy, motionless cold that came from nowhere and yet was there all the time; the stillness of it—if one can imagine "cold" being motionless and still—was what seemed new and strange.

And these—the sky and the air—were overhead; and below was the sea. Here again something uncommon: the surface was like a lake of oil, heaving gently up and down with a quiet motion that rocked our boat dreamily to and fro. We did not need to keep her head to the swell: often I watched her lying broadside on to the tide, and with a boat loaded as we were, this would have been impossible with anything like a swell. The sea slipped away smoothly under the boat, and I think we never heard it lapping on the sides, so oily in appearance was the water. So when one of the stokers said he had been to sea for twenty-six years and never yet seen such a calm night, we accepted it as true without comment. Just as expressive was the remark of another— "It reminds me of a bloomin' picnic!" It was quite true; it did: a picnic on a lake, or a quiet inland river like the Cam, or a backwater on the Thames.

And so in these conditions of sky and air and sea, we gazed broadside on the *Titanic* from a short distance. She was absolutely still—indeed from the first it seemed as if the blow from the iceberg had taken all the courage out of her and she had just come quietly to rest and was settling down without an effort to save herself, without a murmur of protest against such a foul blow. For the sea could not rock her: the wind was not there to howl noisily round the decks, and make the ropes hum; from the first what must have impressed all as they watched was the sense of stillness about her and the slow, insensible way she sank lower and lower in the sea, like a stricken animal.

The mere bulk alone of the ship viewed from the sea below was an awe-inspiring sight. Imagine a ship nearly a sixth of a mile long, 75 feet [*c.* 23 metres] high to the top decks, with four enormous funnels above the decks, and masts again high above the funnels; with her hundreds of portholes, all her saloons and other rooms brilliant with light, and all round her, little boats filled with those who until a few hours before had trod her decks and read in her libraries and listened to the music of her band in happy content; and who were now looking up in amazement at the enormous mass above them and rowing away from her because she was sinking.

I had often wanted to see her from some distance away, and only a few hours before, in conversation at lunch with a fellow-passenger, had registered a vow to get a proper view of her lines and dimensions when we landed at New York: to stand some distance away to take in a full view of her beautiful proportions, which the narrow approach to the dock at Southampton made impossible. Little did I think that the opportunity was to be found so quickly and so dramatically. The background, too, was a different one from what I had planned for her: the black outline of her profile against the sky was bordered all round by stars studded in the sky, and all her funnels and masts were picked out in the same way: her bulk was seen where the stars were blotted out. And one other thing was different from expectation: the thing that ripped away from us instantly, as we saw it, all sense of the beauty of the night, the beauty of the ship's lines, and the beauty of her lights—and all these taken in themselves were intensely beautiful—that thing was the awful angle made by the level of the sea with the rows of porthole lights along her side in dotted lines, row above row. The sea level and the rows of lights should have been parallel—should never have met—and now they met at an angle inside the black hull of the ship. There was nothing else to indicate she was injured; nothing but this apparent violation of a simple geometrical law—that parallel lines should "never meet even if produced ever so far both ways"; but it meant the *Titanic* had sunk by the head until the lowest portholes in the bows were under the sea, and the portholes in the stern were lifted above the normal height. We rowed away from her in the quietness of the night, hoping and praying with all our hearts that she would sink no more and the day would find her still in the same position as she was then. The crew, however, did not think so. It has been said frequently that the officers and crew felt assured that she would remain afloat even after they knew the extent of the damage. Some of them may have done so—and perhaps, from their scientific knowledge of her construction, with more reason at the time than those who said she would sink—but at any rate the stokers in our boat had no such illusion. One of them—I think he was the same man that cut us free from the pulley ropes—told us how he was at work in the stoke-hole, and in anticipation of going off duty in quarter of an hour—thus confirming the time of the collision as 11:45—had near him a pan of soup keeping hot on some part of the machinery; suddenly the whole side of the compartment came in, and the water rushed him off his feet. Picking himself up, he sprang for the compartment doorway and was just through the aperture when the watertight door came down behind him, "like a knife," as he said; "they work them from the bridge." He had gone up on deck but was ordered down again at once and with others was told to draw the fires from under the boiler, which they did, and were then at liberty to come on deck again. It seems that this particular knot of stokers must have known almost as soon as any one of the extent of in-jury. He added mournfully, "I could do with that hot soup now"—and indeed he could: he was clad at the time of the colli-sion, he said, in trousers and singlet, both very thin on account of the intense heat in the stoke-hole; and although he had added a short jacket later, his teeth were chattering with the cold. He found a place to lie down underneath the tiller on the little plat-form where our captain stood, and there he lay all night with a coat belonging to another stoker thrown over him and I think he must have been almost unconscious. A lady next to him, who was warmly clad with several coats, tried to insist on his having one of hers—a fur-lined one—thrown over him, but he absolutely refused while some of the women were insufficiently clad; and so the coat was given to an Irish girl with pretty auburn hair standing near, leaning against the gunwale—with an "outside berth" and so more exposed to the cold air. This same lady was able to distribute more of her wraps to the passengers, a rug to one, a fur boa to another; and she has related with amusement that at the moment of climbing up the *Carpathia*'s side, those to whom these articles had been lent offered them all back to her; but as, like the rest of us, she was encumbered with a lifebelt, she had to say she would receive them back at the end of the climb. I had not seen my dressing-gown since I dropped into the boat, but some time in the night a steerage passenger found it on the floor and put it on.

It is not easy at this time to call to mind who were in the boat, because in the night it was not possible to see more than a few feet away, and when dawn came we had eyes only for the rescue ship and the icebergs; but so far as my memory serves the list was as follows: no first class passengers; three women, one baby, two men from the second cabin; and the other passengers steerage—mostly women; a total of about 35 passengers. The rest, about 25 (and possibly more), were crew and stokers. Near to me all night was a group of three Swedish girls, warmly clad, standing close together to keep warm, and very silent; indeed there was very little talking at any time.

One conversation took place that is, I think, worth repeating: one more proof that the world after all is a small place. The ten-months' old baby which was handed down at the last moment was received by a lady next to me—the same who shared her wraps and coats. The mother had found a place in the middle and was too tightly packed to come through to the child, and so it slept contentedly for about an hour in a stranger's arms; it then began to cry and the temporary nurse said: "Will you feel down and see if the baby's feet are out of the blanket! I don't

THE SINKING OF THE *TITANIC* SEEN FROM A LIFEBOAT

know much about babies but I think their feet must be kept warm." Wriggling down as well as I could, I found its toes exposed to the air and wrapped them well up, when it ceased crying at once: it was evidently a successful diagnosis! Having recognized the lady by her voice—it was much too dark to see faces—as one of my vis-à-vis at the purser's table, I said—"Surely you are Miss——?" "Yes," she replied, "and you must be Mr. Beesley; how curious we should find ourselves in the same boat!" Remembering that she had joined the boat at Queenstown, I said, "Do you know Clonmel? A letter from a great friend of mine who is staying there at——[giving the address] came aboard at Queenstown." "Yes, it is my home: and I was dining at——just before I came away." It seemed that she knew my friend, too; and we agreed that of all places in the world to recognise mutual friends, a crowded lifeboat afloat in mid-ocean at 2 a.m. 1,200 miles from our destination was one of the most unexpected.

And all the time, as we watched, the *Titanic* sank lower and lower by the head and the angle became wider and wider as the stern porthole lights lifted and the bow lights sank, and it was evident she was not to stay afloat much longer. The captain-stoker now told the oarsmen to row away as hard as they could. Two reasons seemed to make this a wise decision: one that as she sank she would create such a wave of suction that boats, if not sucked under by being too near, would be in danger of being swamped by the wave her sinking would create—and we all knew our boat was in no condition to ride big waves, crowded as it was and manned with untrained oarsmen. The second was that an explosion might result from the water getting to the boilers, and debris might fall within a wide radius. And yet, as it turned out, neither of these things happened.

At about 2:15 a.m. I think we were any distance from a mile to two miles away. It is difficult for a landsman to calculate distance at sea but we had been afloat an hour and a half, the boat was heavily loaded, the oarsmen unskilled, and our course erratic: following now one light and now another, sometimes a star and sometimes a light from a port lifeboat which had turned

away from the *Titanic* in the opposite direction and lay almost
on our horizon; and so we could not have gone very far away.

About this time, the water had crept up almost to her sidelight
and the captain's bridge, and it seemed a question only of minutes before she sank. The oarsmen lay on their oars, and all in
the lifeboat were motionless as we watched her in absolute
silence—save some who would not look and buried their heads
on each other's shoulders. The lights still shone with the same
brilliance, but not so many of them: many were now below the
surface. I have often wondered since whether they continued to
light up the cabins when the portholes were under water; they
may have done so.

And then, as we gazed awestruck, she tilted slowly up, revolving apparently about a center of gravity just astern of amidships, until she attained a vertically upright position; and there
she remained—motionless! As she swung up, her lights, which
had shone without a flicker all night, went out suddenly, came
on again for a single flash, then went out altogether. And as they
did so, there came a noise which many people, wrongly I think,
have described as an explosion; it has always seemed to me that
it was nothing but the engines and machinery coming loose from
their bolts and bearings, and falling through the compartments,
smashing everything in their way. It was partly a roar, partly a
groan, partly a rattle, and partly a smash, and it was not a sudden roar as an explosion would be: it went on successively for
some seconds, possibly fifteen to twenty, as the heavy machinery
dropped down to the bottom (now the bows) of the ship: I suppose it fell through the end and sank first, before the ship. But it
was a noise no one had heard before, and no one wishes to hear
again: it was stupefying, stupendous, as it came to us along the
water. It was as if all the heavy things one could think of had
been thrown downstairs from the top of a house, smashing each
other and the stairs and everything in the way.

Several apparently authentic accounts have been given, in which
definite stories of explosions have been related—in some cases
even with wreckage blown up and the ship broken in two; but I
think such accounts will not stand close analysis. In the first

place the fires had been withdrawn and the steam allowed to escape some time before she sank, and the possibility of explosion from this cause seems very remote. Then, as just related, the noise was not sudden and definite, but prolonged—more like the roll and crash of thunder. The probability of the noise being caused by engines falling down will be seen by referring to illustration 57, where the engines are placed in compartments 3, 4, and 5. As the *Titanic* tilted up they would almost certainly fall loose from their bed and plunge down through the other compartments.

No phenomenon like that pictured in some American and English papers occurred—that of the ship breaking in two, and the two ends being raised above the surface. I saw these drawings in preparation on board the *Carpathia*, and said at the time that they bore no resemblance to what actually happened.

When the noise was over the *Titanic* was still upright like a column: we could see her now only as the stern and some 150 feet [*c.* 45 metres] of her stood outlined against the star-specked sky, looming black in the darkness, and in this position she continued for some minutes—I think as much as five minutes, but it may have been less. Then, first sinking back a little at the stern, I thought, she slid slowly forwards through the water and dived slantingly down; the sea closed over her and we had seen the last of the beautiful ship on which we had embarked four days before at Southampton.

And in place of the ship on which all our interest had been concentrated for so long and towards which we looked most of the time because it was still the only object on the sea which was a fixed point to us—in place of the *Titanic*, we had the level sea now stretching in an unbroken expanse to the horizon: heaving gently just as before, with no indication on the surface that the waves had just closed over the most wonderful vessel ever built by man's hand; the stars looked down just the same and the air was just as bitterly cold.

There seemed a great sense of loneliness when we were left on the sea in a small boat without the *Titanic*: not that we were uncomfortable (except for the cold) nor in danger: we did not think we were either, but the *Titanic* was no longer there.

We waited head on for the wave which we thought might come—the wave we had heard so much of from the crew and which they said had been known to travel for miles—and it never came. But although the *Titanic* left us no such legacy of a wave as she went to the bottom, she left us something we would willingly forget forever, something which it is well not to let the imagination dwell on—the cries of many hundreds of our fellow-passengers struggling in the ice-cold water.

I would willingly omit any further mention of this part of the disaster from this book, but for two reasons it is not possible—first, that as a matter of history it should be put on record; and secondly, that these cries were not only an appeal for help in the awful conditions of danger in which the drowning found themselves—an appeal that could never be answered—but an appeal to the whole world to make such conditions of danger and hopelessness impossible ever again; a cry that called to the heavens for the very injustice of its own existence: a cry that clamored for its own destruction.

We were utterly surprised to hear this cry go up as the waves closed over the *Titanic*: we had heard no sound of any kind from her since we left her side; and, as mentioned before, we did not know how many boats she had or how many rafts. The crew may have known, but they probably did not, and if they did, they never told the passengers: we should not have been surprised to know all were safe on some life-saving device.

So that unprepared as we were for such a thing, the cries of the drowning floating across the quiet sea filled us with stupefaction: we longed to return and rescue at least some of the drowning, but we knew it was impossible. The boat was filled to standing-room, and to return would mean the swamping of us all, and so the captain-stoker told his crew to row away from the cries. We tried to sing to keep all from thinking of them; but there was no heart for singing in the boat at that time.

The cries, which were loud and numerous at first, died away gradually one by one, but the night was clear, frosty and still, the water smooth, and the sounds must have carried on its level surface free from any obstruction for miles, certainly much farther from the ship than we were situated. I think the last of them must have been heard nearly forty minutes after the *Titanic* sank. Lifebelts would keep the survivors afloat for hours; but the cold water was what stopped the cries.

There must have come to all those safe in the lifeboats, scattered round the drowning at various distances, a deep resolve that, if anything could be done by them in the future to prevent the repetition of such sounds, they would do it—at whatever cost of time or other things. And not only to them are those cries an imperative call, but to every man and woman who has known of them. It is not possible that ever again can such conditions exist; but it is a duty imperative on one and all to see that they do not. Think of it! A few more boats, a few more planks of wood nailed together in a particular way at a trifling cost, and all those men and women whom the world can so ill afford to lose would be with us to-day, there would be no mourning in thousands of homes which now are desolate, and these words need not have been written.

Archibald Gracie's
The Truth About the Titanic

CHAPTER I

The Last Day Aboard Ship

There is that Leviathan.—Ps. 104: 26

As the sole survivor of all the men passengers of the *Titanic* stationed during the loading of six or more lifeboats with women and children on the port side of the ship, forward on the glass-sheltered Deck A, and later on the Boat Deck above, it is my duty to bear testimony to the heroism on the part of all concerned. First, to my men companions who calmly stood by until the lifeboats had departed loaded with women and the available complement of crew, and who, fifteen to twenty minutes later, sank with the ship, conscious of giving up their lives to save the weak and the helpless.

Second, to Second Officer Lightoller and his ship's crew, who did their duty as if similar occurrences were matters of daily routine; and thirdly, to the women, who showed no signs of fear or panic whatsoever under conditions more appalling than were ever recorded before in the history of disasters at sea.

I think those of my readers who are accustomed to tales of thrilling adventure will be glad to learn first-hand of the heroism displayed on the *Titanic* by those to whom it is my privilege and sad duty to pay this tribute. I will confine the details of my narrative for the most part to what I personally saw, and did, and heard during that never-to-be-forgotten maiden trip of the *Titanic*, which ended with shipwreck and her foundering about 2:22 a.m., Monday, April 15, 1912, after striking an iceberg "in or near latitude 41 degrees, 46 minutes N., longitude 50 degrees,

14 minutes W., North Atlantic Ocean," whereby the loss of 1,490 lives ensued.

On Sunday morning, April 14th, this marvelous ship, the perfection of all vessels hitherto conceived by the brain of man, had, for three and one-half days, proceeded on her way from Southampton to New York over a sea of glass, so level it appeared, without encountering a ripple brought on the surface of the water by a storm.

The Captain had each day improved upon the previous day's speed, and prophesied that, with continued fair weather, we should make an early arrival record for this maiden trip. But his reckoning never took into consideration that Protean monster of the Northern seas which, even before this, had been so fatal to the navigator's calculations and so formidable a weapon of destruction.

Our explorers have pierced to the furthest north and south of the icebergs' retreat, but the knowledge of their habitat, insuring our great ocean liners in their successful efforts to elude them, has not reached the detail of time and place where they become detached and obstruct their path.

In the twenty-four hours' run ending the 14th, according to the posted reckoning, the ship had covered 546 miles, and we were told that the next twenty-four hours would see even a better record made.

Towards evening the report, which I heard, was spread that wireless messages from passing steamers had been received advising the officers of our ship of the presence of icebergs and icefloes. The increasing cold and the necessity of being more warmly clad when appearing on deck were outward and visible signs in corroboration of these warnings. But despite them all no diminution of speed was indicated and the engines kept up their steady running.

Not for fifty years, the old sailors tell us, had so great a mass of ice and icebergs at this time of the year been seen so far south.

The pleasure and comfort which all of us enjoyed upon this floating palace, with its extraordinary provisions for such purposes, seemed an ominous feature to many of us, including myself, who felt it almost too good to last without some terrible retribution inflicted by the hand of an angry omnipotence. Our sentiment in this respect was voiced by one of the most able and distinguished of our fellow passengers, Mr. Charles M. Hays, President of the Canadian Grand Trunk Railroad. Engaged as he then was in studying and providing the hotel equipment along the line of new extensions to his own great railroad system, the consideration of the subject and of the magnificence of the *Titanic*'s accommodations was thus brought home to him. This was the prophetic utterance with which, alas, he sealed his fate a few hours thereafter: "The White Star, the Cunard and the Hamburg-American lines," said he, "are now devoting their attention to a struggle for supremacy in obtaining the most luxurious appointments for their ships, but the time will soon come when the greatest and most appalling of all disasters at sea will be the result."

In the various trips which I have made across the Atlantic, it has been my custom aboard ship, whenever the weather permitted, to take as much exercise every day as might be needful to put myself in prime physical condition, but on board the *Titanic*, during the first days of the voyage, from Wednesday to Saturday, I had departed from this, my usual self-imposed regimen, for during this interval I had devoted my time to social enjoyment and to the reading of books taken from the ship's well-supplied library. I enjoyed myself as if I were in a summer palace on the seashore, surrounded with every comfort—there was nothing to indicate or suggest that we were on the stormy Atlantic Ocean. The motion of the ship and the noise of its machinery were scarcely discernible on deck or in the saloons, either day or night. But when Sunday morning came, I considered it high time to begin my customary exercises, and determined for the rest of the voyage to patronize the squash racquet court, the gymnasium, the swimming pool, etc. I was up early before breakfast and met the professional racquet player in a half hour's warming up, preparatory for a swim in the six-foot deep tank of salt water, heated to a refreshing temperature. In no swimming bath had I ever enjoyed such pleasure before. How curtailed that enjoyment would have been had the presentiment come to me telling how near it was to being my last plunge, and that before dawn of another day I would be swimming for my life in mid-ocean, under water and on the surface, in a temperature of 28 degrees Fahrenheit!

Impressed on my memory as if it were but yesterday, my mind pictures the personal appearance and recalls the conversation which I had with each of these employees of the ship. The racquet professional, F. Wright, was a clean-cut typical young Englishman, similar to hundreds I have seen and with whom I have played, in bygone years, my favorite game of cricket, which has done more than any other sport for my physical development. I have not seen his name mentioned in any account of the disaster, and therefore take this opportunity of speaking of him, for I am perhaps the only survivor able to relate anything about his last days on earth.

Hundreds of letters have been written to us survivors, many containing photographs for identification of some lost loved one, whom perchance we may have seen or talked to before he met his fate. To these numerous inquiries I have been able to reply satisfactorily only in rare instances. The next and last time I saw Wright was on the stairway of Deck C within three-quarters of an hour after the collision. I was going to my cabin when I met him on the stairs going up. "Hadn't we better cancel that appointment for to-morrow morning?" I said rather jocosely to him. "Yes," he replied, but did not stop to tell what he then must have known of the conditions in the racquet court on G Deck, which, according to other witnesses, had at that time become flooded. His voice was calm, without enthusiasm, and perhaps his face was a little whiter than usual.

To the swimming pool attendant I also made promise to be on hand earlier the next morning, but I never saw him again.

One of the characters of the ship, best known to us all, was the gymnasium instructor, T. W. McCawley. He, also, expected me to make my first appearance for real good exercise on the morrow, but alas, he, too, was swallowed up by the sea. How well we survivors all remember this sturdy little man in white flannels and with his broad English accent! With what tireless enthusiasm he showed us the many mechanical devices under his charge and urged us to take advantage of the opportunity of using them, going through the motions of bicycle racing, rowing, boxing, camel and horseback riding, etc.

Such was my morning's preparation for the unforeseen physical exertions I was compelled to put forth for dear life at midnight, a few hours later. Could any better training for the terrible ordeal have been planned?

The exercise and the swim gave me an appetite for a hearty breakfast. Then followed the church service in the dining saloon, and I remember how much I was impressed with the "Prayer for those at Sea," also the words of the hymn, which we sang, No. 418 of the Hymnal. About a fortnight later, when I next heard it sung, I was in the little church at Smithtown, Long Island, attending the memorial service in honor of my old friend and fellow member of the Union Club, James Clinch Smith. To his sister, who sat next to me in the pew, I called attention to the fact that it was the last hymn we sang on this Sunday morning on board the *Titanic*. She was much affected, and gave the reason for its selection for the memorial service to her brother because it was known as Jim's favorite hymn, being the first piece set to music ever played by him as a child and for which he was rewarded with a promised prize, donated by his father.

What a remarkable coincidence that at the first and last ship's service on board the *Titanic*, the hymn we sang began with these impressive lines:

> O God our help in ages past,
> Our hope for years to come,
> Our shelter from the stormy blast
> And our eternal home.

One day was so like another that it is difficult to differentiate in our description all the details of this last day's incidents aboard ship.

The book that I finished and returned to the ship's library was

Mary Johnston's *Old Dominion*. While peacefully reading the tales of adventure and accounts of extraordinary escapes therein, how little I thought that in the next few hours I should be a witness and a party to a scene to which this book could furnish no counterpart, and that my own preservation from a watery grave would afford a remarkable illustration of how ofttimes "truth is stranger than fiction."

During this day I saw much of Mr. and Mrs. Isidor Straus. In fact, from the very beginning to the end of our trip on the *Titanic*, we had been together several times each day. I was with them on the deck the day we left Southampton and witnessed that ominous accident to the American liner, *New York*, lying at her pier, when the displacement of water by the movement of our gigantic ship caused a suction which pulled the smaller ship from her moorings and nearly caused a collision. At the time of this, Mr. Straus was telling me that it seemed only a few years back that he had taken passage on this same ship, the *New York*, on her maiden trip and when she was spoken of as the "last word in shipbuilding." He then called the attention of his wife and myself to the progress that had since been made, by comparison of the two ships then lying side by side. During our daily talks thereafter, he related much of special interest concerning incidents in his remarkable career, beginning with his early manhood in Georgia when, with the Confederate Government Commissioners, as an agent for the purchase of supplies, he ran the blockade of Europe. His friendship with President Cleveland, and how the latter had honored him, were among the topics of daily conversation that interested me most.

On this Sunday, our last day aboard ship, he finished the reading of a book I had loaned him, in which he expressed intense interest. This book was *The Truth About Chickamauga*, of which I am the author, and it was to gain a much-needed rest after seven years of work thereon, and in order to get it off my mind, that I had taken this trip across the ocean and back. As a counter-irritant, my experience was a dose which was highly efficacious.

I recall how Mr. and Mrs. Straus were particularly happy about noon time on this same day in anticipation of communicating by wireless telegraphy with their son and his wife on their way to Europe on board the passing ship *Amerika*. Some time before six o'clock, full of contentment, they told me of the message of greeting received in reply. This last good-bye to their loved ones must have been a consoling thought when the end came a few hours thereafter.

That night after dinner, with my table companions, Messrs. James Clinch Smith and Edward A. Kent, according to usual custom, we adjourned to the palm room, with many others, for the usual coffee at individual tables where we listened to the always delightful music of the *Titanic*'s band. On these occasions, full dress was always *en règle*; and it was a subject both of observation and admiration, that there were so many beautiful women—then especially in evidence—aboard the ship.

I invariably circulated around during these delightful evenings, chatting with those I knew, and with those whose acquaintance I had made during the voyage. I might specify names and particularize subjects of conversation, but the details, while interesting to those concerned, might not be so to all my readers. The recollections of those with whom I was thus closely associated in this disaster, including those who suffered the death from which I escaped and those who survived with me, will be a treasured memory and bond of union until my dying day. From the palm room, the men of my coterie would always go to the smoking-room, and almost every evening join in conversation with some of the well-known men whom we met there, including within my own recollections Major Archie Butt, President Taft's Military Aid, discussing politics; Clarence Moore, of Washington, D. C., relating his venturesome trip some years ago through the West Virginia woods and mountains, helping a newspaper reporter in obtaining an interview with the outlaw, Captain Anse Hatfield; Frank D. Millet, the well-known artist, planning a journey west; Arthur Ryerson and others.

During these evenings I also conversed with Mr. John B. Thayer, Second Vice-President of the Pennsylvania Railroad, and with Mr. George D. Widener, a son of the Philadelphia street-car magnate, Mr. P. A. B. Widener.

My stay in the smoking-room on this particular evening for the first time was short, and I retired early with my cabin steward Cullen's promise to awaken me betimes next morning to get ready for the engagements I had made before breakfast for the game of racquets, work in the gymnasium and the swim that was to follow.

I cannot regard it as a mere coincidence that on this particular Sunday night I was thus prompted to retire early for nearly three hours of invigorating sleep, whereas an accident occurring at midnight of any of the four preceding days would have found me mentally and physically tired. That I was thus strengthened for the terrible ordeal, better even than had I been forewarned of it, I regard on the contrary as the first provision for my safety (answering the constant prayers of those at home), made by the guardian angel to whose care I was entrusted during the series of miraculous escapes presently to be recorded.

CHAPTER II

Struck by an Iceberg

Watchman, what of the night?—Isaiah 21: 11

My stateroom was an outside one on Deck C on the starboard quarter, somewhat abaft amidships. It was No. C, 51. I was enjoying a good night's rest when I was aroused by a sudden shock and noise forward on the starboard side, which I at once concluded was caused by a collision, with some other ship perhaps. I jumped from my bed, turned on the electric light, glanced at my watch nearby on the dresser, which I had changed to agree with ship's time on the day before and which now registered twelve o'clock. Correct ship's time would make it about 11:45. I opened the door of my cabin, looked out into the corridor, but could not see or hear anyone—there was no commotion whatever; but immediately following the collision came a great noise of escaping steam. I listened intently, but could hear no machinery. There was no mistaking that something wrong had happened, because of the ship stopping and the blowing off of steam.

Removing my night clothing I dressed myself hurriedly in underclothing, shoes and stockings, trousers and a Norfolk coat. I give these details in order that some idea of the lapse of time may be formed by an account of what I did during the interval. From my cabin, through the corridor to the stairway was but a short distance, and I ascended to the third deck above, that is, to the Boat Deck. I found here only one young lad, seemingly bent on the same quest as myself.

From the first cabin quarter, forward on the port side, we strained our eyes to discover what had struck us. From vantage points where the view was not obstructed by the lifeboats on this deck I sought the object, but in vain, though I swept the horizon near and far and discovered nothing.

It was a beautiful night, cloudless, and the stars shining brightly. The atmosphere was quite cold, but no ice or iceberg was in sight. If another ship had struck us there was no trace of it, and it did not yet occur to me that it was an iceberg with which we had collided. Not satisfied with a partial investigation, I made a complete tour of the deck, searching every point of the compass with my eyes. Going toward the stern, I vaulted over the iron gate and fence that divide the first and second cabin passengers. I disregarded the "not allowed" notice. I looked about me towards the officers' quarters in expectation of being challenged for non-observance of rules. In view of the collision I had expected to see some of the ship's officers on the Boat Deck, but there was no sign of an officer anywhere, and no one from whom to obtain any information about what had happened. Making my tour of the Boat Deck, the only other beings I saw were a middle-aged couple of the second cabin promenading unconcernedly, arm in arm, forward on the starboard quarter, against the wind, the man in a gray overcoat and outing cap.

Having gained no satisfaction whatever, I descended to the glass-enclosed Deck A, port side, and looked over the rail to see whether the ship was on an even keel, but I still could see nothing wrong. Entering the companionway, I passed Mr. Ismay with a member of the crew hurrying up the stairway. He wore a day suit, and, as usual, was hatless. He seemed too much preoccupied to notice anyone. Therefore I did not speak to him, but regarded his face very closely, perchance to learn from his manner how serious the accident might be. It occurred to me then that he was putting on as brave a face as possible so as to cause no alarm among the passengers.

At the foot of the stairway were a number of men passengers, and I now for the first time discovered that others were aroused as well as myself, among them my friend, Clinch Smith, from whom I first learned that an iceberg had struck us. He opened his hand and showed me some ice, flat like my watch, coolly suggesting that I might take it home for a souvenir. All of us will remember the way he had of cracking a joke without a smile. While we stood there, the story of the collision came to us— how someone in the smoking-room, when the ship struck, rushed out to see what it was, and returning, told them that he had a glimpse of an iceberg towering fifty feet above Deck A, which, if true, would indicate a height of over one hundred feet. Here, too, I learned that the mail room was flooded and that the plucky postal clerks, in two feet of water, were at their posts. They were engaged in transferring to the upper deck, from the ship's post-office, the two hundred bags of registered mail containing four hundred thousand letters. The names of these men, who all sank with the ship, deserve to be recorded. They were: John S. Marsh, William L. Gwynn, Oscar S. Woody, Iago Smith and E. D. Williamson. The first three were Americans, the others Englishmen, and the families of the former were provided for by their Government.

And now Clinch Smith and myself noticed a list on the floor of the companionway. We kept our own counsel about it, not wishing to frighten anyone or cause any unnecessary alarm, especially among the ladies, who then appeared upon the scene. We did not consider it our duty to express our individual opinion upon the serious character of the accident which now appealed to us with the greatest force. He and I resolved to stick together in the final emergency, united in the silent bond of friendship, and lend a helping hand to each other whenever required. I recall having in my mind's eye at this moment all that I had read and heard in days gone by about shipwrecks, and pictured Smith and myself clinging to an overloaded raft in an open sea with a scarcity of food and water. We agreed to visit our respective staterooms and join each other later. All possessions in my stateroom were hastily packed into three large traveling bags so that the luggage might be ready in the event of a hasty transfer to another ship.

Fortunately I put on my long Newmarket overcoat that

reached below my knees, and as I passed from the corridor into the companionway my worst fears were confirmed. Men and women were slipping on life-preservers, the stewards assisting in adjusting them. Steward Cullen insisted upon my returning to my stateroom for mine. I did so and he fastened one on me while I brought out the other for use by someone else.

Out on Deck A, port side, towards the stern, many men and women had already collected. I sought and found the unprotected ladies to whom I had proffered my services during the voyage when they boarded the ship at Southampton, Mrs. E. D. Appleton, wife of my St. Paul's School friend and schoolmate; Mrs. R. C. Cornell, wife of the well-known New York Justice, and Mrs. J. Murray Brown, wife of the Boston publisher, all old friends of my wife. These three sisters were returning home from a sad mission abroad, where they had laid to rest the remains of a fourth sister, Lady Victor Drummond, of whose death I had read accounts in the London papers, and all the sad details connected therewith were told me by the sisters themselves. That they would have to pass through a still greater ordeal seemed impossible, and how little did I know of the responsibility I took upon myself for their safety! Accompanying them, also unprotected, was their friend, Miss Edith Evans, to whom they introduced me. Mr. and Mrs. Straus, Colonel and Mrs. Astor and others well known to me were among those here congregated on the port side of Deck A, including, besides Clinch Smith, two of our coterie of after-dinner companions, Hugh Woolner, son of the English sculptor, whose works are to be seen in Westminster Abbey, and H. Björnström Steffanson, the young lieutenant of the Swedish army, who, during the voyage, had told me of his acquaintance with Mrs. Gracie's relatives in Sweden.

It was now that the band began to play, and continued while the boats were being lowered. We considered this a wise provision tending to allay excitement. I did not recognize any of the tunes, but I know they were cheerful and were not hymns. If, as has been reported, "Nearer My God to Thee" was one of the selections, I assuredly should have noticed it and regarded it as a tactless warning of immediate death to us all and one likely to create a panic that our special efforts were directed towards avoiding, and which we accomplished to the fullest extent. I know of only two survivors whose names are cited by the newspapers as authority for the statement that this hymn was one of those played. On the other hand, all whom I have questioned or corresponded with, including the best qualified, testified emphatically to the contrary.

Our hopes were buoyed with the information, imparted through the ship's officers, that there had been an interchange of wireless messages with passing ships, one of which was certainly coming to our rescue. To reassure the ladies of whom I had assumed special charge, I showed them a bright white light of what I took to be a ship about five miles off and which I felt sure was coming to our rescue. Colonel Astor heard me telling this to them and he asked me to show it and I pointed the light out to him. In so doing we both had now to lean over the rail of the ship and look close in towards the bow, avoiding a lifeboat even then made ready with its gunwale lowered to the level of the floor of the Boat Deck above us and obstructing our view; but instead of growing brighter the light grew dim and less and less distinct and passed away altogether. The light, as I have since learned, with tearful regret for the lost who might have been saved, belonged to the steamer *Californian* of the Leyland line, Captain Stanley Lord, bound from London to Boston. She belonged to the International Mercantile Marine Company, the owners of the *Titanic*.

This was the ship from which two of the six "ice messages" were sent. The first one received and acknowledged by the *Titanic* was one at 7:30 p.m., an intercepted message to another ship. The next was about 11 p.m., when the Captain of the *Californian* saw a ship approaching from the eastward, which he was advised to be the *Titanic*, and under his orders this message was sent: "We are stopped and surrounded by ice." To this the *Titanic*'s wireless operator brusquely replied, "Shut up, I am busy. I am working Cape Race." The business here referred to was the sending of wireless messages for passengers on the *Titanic*; and the stronger current of the *Californian* eastward interfered therewith. Though the navigation of the ship and the issues of life and death were at stake, the right of way was given to communication with Cape Race until within a few minutes of the *Titanic*'s collision with the iceberg.

Nearly all this time, until 11:30 p.m., the wireless operator of the *Californian* was listening with 'phones on his head, but at 11:30 p.m., while the *Titanic* was still talking to Cape Race, the former ship's operator "put the 'phones down, took off his clothes and turned in."

The fate of thousands of lives hung in the balance many times that ill-omened night, but *the circumstances in connection with the S. S. Californian* (Br. Rep. pp. 43–46), furnish the evidence corroborating that of the American Investigation, viz., that it was not chance, but the grossest negligence alone which sealed the fate of all the noble lives, men and women, that were lost.

It appears from the evidence referred to, information in regard to which we learned after our arrival in New York, that the Captain of the *Californian* and his crew were watching our lights from the deck of their ship, which remained approximately stationary until 5:15 a.m. on the following morning. During this interval it is shown that they were never distant more than six or seven miles. In fact, at 12 o'clock, the *Californian* was only four or five miles off at the point and in the general direction where she was seen by myself and at least a dozen others, who bore testimony before the American Committee, from the decks of the *Titanic*. The white rockets which we sent up, referred to presently, were also plainly seen at the time. Captain Lord was completely in possession of the knowledge that he was in proximity to a ship in distress. He could have put himself into immediate communication with us by wireless had he desired confirmation of the name of the ship and the disaster which had befallen it. His indifference is made apparent by his orders to "go on Morseing," instead of utilizing the more modern method of the inventive genius and gentleman, Mr. Marconi, which eventually saved us all. "The night was clear and the sea was smooth. The ice by which the *Californian* was surrounded," says the British Report, "was loose ice extending for a distance of not more than two or three miles in the direction of the *Titanic*." When she first saw the rockets, the *Californian* could have pushed through the ice to the open water without any serious risk and so have come to the assistance of the *Titanic*. A discussion of this subject is the most painful of all others for those who lost their loved ones aboard our ship.

When we realized that the ship whose lights we saw was not coming towards us, our hopes of rescue were correspondingly depressed, but the men's counsel to preserve calmness prevailed; and to reassure the ladies they repeated the much advertised fiction of "the unsinkable ship" on the supposed highest qualified authority. It was at this point that Miss Evans related to me the story that years ago in London she had been told by a fortune-teller to "beware of water," and now "she knew she would be drowned." My efforts to persuade her to the contrary were futile. Though she gave voice to her story, she presented no evidence whatever of fear, and when I saw and conversed with her an hour later when conditions appeared especially desperate, and the last lifeboat was supposed to have departed, she was perfectly calm and did not revert again to the superstitious tale.

From my own conclusions, and those of others, it appears that about forty-five minutes had now elapsed since the collision when Captain Smith's orders were transmitted to the crew to lower the lifeboats, loaded with women and children first. The self-abnegation of Mr. and Mrs. Isidor Straus here shone forth heroically when she promptly and emphatically exclaimed: "No! I will not be separated from my husband; as we have lived, so will we die together;" and when he, too, declined the assistance proffered on my earnest solicitation that, because of his age and helplessness, exception should be made and he be allowed to accompany his wife in the boat. "No!" he said, "I do not wish any distinction in my favor which is not granted to others." As near as I can recall them these were the words which they addressed to me. They expressed themselves as fully prepared to die, and calmly sat down in steamer chairs on the glass-enclosed Deck A, prepared to meet their fate. Further entreaties to make them change their decision were of no avail. Later they moved to the

Boat Deck above, accompanying Mrs. Straus's maid, who entered a lifeboat.

When the order to load the boats was received I had promptly moved forward with the ladies in my charge toward the boats then being lowered from the Boat Deck above to Deck A on the port side of the ship, where we then were. A tall, slim young Englishman, Sixth Officer J. P. Moody, whose name I learned later, with other members of the ship's crew, barred the progress of us men passengers any nearer to the boats. All that was left me was then to consign these ladies in my charge to the protection of the ship's officer, and I thereby was relieved of their responsibility and felt sure that they would be safely loaded in the boats at this point. I remember a steward rolling a small barrel out of the door of the companionway. "What have you there?" said I. "Bread for the lifeboats," was his quick and cheery reply, as I passed inside the ship for the last time, searching for two of my table companions, Mrs. Churchill Candee of Washington and Mr. Edward A. Kent. It was then that I met Wright, the racquet player, and exchanged the few words on the stairway already related.

Considering it well to have a supply of blankets for use in the open boats exposed to the cold, I concluded, while passing, to make another, and my last, descent to my stateroom for this purpose, only to find it locked, and on asking the reason why was told by some other steward than Cullen that it was done "to prevent looting." Advising him of what was wanted, I went with him to the cabin stewards' quarters nearby, where extra blankets were stored, and where I obtained them. I then went the length of the ship inside on this glass-enclosed Deck A from aft, forwards, looking in every room and corner for my missing table companions, but no passengers whatever were to be seen except in the smoking-room, and there all alone by themselves, seated around a table, were four men, three of whom were personally well known to me, Major Butt, Clarence Moore and Frank Millet, but the fourth was a stranger, whom I therefore cannot identify. All four seemed perfectly oblivious of what was going on on the decks outside. It is impossible to suppose that they did not know of the collision with an iceberg and that the room they were in had been deserted by all others, who had hastened away. It occurred to me at the time that these men desired to show their entire indifference to the danger and that if I advised them as to how seriously I regarded it, they would laugh at me. This was the last I ever saw of any of them, and I know of no one who testifies to seeing them later, except a lady who mentions having seen Major Butt on the bridge five minutes before the last boat left the ship. There is no authentic story of what they did when the water reached this deck, and their ultimate fate is only a matter of conjecture. That they went down in the ship on this Deck A, when the steerage passengers (as described later) blocked the way to the deck above, is my personal belief, founded on the following facts, to wit: First, that neither I nor anyone else, so far as I know, ever saw any of them on the Boat Deck, and second, that the bodies of none of them were ever recovered, indicating the possibility that all went down inside the ship or the enclosed deck.

I next find myself forward on the port side, part of the time on the Boat Deck, and part on the deck below it, called Deck A, where I rejoined Clinch Smith, who reported that Mrs. Candee had departed on one of the boats. We remained together until the ship went down. I was on the Boat Deck when I saw and heard the first rocket, and then successive ones sent up at intervals thereafter. These were followed by the Morse red and blue lights, which were signaled near by us on the deck where we were; but we looked in vain for any response. These signals of distress indicated to every one of us that the ship's fate was sealed, and that she might sink before the lifeboats could be lowered.

And now I am on Deck A again, where I helped in the loading of two boats lowered from the deck above. There were twenty boats in all on the ship: 14 wooden lifeboats, each thirty feet long by nine feet one inch broad, constructed to carry sixty-five persons each: 2 wooden cutters, emergency boats, twenty-five feet two inches long by seven feet two inches broad, constructed to carry forty persons each; and 4 Engelhardt "surf-boats" with canvas collapsible sides extending above the gunwales, twenty-five feet five inches long by eight feet broad, constructed to carry forty-seven persons each. The lifeboats were ranged along the ship's rail, or its prolongation forward and aft on the Boat Deck, the odd numbered on the starboard and the even numbered on the port side. Two of the Engelhardt boats were on the Boat Deck forward beneath the Emergency boats suspended on davits above. The other Engelhardt boats were on the roof of the officers' house forward of the first funnel. They are designated respectively by the letters, A, B, C, D; A and C on the starboard, B and D on the port sides. They have a rounded bottom like a canoe. The name "collapsible boat" generally applied has given rise to mistaken impressions in regard to them, because of the adjustable canvas sides above-mentioned.

At this quarter I was no longer held back from approaching near the boats, but my assistance and work as one of the crew in the loading of boats and getting them away as quickly as possible were accepted, for there was now no time to spare. The Second Officer, Lightoller, was in command on the port side forward, where I was. One of his feet was planted in the lifeboat, and the other on the rail of Deck A, while we, through the wood frames of the lowered glass windows on this deck, passed women, children, and babies in rapid succession without any confusion whatsoever. Among this number was Mrs. Astor, whom I lifted over the four-feet high rail of the ship through the frame. Her husband held her left arm as we carefully passed her to Lightoller, who seated her in the boat. A dialogue now ensued between Colonel Astor and the officer, every word of which I listened to with intense interest. Astor was close to me in the adjoining window-frame, to the left of mine. Leaning out over the rail he asked permission of Lightoller to enter the boat to protect his wife, which, in view of her delicate condition, seems to have been a reasonable request, but the officer, intent upon his duty, and obeying orders, and not knowing the millionaire from the rest of us, replied: "No, sir, no men are allowed in these boats until women are loaded first." Colonel Astor did not demur, but bore the refusal bravely and resignedly, simply asking the num-

ber of the boat to help find his wife later in case he also was rescued. "Number 4," was Lightoller's reply. Nothing more was
said. Colonel Astor moved away from this point and I never saw
him again. I do not for a moment believe the report that he attempted to enter, or did enter, a boat and it is evident that if any
such thought occurred to him at all it must have been at this
present time and in this boat with his wife. Second Officer Lightoller recalled the incident perfectly when I reminded him of it.
It was only through me that Colonel Astor's identity was established in his mind. "I assumed," said he, "that I was asked to
give the number of the lifeboat as the passenger intended, for
some unknown cause, to make complaint about me." From the
fact that I never saw Colonel Astor on the Boat Deck later, and
also because his body, when found, was crushed (according to
the statement of one who saw it at Halifax, Mr. Harry K. White,
of Boston, Mr. Edward A. Kent's brother-in-law, my schoolmate
and friend from boyhood), I am of the opinion that he met his
fate on the ship when the boilers tore through it, as described
later.

One of the incidents I recall when loading the boats at this
point was my seeing a young woman clinging tightly to a baby
in her arms as she approached near the ship's high rail, but un-
willing even for a moment to allow anyone else to hold the little
one while assisting her to board the lifeboat. As she drew back
sorrowfully to the outer edge of the crowd on the deck, I followed and persuaded her to accompany me to the rail again,
promising if she would entrust the baby to me I would see that
the officer passed it to her after she got aboard. I remember her
trepidation as she acceded to my suggestion and the happy expression of relief when the mother was safely seated with the
baby restored to her. "Where is my baby?" was her anxious
wail. "I have your baby," I cried, as it was tenderly handed
along. I remember this incident well because of my feeling at the
time, when I had the babe in my care; though the interval was
short, I wondered how I should manage with it in my arms if the
lifeboats got away and I should be plunged into the water with it
as the ship sank.

According to Lightoller's testimony before the Senate Committee he put twenty to twenty-five women, with two seamen to row, in the first boat and thirty, with two seamen in the second.

Our labors in loading the boats were now shifted to the Boat Deck above, where Clinch Smith and I, with others, followed Lightoller and the crew. On this deck some difficulty was experienced in getting the boats ready to lower. Several causes may have contributed to this, viz., lack of drill and insufficient number of seamen for such emergency, or because of the new tackle not working smoothly. We had the hardest time with the Engelhardt boat, lifting and pushing it towards and over the rail. My shoulders and the whole weight of my body were used in assisting the crew at this work. Lightoller's testimony tells us that as the situation grew more serious he began to take chances and in loading the third boat he filled it up as full as he dared to, with about thirty-five persons. By this time he was short of seamen, and in the fourth boat he put the first man passenger. "Are you a sailor?" Lightoller asked, and received the reply from the gentleman addressed that he was "a yachtsman." Lightoller told him if he was "sailor enough to get out over the bulwarks to the lifeboats, to go ahead." This passenger was Major Arthur Peuchen, of Toronto, who acquitted himself as a brave man should. My energies were so concentrated upon this work of loading the boats at this quarter that lapse of time, sense of sight and sense of hearing recorded no impressions during this interval until the last boat was loaded; but there is one fact of which I am positive, and that is that every man, woman, officer and member of the crew did their full duty without a sign of fear or confusion. Lightoller's strong and steady voice rang out his orders in clear firm tones, inspiring confidence and obedience. There was not one woman who shed tears or gave any sign of fear or distress. There was not a man at this quarter of the ship who indicated a desire to get into the boats and escape with the women. There was not a member of the crew who shirked, or left his post. The coolness, courage, and sense of duty that I here witnessed made me thankful to God and proud of my Anglo-Saxon race that gave this perfect and superb exhibition of self-control at this hour of severest trial. "The boat's deck was only ten feet from the water when I lowered the sixth boat," testified Lightoller, "and when we lowered the first, the distance to the water was seventy feet. We had now loaded all the women who were in sight at that quarter of the ship, and I ran along the deck with Clinch Smith on the port side some distance aft shouting, "Are there any more women?" "Are there any more women?" On my return there was a very palpable list to port as if the ship was about to topple over. The deck was on a corresponding slant. "All passengers to the starboard side," was Lightoller's loud command, heard by all of us. Here I thought the final crisis had come, with the boats all gone, and when we were to be precipitated into the sea.

Prayerful thoughts now began to rise in me that my life might be preserved and I be restored to my loved ones at home. I weighed myself in the balance, doubtful whether I was thus deserving of God's mercy and protection. I questioned myself as to the performance of my religious duties according to the instructions of my earliest Preceptor, the Rev. Henry A. Coit, whose St. Paul's School at Concord, N. H., I had attended. My West Point training in the matter of recognition of constituted authority and maintenance of composure stood me in good stead.

My friend, Clinch Smith, urged immediate obedience to Lightoller's orders, and, with other men passengers, we crossed over to the starboard quarter of the ship, forward on the same Boat Deck where, as I afterwards learned, the officer in command was First Officer Murdoch, who had also done noble work, and was soon thereafter to lose his life. Though the deck here was not so noticeably aslant as on the port side, the conditions appeared fully as desperate. All the lifeboats had been lowered and had departed. There was somewhat of a crowd congregated along the rail. The light was sufficient for me to recognize distinctly many of those with whom I was well acquainted. Here, pale and determined, was Mr. John B. Thayer, Second Vice-President of the Pennsylvania Railroad, and Mr. George D. Widener. They were looking over the ship's gunwale, talking earnestly as if debating what to do. Next to them it pained me to discover

Mrs. J. M. Brown and Miss Evans, the two ladies whom more than an hour previous I had, as related, consigned to the care of Sixth Officer Moody on Deck A, where he, as previously described, blocked my purpose of accompanying these ladies and personally assisting them into the boat. They showed no signs of perturbation whatever as they conversed quietly with me. Mrs. Brown quickly related how they became separated, in the crowd, from her sisters, Mrs. Appleton and Mrs. Cornell. Alas! that they had not remained on the same port side of the ship, or moved forward on Deck A, or the Boat Deck! Instead, they had wandered in some unexplained way to the very furthest point diagonally from where they were at first. At the time of introduction I had not caught Miss Evans' name, and when we were here together at this critical moment I thought it important to ask, and she gave me her name. Meantime the crew were working on the roof of the officers' quarters to cut loose one of the Engelhardt boats. All this took place more quickly than it takes to write it.

Meantime, I will describe what was going on at the quarter where I left Lightoller loading the last boat on the port side. The information was obtained personally from him, in answer to my careful questioning during the next few days on board the *Carpathia*, when I made notes thereof, which were confirmed again the next week in Washington, where we were both summoned before the Senate Investigating Committee. "Men from the steerage," he said, "rushed the boat." "Rush" is the word he used, meaning they got in without his permission. He drew his pistol and ordered them out, threatening to shoot if they attempted to enter the boat again. I presume it was in consequence of this incident that the crew established the line which I encountered, presently referred to, which blocked the men passengers from approaching the last boat loaded on the port side forward, where we had been, and the last one that was safely loaded from the ship.

During this very short interval I was on the starboard side, as described, next to the rail, with Mrs. Brown and Miss Evans, when I heard a member of the crew, coming from the quarter where the last boat was loaded, say that there was room for more ladies in it. I immediately seized each lady by the arm, and, with Miss Evans on my right and Mrs. Brown on my left, hurried, with three other ladies following us, toward the port side; but I had not proceeded half-way, and near amidship, when I was stopped by the aforesaid line of the crew barring my progress, and one of the officers told me that only the women could pass.

The story of what now happened to Mrs. Brown and Miss Evans after they left me must be told by Mrs. Brown, as related to me by herself when I rejoined her next on board the *Carpathia*. Miss Evans led the way, she said, as they neared the rail where what proved to be the last lifeboat was being loaded, but in a spirit of most heroic self-sacrifice Miss Evans insisted upon Mrs. Brown's taking precedence in being assisted aboard the boat. "You go first," she said. "You are married and have children." But when Miss Evans attempted to follow after, she was unable to do so for some unknown cause. The women in the boat were not able, it would appear, to pull Miss Evans in. It was necessary for her first to clear the four feet high ship's gunwale, and no man or member of the crew was at this particular point to lift her over. I have questioned Mr. Lightoller several times about this, but he has not been able to give any satisfactory explanation and cannot understand it, for when he gave orders to lower away, there was no woman in sight. I have further questioned him as to whether there was an interval between the ship's rail and the lifeboat he was loading, but he says, "No," for until the very last boat he stood, as has already been described, with one foot planted on the ship's gunwale and the other in the lifeboat. I had thought that the list of the ship might have caused too much of an interval for him to have done this. Perhaps what I have read in a letter of Mrs. Brown may furnish some reason why Miss Evans' efforts to board the lifeboat, in which there was plenty of room for her, were unavailing. "Never mind," she is said to have called out, "I will go on a later boat." She then ran away and was not seen again; but there was no later boat, and it would seem that after a momentary impulse, being disappointed and being unable to get into the boat, she went aft on the port side, and no one saw her again. Neither the second officer nor I saw any women on the deck during the interval thereafter of fifteen or twenty minutes before the great ship sank.

An inspection of the American and British Reports shows that all women and children of the first cabin were saved except five. Out of the one hundred and fifty these were the five lost: (1) Miss Evans; (2) Mrs. Straus; (3) Mrs. H. J. Allison, of Montreal; (4) her daughter, Miss Allison, and (5) Miss A. E. Isham, of New York. The first two have already been accounted for. Mrs. Allison and Miss Allison could have been saved had they not chosen to remain on the ship. They refused to enter the lifeboat unless Mr. Allison was allowed to go with them. This statement was made in my presence by Mrs. H. A. Cassobeer, of New York, who related it to Mrs. Allison's brother, Mr. G. F. Johnston, and myself. Those of us who survived among the first cabin passengers will remember this beautiful Mrs. Allison, and will be glad to know of the heroic mould in which she was cast, as exemplified by her fate, which was similar to that of another, Mrs. Straus, who has been memorialized the world over. The fifth lady lost was Miss A. E. Isham, and she is the only one of whom no survivor, so far as I can learn, is able to give any information whatever as to where she was or what she did on that fateful Sunday night. Her relatives, learning that her stateroom, No. C, 49, adjoined mine, wrote me in the hope that I might be able to furnish some information to their sorrowing hearts about her last hours on the shipwrecked *Titanic*. It was with much regret that I replied that I had not seen my neighbor at any time, and, not having the pleasure of her acquaintance, identification was impossible. I was, however, glad to be able to assure her family of one point, viz., that she did not meet with the horrible fate which they feared, in being locked in her stateroom and drowned. I had revisited my stateroom twice after being aroused by the collision, and am sure that she was fully warned of what had happened, and after she left her stateroom it was locked behind her, as was mine.

The simple statement of fact that all of the first cabin women were sent off in the lifeboats and saved, except five—three of whom met heroic death through choice and two by some mischance—is in itself the most sublime tribute that could be paid to the self-sacrifice and the gallantry of the first cabin men, including all the grand heroes who sank with the ship and those of us who survived their fate. All authentic testimony of both first and second cabin passengers is also in evidence that the Captain's order for women and children to be loaded first met with the unanimous approval of us all, and in every instance was carried out both in letter and in spirit. In Second Officer Lightoller's testimony before the Senate Committee, when asked whether the Captain's order was a rule of the sea, he answered that it was "the rule of human nature." There is no doubt in my mind that the men at that quarter where we were would have adopted the same rule spontaneously whether ordered by the Captain, or not. Speaking from my own personal observation, which by comparison with that of the second officer I find in accord with his, all six boat loads, including the last, departed with women and children only, with not a man passenger except Major Peuchen, whose services were enlisted to replace the lack of crew. I may say further that with the single exception of Colonel Astor's plea for the protection of his wife, in delicate condition, there was not one who made a move or a suggestion to enter a boat.

While the light was dim on the decks it was always sufficient for me to recognize anyone with whom I was acquainted, and I am happy in being able to record the names of those I know beyond any doubt whatever, as with me in these last terrible scenes when Lightoller's boats were being lowered and after the last lifeboat had left the ship. The names of these were: James Clinch Smith, Colonel John Jacob Astor, Mr. John B. Thayer and Mr. George D. Widener. So far as I know, and my research has been exhaustive, I am the sole surviving passenger who was with or assisted Lightoller in the loading of the last boats. When I first saw and realized that every lifeboat had left the ship, the sensation felt was not an agreeable one. No thought of fear entered my head, but I experienced a feeling which others may recall when holding the breath in the face of some frightful emergency and when "vox faucibus hæsit," as frequently happened to the old Trojan hero of our school days. This was the nearest approach to fear, if it can be so characterized, that is discernible in an analysis of my actions or feelings while in the midst of the many dangers which beset me during that night of terror. Though still worse and seemingly many hopeless conditions soon prevailed, and unexpected ones, too, when I felt that "any moment might be my last," I had no time to contemplate danger when there was continuous need of quick thought, action and composure withal. Had I become rattled for a moment, or in the slightest degree been undecided during the several emergencies presently cited, I am certain that I never should have lived to tell the tale of my miraculous escape. For it is eminently fitting, in gratitude to my Maker, that I should make the acknowledgment that I know of no recorded instance of Providential deliverance more directly attributable to cause and effect, illustrating the efficacy of prayer and how "God helps those who help themselves." I should have only courted the fate of many hundreds of others had I supinely made no effort to supplement my prayers with all the strength and power which He has granted to me. While I said to myself, "Good-bye to all at home," I hoped and prayed for escape. My mind was nerved to do the duty of the moment, and my muscles seemed to be hardened in preparation for any struggle that might come. When I learned that there was still another boat, the Engelhardt, on the roof of the officers' quarters, I felt encouraged with the thought that here was a chance of getting away before the ship sank; but what was one boat among so many eager to board her?

During my short absence in conducting the ladies to a position of safety, Mr. Thayer and Mr. Widener had disappeared, but I know not whither. Mr. Widener's son, Harry, was probably with them, but Mr. Thayer supposed that his young son, Jack, had left the ship in the same boat with his mother. Messrs. Thayer and Widener must have gone toward the stern during the short interval of my absence. No one at this point had jumped into the sea. If there had been any, both Clinch Smith and I would have known it. After the water struck the bridge forward there were many who rushed aft, climbed over the rail and jumped, but I never saw one of them.

I was now working with the crew at the davits on the starboard side forward, adjusting them, ready for lowering the Engelhardt boat from the roof of the officers' house to the Boat Deck below. Some one of the crew on the roof, where it was, sang out, "Has any passenger a knife?" I took mine out of my pocket and tossed it to him, saying, "Here is a small penknife, if that will do any good." It appeared to me then that there was more trouble than there ought to have been in removing the canvas cover and cutting the boat loose, and that some means should have been available for doing this without any delay. Meantime, four or five long oars were placed aslant against the walls of the officers' house to break the fall of the boat, which was pushed from the roof and slipped with a crash down on the Boat Deck, smashing several of the oars. Clinch Smith and I scurried out of the way and stood leaning with our backs against the rail, watching this procedure and feeling anxious lest the boat might have been stove in, or otherwise injured so as to cause her to leak in the water. The account of the junior Marconi operator, Harold S. Bride, supplements mine. "I saw a collapsible boat," he said, "near a funnel, and went over to it. Twelve men were trying to boost it down to the Boat Deck. They were having an awful time. It was the last boat left. I looked at it longingly a few minutes; then I gave a hand and over she went."

About this time I recall that an officer on the roof of the house called down to the crew at this quarter, "Are there any seamen down there among you?" "Aye, aye, sir," was the response, and quite a number left the Boat Deck to assist in what I supposed to have been the cutting loose of the other Engelhardt boat up there on the roof. Again I heard an inquiry for another knife. I thought I recognized the voice of the second officer working up there with the crew. Lightoller has told me, and has written me as well, that "boat A on the starboard side did not leave the ship,"[1]

---

1. With the evidence on the subject presented later he recognizes that Boat A floated away and was afterwards utilized.

while "B was thrown down to the Boat Deck," and was the one on which he and I eventually climbed. The crew had thrown the Engelhardt boat to the deck, but I did not understand why they were so long about launching it, unless they were waiting to cut the other one loose and launch them both at the same time. Two young men of the crew, nice looking, dressed in white, one tall and the other smaller, were coolly debating as to whether the compartments would hold the ship afloat. They were standing with their backs to the rail looking on at the rest of the crew, and I recall asking one of them why he did not assist.

At this time there were other passengers around, but Clinch Smith was the only one associated with me here to the last. It was about this time, fifteen minutes after the launching of the last lifeboat on the port side, that I heard a noise that spread consternation among us all. This was no less than the water striking the bridge and gurgling up the hatchway forward. It seemed momentarily as if it would reach the Boat Deck. It appeared as if it would take the crew a long time to turn the Engelhardt boat right side up and lift it over the rail, and there were so many ready to board her that she would have been swamped. Probably taking these points into consideration, Clinch Smith made the proposition that we should leave and go toward the stern, still on the starboard side, so he started and I followed immediately after him. We had taken but a few steps in the direction indicated when there arose before us from the decks below, a mass of humanity several lines deep, covering the Boat Deck, facing us, and completely blocking our passage toward the stern.

There were women in the crowd, as well as men, and they seemed to be steerage passengers who had just come up from the decks below. Instantly, when they saw us and the water on the deck chasing us from behind, they turned in the opposite direction towards the stern. This brought them at that point plumb against the iron fence and railing which divide the first and second cabin passengers. Even among these people there was no hysterical cry, or evidence of panic, but oh, the agony of it! Clinch Smith and I instantly saw that we could make no progress ahead, and with the water following us behind over the deck, we were in a desperate place. I can never forget the exact point on the ship where he and I were located, viz., at the opening of the angle made by the walls of the officers' house and only a short distance abaft the *Titanic*'s forward "expansion joint." Clinch Smith was immediately on my left, nearer the apex of the angle, and our backs were turned toward the ship's rail and the sea. Looking up toward the roof of the officers' house I saw a man to the right of me and above lying on his stomach on the roof, with his legs dangling over. Clinch Smith jumped to reach this roof, and I promptly followed. The efforts of both of us failed. I was loaded down with heavy long-skirted overcoat and Norfolk coat beneath, with clumsy life-preserver over all, which made my jump fall short. As I came down, the water struck my right side. I crouched down into it preparatory to jumping with it, and rose as if on the crest of a wave on the seashore. This expedient brought the attainment of the object I had in view. I was able to reach the roof and the iron railing that is along the edge of it, and pulled myself over on top of the officers' house on my stomach near the base of the second funnel. The feat which I instinctively accomplished was the simple one, familiar to all bathers in the surf at the seashore. I had no time to advise Clinch Smith to adopt it. To my utter dismay, a hasty glance to my left and right showed that he had not followed my example, and that the wave, if I may call it such, which had mounted me to the roof, had completely covered him, as well as all people on both sides of me, including the man I had first seen athwart the roof.

I was thus parted forever from my friend, Clinch Smith, with whom I had agreed to remain to the last struggle. I felt almost a pang of responsibility for our separation; but he was not in sight and there was no chance of rendering assistance. His ultimate fate is a matter of conjecture. Hemmed in by the mass of people toward the stern, and cornered in the locality previously described, it seems certain that as the ship keeled over and sank, his body was caught in the angle or in the coils of rope and other appurtenances on the deck and borne down to the depths below. There could not be a braver man than James Clinch Smith. He was the embodiment of coolness and courage during the whole period of the disaster. While in constant touch and communication with him at the various points on the ship when we were together on this tragic night, he never showed the slightest sign of fear, but manifested the same quiet imperturbable manner so well known to all of his friends, who join with his family in mourning his loss. His conduct should be an inspiration to us all, and an appropriate epitaph to his memory taken from the words of Christ would be: "Greater love hath no man than this, that a man lay down his life for his friend."

CHAPTER III

The Foundering of the *Titanic*

There is sorrow on the sea; it cannot be quiet.—Jeremiah 49: 23

Before I resume the story of my personal escape it is pertinent that I should, at this juncture, discuss certain points wherein the statements of survivors are strangely at variance.

First: Was there an explosion of the ship's boilers?

I am of opinion that there was none, because I should have been conscious of it. When aboard ship I should have heard it and felt it, but I did not. As my senses were on the lookout for every danger, I cannot conceive it possible that an explosion occurred without my being made aware of it. When I went down holding on to the ship and was under water, I heard no sound indicating anything of the sort, and when I came to the surface there was no ship in sight. Furthermore, there was no perceptible wave which such a disturbance would have created.

The two ranking surviving officers of the *Titanic*, viz., Second Officer Lightoller and Third Officer Pitman, with whom I had a discussion on this and other points in almost daily conversation in my cabin on the *Carpathia*, agreed with me that there was no explosion of the boilers. The second officer and myself had various similar experiences, and, as will be noticed in the course of this narrative, we were very near together during all the perils of that awful night. The only material difference worth noting was the manner in which each parted company with the ship, and finally reached the bottom-up Engelhardt boat on top of which we made our escape. According to his testimony before the

Senate Committee, he stood on the roof of the officers' quarters in front of the first funnel, facing forward, and as the ship dived, he dived also, while I held on to the iron railing on the same roof, near the second funnel, as has been described, and as the ship sank I was pulled down with it. The distance between us on the ship was then about fifteen yards.

There are so many newspaper and other published reports citing the statements of certain survivors as authority for this story of an explosion of the boilers that the reading world generally has been made to believe it. Among the names of passengers whose alleged statements (I have received letters repudiating some of these interviews) are thus given credence, I have read those of Miss Cornelia Andrews, of Hudson, N. Y.; Mrs. W. E. Carter, of Philadelphia, Pa.; Mr. John Pillsbury Snyder, of Minneapolis, Minn.; Miss Minahan, of Fond du Lac, Wis., and Lady Duff Gordon, of England, all of whom, according to the newspaper reports, describe their position in the lifeboats around the ship and how they heard, or saw, the "ship blow up," or "the boilers explode" with one or two explosions just before the ship sank out of their sight. On the other hand, Mr. Hugh Woolner told me on the *Carpathia* that from his position in the lifeboat, which he claims was the nearest one to the *Titanic* when she sank some seventy-five yards away, there was a terrific noise on the ship, as she slanted towards the head before the final plunge, which sounded like the crashing of millions of dishes of crockery. Woolner and I when on board the *Carpathia*, as presently described, had our cabin together, where we were visited by Officers Lightoller and Pitman. This was one of the points we discussed together, and the conclusion was at once reached as to the cause of this tremendous crash. Since then, Lightoller has been subjected to rigid examination before this country's and England's Investigating Committees, and has been a party to discussions with experts, including the designers and builders of the *Titanic*. His conclusion expressed on the *Carpathia* is now strengthened, and he says that there was no explosion of the boilers and that the great noise which was mistaken for it was due to "the boilers leaving their beds" on E Deck when the ship was aslant and, with their great weight, sliding along the deck, crushing and tearing through the doomed vessel forward toward the bow. Third Officer Pitman also gave his testimony on this, as well as the next point considered. Before the Senate Committee he said: "Then she turned right on end and made a big plunge forward. The *Titanic* did not break asunder. I heard reports like big guns in the distance. I assumed the great bulkheads had gone to pieces." Cabin-steward Samuel Rule said: "I think the noise we heard was that of the boilers and engines breaking away from their seatings and falling down through the forward bulkhead. At the time it occurred, the ship was standing nearly upright in the water."

The peculiar way in which the *Titanic* is described as hesitating and assuming a vertical position before her final dive to the depths below can be accounted for only on this hypothesis of the sliding of the boilers from their beds. A second-cabin passenger, Mr. Lawrence Beesley, a Cambridge University man, has written an excellent book about the *Titanic* disaster, dwelling especially upon the lessons to be learned from it. His account given to the newspapers also contains the most graphic description from the viewpoint of those in the lifeboats, telling how the great ship looked before her final plunge. He "was a mile or two miles away," he writes, "when the oarsmen lay on their oars and all in the lifeboat were motionless as we watched the ship in absolute silence—save some who would not look and buried their heads on each other's shoulders. . . . As we gazed awestruck, she tilted slightly up, revolving apparently about a centre of gravity just astern of amidships until she attained a vertical upright position, and there she remained—motionless! As she swung up, her lights, which had shone without a flicker all night, went out suddenly, then came on again for a single flash and then went out altogether; and as they did so there came a noise which many people, wrongly, I think, have described as an explosion. It has always seemed to me that it was nothing but the engines and machinery coming loose from their place and bearings and falling through the compartments, smashing everything in their way. It was partly a roar, partly a groan, partly a rattle and partly a smash, and it was not a sudden roar as an explosion would be; it went on successively for some seconds, possibly fifteen or twenty, as the heavy machinery dropped down to the bottom (now the bows) of the ship; I suppose it fell through the end and sank first before the ship. (For evidence of shattered timbers, see Hagan's testimony, p. 156.) But it was a noise no one had heard before and no one wishes to hear again. It was stupefying, stupendous, as it came to us along the water. It was as if all the heavy things one could think of had been thrown downstairs from the top of a house, smashing each other, and the stairs and everything in the way.

"Several apparently authentic accounts have been given in which definite stories of explosions have been related—in some cases even with wreckage blown up and the ship broken in two; but I think such accounts will not stand close analysis. In the first place, the fires had been withdrawn and the steam allowed to escape some time before she sank, and the possibility from explosion from this cause seems very remote."

Second: Did the ship break in two?

I was on the *Carpathia* when I first heard any one make reference to this point. The seventeen-year-old son of Mr. John B. Thayer, "Jack" Thayer, Jr., and his young friend from Philadelphia, R. N. Williams, Jr., the tennis expert, in describing their experiences to me were positive that they saw the ship split in two. This was from their position in the water on the starboard quarter. "Jack" Thayer gave this same description to an artist, who reproduced it in an illustration in the New York *Herald*, which many of us have seen. Some of the passengers, whose names I have just mentioned, are also cited by the newspapers as authority for the statements that the ship "broke in two," that she "buckled amidships," that she "was literally torn to pieces," etc. On the other hand, there is much testimony available which is at variance with this much-advertised sensational newspaper account. Summing up its investigation of this point the Senate Committee's Report reads: "There have been many conflicting statements as to whether the ship broke in two, but the preponderance of evidence is to the effect that she assumed an almost end-on position and sank intact." This was as Lightoller testified before the Committee, that the *Titanic*'s decks were "absolutely intact" when she went down. On this point, too, Beesley is in accord, from his viewpoint in the lifeboat some distance away out of danger, whence, more composedly than others, he could see the last of the ill-fated ship as the men lay on their oars watching until she disappeared. "No phenomenon," he continues, "like that pictured in some American and English papers occurred—that of the ship breaking in two, and the two ends being raised above the surface. When the noise was over, the *Titanic* was still upright like a column; we could see her now only as the stern and some 150 feet of her stood outlined against the star-specked sky, looming black in the darkness, and in this position she continued for some minutes—I think as much as five minutes—but it may have been less. Then, as sinking back a little at the stern, I thought she slid slowly forwards through the water and dived slantingly down."

From my personal viewpoint I also know that the *Titanic*'s decks were intact at the time she sank, and when I sank with her, there was over seven-sixteenths of the ship already under water, and there was no indication then of any impending break of the deck or ship. I recently visited the sister ship of the *Titanic*, viz., the *Olympic*, at her dock in New York harbor. This was for the purpose of still further familiarizing myself with the corresponding localities which were the scene of my personal experiences on the *Titanic*, and which are referred to in this narrative. The only difference in the deck plan of the sister ship which I noted, and which the courteous officers of the *Olympic* mentioned, is that the latter ship's Deck A is not glass-enclosed like the *Titanic*'s; but one of the principal points of discovery that I made during my investigation concerns this matter of the alleged breaking in two of this magnificent ship. The White Star Line officers pointed out to me what they called the ship's "forward expansion joint," and they claimed the *Titanic* was so constructed that she must have split in two at this point, if she did so at all. I was interested in observing that this "expansion joint" was less than twelve feet forward from that point on the Boat

Deck whence I jumped, as described (to the iron railing on the roof of the officers' quarters). It is indicated by a black streak of leather-covering running transversely across the deck and then up the vertical white wall of the officers' house. This "joint" extends, however, only through the Boat Deck and Decks A and B, which are superimposed on Deck C. If there was any splitting in two, it seems to me also that this superstructure, weakly joined, would have been the part to split; but it certainly did not. It was only a few seconds before the time of the alleged break that I stepped across this dividing line of the two sections and went down with the after section about twelve feet from this "expansion joint."

One explanation which I offer of what must be a delusion on the part of the advocates of the "break-in-two" theory is that when the forward funnel fell, as hereafter described, it may have looked as if the ship itself was splitting in two, particularly to the young men who are cited as authority.

Third: Did either the Captain or the First Officer shoot himself?

Notwithstanding all the current rumors and newspaper statements answering this question affirmatively, I have been unable to find any passenger or member of the crew cited as authority for the statement that either Captain Smith or First Officer Murdoch did anything of the sort. On the contrary, so far as relates to Captain Smith, there are several witnesses, including Harold S. Bride, the junior Marconi operator, who saw him at the last on the bridge of his ship, and later, when sinking and struggling in the water. Neither can I discover any authentic testimony about First Officer Murdoch's shooting himself. On the contrary, I find fully sufficient evidence that he did not. He was a brave and efficient officer and no sufficient motive for self-destruction can be advanced. He performed his full duty under difficult circumstances, and was entitled to praise and honor. During the last fifteen minutes before the ship sank, I was located at that quarter forward on the Boat Deck, starboard side, where Murdoch was in command and where the crew under him were engaged in the vain attempt of launching the Engelhardt boat. The report of a pistol shot during this interval ringing in my ears within a few feet of me would certainly have attracted my attention, and later, when I moved astern, the distance between us was not so great as to prevent my hearing it. The "big wave" or "giant wave," described by Harold Bride, swept away Murdoch and the crew from the Boat Deck first before it struck me, and when I rose with it to the roof of the officers' house, Bride's reported testimony fits in with mine so far as relates to time, place, and circumstance, and I quote his words as follows: "About ten minutes before the ship sank, Captain Smith gave word for every man to look to his own safety. I sprang to aid the men struggling to launch the life raft (Engelhardt boat), and we had succeeded in getting it to the edge of the ship when a giant wave carried it away." Lightoller also told me on board the *Carpathia* that he saw Murdoch when he was engulfed by the water and that if before this a pistol had been fired within the short distance that separated them, he also is confident that he would have heard it.

Fourth: On which side did the ship list?

The testimony on this point, which at first blush appears conflicting, proves on investigation not at all so, but just what was to be expected from the mechanical construction of the ship. We find the most authoritative testimony in evidence that the *Titanic* listed on the starboard side, and again, on equally authoritative testimony, that she listed on the port side. Quartermaster Hitchens, who was at the wheel when the iceberg struck the ship, testified on this point before the Senate Committee as follows: "The Captain came back to the wheel house and looked at the commutator (clinometer) in front of the compass, which is a little instrument like a clock to tell you how the ship is listing. The ship had a list of five degrees to the starboard about five or ten minutes after the impact." Mr. Karl Behr, the well-known tennis player, interviewed by the New York *Tribune* is quoted as saying: "We had just retired when the collision came. I pulled on my clothes and went down the deck to the Beckwith cabin and, after I had roused them, I noted that the ship listed to the starboard, and that was the first thing that made me think that we

were in for serious trouble." On the other hand, the first time I
noticed this list was, as already described in my narrative, when
I met Clinch Smith in the companionway and we saw a slight list
to port, which gave us the first warning of how serious the accident was. The next and last time, as has also been described,
was when Second Officer Lightoller ordered all passengers to
the starboard side because of the very palpable list to port, when
the great ship suddenly appeared to be about to topple over.
Lightoller also corroborates the statement as to this list on the
port side. Other witnesses might be quoted, some of whom tes-
tify to the starboard list, and others to the one to port. The conclusion, therefore, is reached that the *Titanic* listed at one time
to starboard and at another time to port. This is as it should be
because of the transverse water-tight compartments which made
the water, immediately after the compact, rush from the starboard quarter to the port, and then back again, keeping the ship
balancing on her keel until she finally sank. If she had been constructed otherwise, with longitudinal compartments only, it is
evident that after the impact on the starboard side, the *Titanic*
would have listed only to the starboard side, and after a very
much shorter interval would have careened over on that quarter,
and a much smaller proportion of lives would have been saved.

CHAPTER IV

Struggling in the Water for Life

Out of the deep have I called unto Thee, O Lord.—Ps. 130: 1

I now resume the narrative description of my miraculous escape, and it is with considerable diffidence that I do so, for the personal equation monopolizes more attention than may be pleasing to my readers who are not relatives or intimate friends.

As may be noticed in Chapter II, it was Clinch Smith's suggestion and on his initiative that we left that point on the starboard side of the Boat Deck where the crew, under Chief Officer Wilde and First Officer Murdoch, were in vain trying to launch the Engelhardt Boat B which had been thrown down from the roof of the officers' quarters forward of the first funnel. I say "Boat B" because I have the information to that effect in a letter from Second Officer Lightoller. Confirmation of this statement I also find in the reported interview of a Saloon Steward, Thomas Whitely, in the New York *Tribune* the day after the *Carpathia*'s arrival. An analysis of his statement shows that Boat A became entangled and was abandoned, while he saw the other, bottom up and filled with people. It was on this boat that he also eventually climbed and was saved with the rest of us. Clinch Smith and I got away from this point just before the water reached it and drowned Chief Officer Wilde and First Officer Murdoch, and others who were not successful in effecting a lodgment on the boat as it was swept off the deck. This moment was the first fateful crisis of the many that immediately followed. As bearing upon it I quote the reported statement of Harold S. Bride, the junior Marconi operator. His account also helps to determine the fate of Captain Smith. He says: "Then came the Captain's voice [from the bridge to the Marconi operators], 'Men, you have done your full duty. You can do no more. Abandon your cabin. Now, it is every man for himself.'" "Phillips continued to work," he says, "for about ten minutes or about fifteen minutes after the Captain had released him. The water was then coming into our cabin. . . . I went to the place where I had seen the collapsible boat on the Boat Deck and to my surprise I saw the boat, and the men still trying to push it off. They could not do it. I went up to them and was just lending a hand when a large wave came awash of the deck. The big wave carried the boat off. I had hold of an oarlock and I went off with it. The next I knew I was in the boat. But that was not all. I was in the boat and the boat was upside down and I was under it. . . . How I got out from under the boat I do not know, but I felt a breath at last."

From this it appears evident that, so far as Clinch Smith is concerned, it would have been better to have stayed by this Engelhardt boat to the last, for here he had a chance of escape like Bride and others of the crew who clung to it, but which I only reached again after an incredibly long swim under water. The next crisis, which was the fatal one to Clinch Smith and to the great mass of people that suddenly arose before us as I followed him astern, has already been described. The simple expedient of jumping with the "big wave" as demonstrated above carried me to safety, away from a dangerous position to the highest part of the ship; but I was the only one who adopted it successfully. The force of the wave that struck Clinch Smith and the others undoubtedly knocked most of them there unconscious against the walls of the officers' quarters and other appurtenances of the ship on the Boat Deck. As the ship keeled over forward, I believe that their bodies were caught in the angles of this deck, or entangled in the ropes, and in these other appurtenances thereon, and sank with the ship.

My holding on to the iron railing just when I did prevented my being knocked unconscious. I pulled myself over on the roof on my stomach, but before I could get to my feet I was in a whirlpool of water, swirling round and round, as I still tried to cling to the railing as the ship plunged to the depths below. Down, down, I went: it seemed a great distance. There was a very noticeable pressure upon my ears, though there must have been plenty of air that the ship carried down with it. When under water I retained, as it appears, a sense of general direction, and, as soon as I could do so, swam away from the starboard side of the ship, as I knew my life depended upon it. I swam with all my strength, and I seemed endowed with an extra supply for the occasion. I was incited to desperate effort by the thought of boiling water, or steam, from the expected explosion of the ship's boilers, and that I would be scalded to death, like the sailors of whom I had read in the account of the British battle-ship *Victoria* sunk in collision with the *Camperdown* in the Mediterranean in 1893. Second Officer Lightoller told me he also had the same idea, and that if the fires had not been drawn the boilers would explode and the water become boiling hot. As a consequence, the plunge in the icy water produced no sense of coldness whatever, and I had no thought of cold until later on when I climbed on the bottom of the upturned boat. My being drawn down by suction to a greater depth was undoubtedly checked to some degree by the life-preserver which I wore, but it is to the buoyancy of the water, caused by the volume of air rising from the sinking ship, that I attributed the assistance which enabled me to strike out and swim faster and further under water than I ever did before. I held my breath for what seemed an interminable time until I could scarcely stand it any longer, but I congratulated myself then and there that not one drop of sea-water was allowed to enter my mouth. With renewed determination and set jaws, I swam on. Just at the moment I thought that for lack of breath I would have to give in, I seemed to have been provided with a second wind, and it was just then that the thought that this was my last moment came upon me. I wanted to convey the news of how I died to my loved ones at home. As I swam beneath the surface of the ocean, I prayed that my spirit could go to them and say, "Good-bye, until we meet again in heaven." In this connection, the thought was in my mind of a well authenticated experience of mental telepathy that occurred to a member of my wife's family. Here in my case was a similar experience of a shipwrecked loved one, and I thought if I prayed hard enough that this, my last wish to communicate with my wife and daughter, might be granted.

To what extent my prayer was answered let Mrs. Gracie describe in her own written words, as follows: "I was in my room at my sister's house, where I was visiting, in New York. After retiring, being unable to rest I questioned myself several times over, wondering what it was that prevented the customary long and peaceful slumber, lately enjoyed. 'What is the matter?' I uttered. A voice in reply seemed to say, 'On your knees and pray.' Instantly, I literally obeyed with my prayer book in my hand, which by chance opened at the prayer 'For those at Sea.' The thought then flashed through my mind, 'Archie is praying for me.' I continued wide awake until a little before five o'clock a.m., by the watch that lay beside me. About 7 a.m. I dozed a while and then got up to dress for breakfast. At 8 o'clock my sister, Mrs. Dalliba Dutton, came softly to the door, newspaper in hand, to gently break the tragic news that the *Titanic* had sunk, and showed me the list of only twenty names saved, headed with '*Colonel* Archibald Butt'; but my husband's name was not included. My head sank in her protecting arms as I murmured helplessly, 'He is all I have in the whole world.' I could only pray for strength, and later in the day, believing myself a widow, I wrote to my daughter, who was in the care of our housekeeper and servants in our Washington home, 'Cannot you see your father in his tenderness for women and children, helping them all, and then going down with the ship? If he has gone, I will not live long, but I would not have him take a boat.'"

But let me now resume my personal narrative. With this second wind under water there came to me a new lease of life and strength, until finally I noticed by the increase of light that I was drawing near to the surface. Though it was not daylight, the clear star-lit night made a noticeable difference in the degree of light immediately below the surface of the water. As I was rising, I came in contact with ascending wreckage, but the only thing I struck of material size was a small plank, which I tucked under my right arm. This circumstance brought with it the reflection that it was advisable for me to secure what best I could to keep me afloat on the surface until succor arrived. When my head at last rose above the water, I detected a piece of wreckage like a wooden crate, and I eagerly seized it as a nucleus of the projected raft to be constructed from what flotsam and jetsam I might collect. Looking about me, I could see no *Titanic* in sight. She had entirely disappeared beneath the calm surface of the ocean and without a sign of any wave. That the sea had swallowed her up with all her precious belongings was indicated by the slight sound of a gulp behind me as the water closed over her. The length of time that I was under water can be estimated by the fact that I sank with her, and when I came up there was no ship in sight. The accounts of others as to the length of time it took the *Titanic* to sink afford the best measure of the interval I was below the surface.

What impressed me at the time that my eyes beheld the horrible scene was a thin light-gray smoky vapor that hung like a pall a few feet above the broad expanse of sea that was covered with a mass of tangled wreckage. That it was a tangible vapor, and not a product of imagination, I feel well assured. It may have been caused by smoke or steam rising to the surface around the area where the ship had sunk. At any rate it produced a supernatural effect, and the pictures I had seen by Dante and the description I had read in my Virgil of the infernal regions, of Charon, and the River Lethe, were then uppermost in my thoughts. Add to this, within the area described, which was as far as my eyes could reach, there arose to the sky the most horrible sounds ever heard by mortal man except by those of us who survived this terrible tragedy. The agonizing cries of death from over a thousand throats, the wails and groans of the suffering, the shrieks of the terror-stricken and the awful gaspings for breath of those in the last throes of drowning, none of us will ever forget to our dying day. "Help! Help! Boat ahoy! Boat ahoy!" and "My God! My God!" were the heartrending cries and shrieks of men, which floated to us over the surface of the dark waters continuously for the next hour, but as time went on, growing weaker and weaker until they died out entirely.

As I clung to my wreckage, I noticed just in front of me, a few yards away, a group of three bodies with heads in the water, face downwards, and just behind me to my right another body, all giving unmistakable evidence of being drowned. Possibly these had gone down to the depths as I had done, but did not have the lung power that I had to hold the breath and swim under water, an accomplishment which I had practised from my school days. There was no one alive or struggling in the water or calling for aid within the immediate vicinity of where I arose to the surface. I threw my right leg over the wooden crate in an attempt to straddle and balance myself on top of it, but I turned over in a somersault with it under water, and up to the surface again. What may be of interest is the thought that then occurred to me of the accounts and pictures of a wreck, indelibly impressed upon my memory when a boy, because of my acquaintance with some of the victims, of a frightful disaster of that day, namely the wreck of the *Ville de Havre* in the English Channel in 1873, and I had in mind Mrs. Bulkley's description, and the picture of her clinging to some wreckage as a rescue boat caught sight of her, bringing the comforting words over the water, "We are English sailors coming to save you." I looked around, praying for a similar interposition of Fate, but I knew the thought of a rescuing boat was a vain one—for had not all the lifeboats, loaded with women and children, departed from the ship fifteen or twenty minutes before I sank with it? And had I not seen the procession of them on the port side fading away from our sight?

But my prayerful thought and hope were answered in an unexpected direction. I espied to my left, a considerable distance away, a better vehicle of escape than the wooden crate on which my attempt to ride had resulted in a second ducking. What I saw was no less than the same Engelhardt, or "surf-boat," to whose launching I had lent my efforts, until the water broke upon the ship's Boat Deck where we were. On top of this upturned boat, half reclining on her bottom, were now more than a dozen men, whom, by their dress, I took to be all members of the crew of the ship. Thank God, I did not hesitate a moment in discarding the friendly crate that had been my first aid. I struck out through the wreckage and after a considerable swim reached the port side amidships of this Engelhardt boat, which with her companions, wherever utilized, did good service in saving the lives of many others. All honor to the Dane, Captain Engelhardt of Copenhagen, who built them. I say "port side" because this boat as it was propelled through the water had Lightoller in the bow and Bride at the stern, and I believe an analysis of the testimony shows that the actual bow of the boat was turned about by the wave that struck it on the Boat Deck and the splash of the funnel thereafter, so that its bow pointed in an opposite direction to that of the ship. There was one member of the crew on this craft at the bow and another at the stern who had "pieces of boarding," improvised paddles, which were used effectually for propulsion.

When I reached the side of the boat I met with a doubtful reception, and, as no extending hand was held out to me, I grabbed, by the muscle of the left arm, a young member of the crew nearest and facing me. At the same time I threw my right leg over the boat astraddle, pulling myself aboard, with a friendly lift to my foot given by someone astern as I assumed a reclining position with them on the bottom of the capsized boat. Then after me came a dozen other swimmers who clambered around and whom we helped aboard. Among them was one completely exhausted, who came on the same port side as myself. I pulled him in and he lay face downward in front of me for several hours, until just before dawn he was able to stand up with the rest of us. The journey of our craft from the scene of the disaster will be described in the following chapter. The moment of getting aboard this upturned boat was one of supreme mental relief, more so than any other until I reached the deck of the hospitable *Carpathia* on the next morning. I now felt for the first time after the lifeboats left us aboard ship that I had some chance of escape from the horrible fate of drowning in the icy waters of the middle Atlantic. Every moment of time during the many experiences of that night, it seemed as if I had all the God-given physical strength and courage needed for each emergency, and never suffered an instant from any exhaustion, or required the need of a helping hand. The only time of any stress whatever was during the swim, just described, under water, at the moment when I gained my second wind which brought me to the surface gasping somewhat, but full of vigor. I was all the time on the lookout for the next danger that was to be overcome. I kept my presence of mind and courage throughout it all. Had I lost either for one moment, I never could have escaped to tell the tale. This is in answer to many questions as to my personal sensations during these scenes and the successive dangers which I encountered. From a psychological viewpoint also, it may be a study of interest illustrating the power of mind over matter. The sensation of fear has a visible effect upon one. It palsies one's thoughts and actions. One becomes thereby short of breath; the heart actually beats quicker and as one loses one's head one grows desperate and is gone. I have questioned those who have been near drowning and who know this statement to be a fact. It is the same in other emergencies, and the lesson to be learned is that we should—

> Let courage rise with danger,
> And strength to strength oppose.

To attain this courage in the hour of danger is very much a matter of physical, mental and religious training. But courage and strength would have availed me little had I not providentially escaped from being knocked senseless, or maimed, as so many other strong swimmers undoubtedly were. The narrow escapes that I had from being thus knocked unconscious could be recapitulated, and I still bear the scars on my body of wounds received at the moment, or moments, when I was struck by some undefined object. I received a blow on the top of my head, but I did not notice it or the other wounds until I arrived on board the *Carpathia*, when I found inflamed cuts on both my legs and bruises on my knees, which soon became black and blue, and I was sore to the touch all over my body for several days.

It is necessary for me to turn to the accounts of others for a description of what happened during the interval that I was under water. My information about it is derived from many sources and includes various points of general interest, showing how the *Titanic* looked when she foundered, the undisputed facts that there was very little suction and that the forward funnel broke from the ship, falling on the starboard side into the sea. Various points of personal interest are also derived from the same source which the reader can analyze, for estimating the interval that I was below the surface of the ocean and the distance covered in my swim under water; for after I rose to the surface it appears that I had passed under both the falling funnel and then under the upturned boat, and a considerable distance beyond. Had I gone but a short distance under water and arisen straight up, I should have met the horrible fate of being struck by the falling funnel which, according to the evidence submitted, must have killed or drowned a number of unfortunates struggling in the water. I select these accounts of my shipwrecked companions, which supplement my personal experience, particularly the accounts of the same reliable and authoritative witnesses already cited, and from those who were rescued, as I was, on the bottom of the upset Engelhardt boat.

The following is from the account of Mr. Beesley: "The water was by now up to the last row of portholes. We were about two miles from her, and the crew insisted that such a tremendous wave would be formed by suction as she went down, that we ought to get as far as possible away. The 'Captain' (as he calls Stoker Fred Barrett), and all, lay on their oars. Presently, about 2 a.m. (2:15 a.m. per book account), as near as I can remember, we observed her settling very rapidly, with the bow and bridge completely under water, and concluded it was now only a question of minutes before she went; and so it proved. She slowly tilted, straight on end, with the stern vertically upward. . . . To our amazement, she remained in that upright position for a time which I estimate as five minutes." On a previous page of my narrative, I have already quoted from his book account how "the stern and some 150 feet of the ship stood outlined against the star-specked sky, looming black in the darkness, and in this position she continued for some minutes—I think as much as five minutes, but it may have been less." Now, when I disappeared under the sea, sinking with the ship, there is nothing more surely established in my testimony than that about nine-sixteenths of the *Titanic* was still out of the water, and when my head reached the surface she had entirely disappeared.

The New York *Times*, of April 19, 1912, contained the story of Mr. and Mrs. D. H. Bishop, first cabin passengers from Dowagiac, Michigan. Their short account is one of the best I have read. As they wrote it independently of Beesley's account, and from a different point of view, being in another lifeboat (No. 7, the first to leave the ship), the following corroborative testimony, taken from their story, helps to establish the truth:

"We did not begin to understand the situation till we were perhaps a mile away from the *Titanic*. Then we could see the row of lights along the deck begin to slant gradually upward from the bow. Very slowly the lines of light began to point downward at a greater and greater angle. The sinking was so slow that you could not perceive the lights of the deck changing their position. The slant seemed to be greater about every quarter of an hour. That was the only difference.

"In a couple of hours she began to go down more rapidly. . . . Suddenly the ship seemed to shoot up out of the water and stand there perpendicularly. It seemed to us that it stood *upright in the water for four full minutes*.[1] Then it began to slide gently downwards. Its speed increased as it went down head first, so that the stern shot down with a rush."

Harold Bride, who was swept from the Boat Deck, held on to an oarlock of the Engelhardt boat (which Clinch Smith and I had left a few moments before, as has already been described). I have cited his account of coming up under the boat and then clambering upon it. He testifies to there being no suction and adds the following: "I suppose I was 150 feet away when the *Titanic*, on her nose with her after-quarter sticking straight up into the air, began to settle—slowly. When at last the waves

1. Italics are mine. —AUTHOR.

washed over her rudder, there was not the least bit of suction I could feel. She must have kept going just so slowly as she had been." Second Officer Lightoller too, in his conversation with me, verified his testimony before the Senate Committee that, "The last boat, a flat collapsible (the Engelhardt), to put off was the one on top of the officers' quarters. Men jumped upon it on deck and waited for the water to float it off. The forward funnel fell into the water, just missing the raft (as he calls our upset boat). The funnel probably killed persons in the water. This was the boat I eventually got on. About thirty men clambered out of the water on to it."

Seventeen-year-old "Jack" Thayer was also on the starboard side of the ship, and jumped from the rail before the Engelhardt boat was swept from the Boat Deck by the "giant wave." Young Thayer's reported description of this is as follows:

"I jumped out, feet first, went down, and as I came up I was pushed away from the ship by some force. I was sucked down again, and as I came up I was pushed out again and twisted around by a large wave, coming up in the midst of a great deal of small wreckage. My hand touched the canvas fender of an overturned lifeboat. I looked up and saw some men on the top. One of them helped me up. In a short time the bottom was covered with twenty-five or thirty men. The assistant wireless operator (Bride) was right next to me holding on to me and kneeling in the water."

In my conversations with Thayer, Lightoller and others, it appears that the funnel fell in the water between the Engelhardt boat and the ship, washing the former further away from the *Titanic*'s starboard side.

Since the foregoing was written, the testimony before the United States Senate Committee has been printed in pamphlet form, from which I have been able to obtain other evidence, and particularly that of Second Officer Lightoller in regard to the last quarter of an hour or so on board the ship and up to the time we reached the upset boat. I have also obtained and substantiated other evidence bearing upon the same period. Mr. Lightoller testified as follows: "Half an hour, or three-quarters of an hour before I left the ship, when it was taking a heavy list—not a heavy list—a list over to port, the order was called, I think by the chief officer, 'Everyone on the starboard side to straighten her up,' which I repeated. When I left the ship I saw no women or children aboard whatever. All the boats on the port side were lowered with the exception of one—the last boat, which was stowed on top of the officers' quarters. We had not time to launch it, nor yet to open it. When all the other boats were away, I called for men to go up there; told them to cut her adrift and throw her down. It floated off the ship, and I understand the men standing on top, who assisted to launch it down, jumped on to it as it was on the deck and floated off with it. It was the collapsible type of boat, and the bottom-up boat we eventually got on. When this lifeboat floated off the ship, we were thrown off a couple of times. When I came to it, it was bottom-up and there was no one on it. Immediately after finding that overturned lifeboat, and when I came alongside of it, there were quite a lot of us in the water around it preparatory to getting up on it. Then the forward funnel fell down. It fell alongside of the lifeboat about four inches clear of it on all the people there alongside of the boat. Eventually, about thirty of us got on it: Mr. Thayer, Bride, the second Marconi operator, and Col. Gracie. I think all the rest were firemen taken out of the water."

Compare this with the description given by J. Hagan in correspondence which he began with me last May. J. Hagan is a poor chap, who described himself in this correspondence as one who "was working my passage to get to America for the first time," and I am convinced that he certainly earned it, and, moreover, was one of us on that upset boat that night. His name does not appear on the list of the crew and must not be confounded with "John Hagan, booked as fireman on the steamer, who sailed for England April 20th on the *Lapland*," whereas our John Hagan was admitted to St. Vincent's hospital on April 22nd. In describing this period John Hagan says it was by the Captain's orders, when the ship was listing to port, that passengers were sent to the starboard side to straighten the ship. He went half-way and returned to where Lightoller was loading the last boat lowered. Lightoller told him there was another boat on the roof of the officers' house if he cared to get it down. This was the Engelhardt Boat B which, with three others, he could not open until assisted by three more, and then they pushed it, upside down, on the Boat Deck below. Hagan cut the string of the oars and was passing the first oar down to the others, who had left him, when the boat floated into the water, upside down. He jumped to the Boat Deck and into the water after the boat and "clung to the tail end of the keel." The ship was shaking very much, part of it being under water. "On looking up at it, I could see death in a minute for us as the forward funnel was falling and it looked a certainty it would strike our boat and smash it to pieces; but the funnel missed us about a yard, splashing our boat thirty yards outward from the ship, and washing off several who had got on when the boat first floated." Hagan managed to cling to it but got a severe soaking. The cries of distress that he heard near by were an experience he can never forget. It appeared to him that the flooring of the ship forward had broken away and was floating all around. Some of the men on the upset boat made use of some pieces of boarding for paddles with which to help keep clear of the ship.

John Collins, assistant cook on the *Titanic*, also gave his interesting testimony before the Senate Committee. He appears to have come on deck at the last moment on the starboard side and witnessed the Engelhardt boat when it floated off into the sea, he being carried off by the same wave when he was amidships on the bow as the ship sank, and kept down under water for at least two or three minutes. When he came up, he saw this boat again—the same boat on which he had seen men working when the waves washed it off the deck, and the men clinging to it. He was only about four or five yards off and swam over to it and got on to it. He says he is sure there were probably fifteen thereon at the time he got on. Those who were on the boat did not help him to get on. They were watching the ship. After he got on the boat, he did not see any lights on the *Titanic*, though the stern of the ship was still afloat when he first reached the surface. He accounts for the wave that washed him off amidships as due to the suction which took place when the bow went down in the water and the waves washed the decks clear. He saw a mass of people in the wreckage, hundreds in number, and heard their awful cries.

CHAPTER V

All Night on Bottom of Half-Submerged Upturned Boat

*O God of our salvation, Thou who art the hope of them
that remain in the broad sea . . .* —Ps. 65: 5, 7

All my companions in shipwreck who made their escape with
me on top of the bottom-side-up Engelhardt boat, must recall
the anxious moment after the limit was reached when "about 30
men had clambered out of the water on to the boat." The weight
of each additional body submerged our lifecraft more and more
beneath the surface. There were men swimming in the water all
about us. One more clambering aboard would have swamped
our already crowded craft. The situation was a desperate one,
and was only saved by the refusal of the crew, especially those at
the stern of the boat, to take aboard another passenger. After
pulling aboard the man who lay exhausted, face downward in
front of me, I turned my head away from the sights in the water
lest I should be called upon to refuse the pleading cries of those
who were struggling for their lives. What happened at this juncture, therefore, my fellow companions in shipwreck can better
describe. Steward Thomas Whiteley, interviewed by the New
York *Tribune*, said: "I drifted near a boat wrong-side-up. About
30 men were clinging to it. They refused to let me get on. Somebody tried to hit me with an oar, but I scrambled on to her."
Harry Senior, a fireman on the *Titanic*, as interviewed in the
London *Illustrated News* of May 4th, and in the New York
Times of April 19th, is reported as follows: "On the overturned

boat in question were, amongst others, Charles Lightoller, Second Officer of the *Titanic*; Col. Archibald Gracie, and Mr. J. B. Thayer, Jr., all of whom had gone down with the liner and had come to the surface again"; and "I tried to get aboard of her, but some chap hit me over the head with an oar. There were too many on her. I got around to the other side of the boat and climbed on. There were thirty-five of us, including the second officer, and no women. I saw any amount of drowning and dead around us." Bride's story in the same issue of the New York *Times* says: "It was a terrible sight all around—men swimming and sinking. Others came near. Nobody gave them a hand. The bottom-up boat already had more men than it would hold and was sinking. At first the large waves splashed over my clothing; then they began to splash over my head and I had to breathe when I could."

Though I did not see, I could not avoid hearing what took place at this most tragic crisis in all my life. The men with the paddles, forward and aft, so steered the boat as to avoid contact with the unfortunate swimmers pointed out struggling in the water. I heard the constant explanation made as we passed men swimming in the wreckage, "Hold on to what you have, old boy; one more of you aboard would sink us all." In no instance, I am happy to say, did I hear any word of rebuke uttered by a swimmer because of refusal to grant assistance. There was no case of cruel violence. But there was one transcendent piece of heroism that will remain fixed in my memory as the most sublime and coolest exhibition of courage and cheerful resignation to fate and fearlessness of death. This was when a reluctant refusal of assistance met with the ringing response in the deep manly voice of a powerful man, who, in his extremity, replied: "All right, boys; good luck and God bless you." I have often wished that the identity of this hero might be established and an individual tribute to his memory preserved. He was not an acquaintance of mine, for the tones of his voice would have enabled me to recognize him.

Collins in his testimony and Hagan in his letter to me refer to the same incident, the former before the Senate Committee, saying: "All those who wanted to get on and tried to get on got on with the exception of only one. This man was not pushed off by anyone, but those on the boat asked him not to try to get on. We were all on the boat running [shifting our weight] from one side to the other to keep her steady. If this man had caught hold of her he would have tumbled the whole lot of us off. He acquiesced and said, 'that is all right, boys; keep cool; God bless you,' and he bade us good-bye."

Hagan refers to the same man who "swam close to us saying, 'Hello boys, keep calm, boys,' asking to be helped up, and was told he could not get on as it might turn the boat over. He asked for a plank and was told to cling to what he had. It was very hard to see so brave a man swim away saying, 'God bless you.'"

All this time our nearly submerged boat was amidst the wreckage and fast being paddled out of the danger zone whence arose the heartrending cries already described of the struggling swimmers. It was at this juncture that expressions were used by some of the uncouth members of the ship's crew, which grated upon my sensibilities. The hearts of these men, as I presently discovered, were all right and they were far from meaning any offence when they adopted their usual slang, sounding harsh to my ears, and referred to our less fortunate shipwrecked companions as "the blokes swimming in the water." What I thus heard made me feel like an alien among my fellow boatmates, and I did them the injustice of believing that I, as the only passenger aboard, would, in case of diversity of interest, receive short shrift at their hands and for this reason I thought it best to have as little to say as possible. During all these struggles I had been uttering silent prayers for deliverance, and it occurred to me that this was the occasion of all others when we should join in an appeal to the Almighty as our last and only hope in life, and so it remained for one of these men, whom I had regarded as uncouth, a Roman Catholic seaman, to take precedence in suggesting the thought in the heart of everyone of us. He was astern and in arm's length of me. He first made inquiry as to the religion of each of us and found Episcopalians, Roman Catholics and Presbyterians. The suggestion that we should say the Lord's

Prayer together met with instant approval, and our voices with one accord burst forth in repeating that great appeal to the Creator and Preserver of all mankind, and the only prayer that everyone of us knew and could unite in, thereby manifesting that we were all sons of God and brothers to each other whatever our sphere in life or creed might be. Recollections of this incident are embodied in my account as well as those of Bride and Thayer, independently reported in the New York papers on the morning after our arrival. This is what Bride recalls: "Somebody said 'don't the rest of you think we ought to pray?' The man who made the suggestion asked what the religion of the others was. Each man called out his religion. One was a Catholic, one a Methodist, one a Presbyterian. It was decided the most appropriate prayer for all of us was the Lord's Prayer. We spoke it over in chorus, with the man who first suggested that we pray as the leader."

Referring to this incident in his sermon on "The Lessons of the Great Disaster," the Rev. Dr. Newell Dwight Hillis, of Plymouth Church, says: "When Col. Gracie came up, after the sinking of the *Titanic*, he says that he made his way to a sunken raft. The submerged little raft was under water often, but every man, without regard to nationality, broke into instant prayer. There were many voices, but they all had one signification—their sole hope was in God. There were no millionaires, for millions fell away like leaves; there were no poor; men were neither wise nor ignorant; they were simply human souls on the sinking raft; the night was black and the waves yeasty with foam, and the grave where the *Titanic* lay was silent under them, and the stars were silent over them! But as they prayed, each man by that inner light saw an invisible Friend walking across the waves. Henceforth, these need no books on Apologetics to prove there is a God. This man who has written his story tells us that God heard the prayers of some by giving them death, and heard the prayers of others equally by keeping them in life; but God alone is great!"

The lesson thus drawn from the incident described must be well appreciated by all my boatmates who realized the utter helplessness of our position, and that the only hope we then had in life was in our God, and as the Rev. Dr. Hillis says: "In that moment the evanescent, transient, temporary things dissolved like smoke, and the big, permanent things stood out—God, Truth, Purity, Love, and Oh! how happy those who were good friends with God, their conscience and their record."

We all recognize the fact that our escape from a watery grave was due to the conditions of wind and weather. All night long we prayed that the calm might last. Towards morning the sea became rougher, and it was for the two-fold purpose of avoiding the ice-cold water,[1] and also to attract attention, that we all stood up in column, two abreast, facing the bow. The waves at this time broke over the keel, and we maintained a balance to prevent the escape of the small volume of air confined between sea and upset boat by shifting the weight of our bodies first to port and then to starboard. I believe that the life of everyone of us depended upon the preservation of this confined air-bubble, and our anxious thought was lest some of this air might escape and deeper down our overloaded boat would sink. Had the boat been completely turned over, compelling us to cling to the submerged gunwale, it could not have supported our weight, and we should have been frozen to death in the ice-cold water before rescue could reach us. My exertions had been so continuous and so strenuous before I got aboard this capsized boat that I had taken no notice of the icy temperature of the water. We all suffered severely from cold and exposure. The boat was so loaded down with the heavy weight it carried that it became partly submerged, and the water washed up to our waists as we lay in our reclining position. Several of our companions near the stern of the boat, unable to stand the exposure and strain, gave up the struggle and fell off.

After we had left the danger zone in the vicinity of the wreck, conversation between us first developed, and I heard the men aft of me discussing the fate of the Captain. At least two of them,

1. Temperature of water 28 degrees, of air 27 degrees Fahrenheit, at midnight, April 14th (American Inquiry, p. 1142).

according to their statements made at the time, had seen him on this craft of ours shortly after it was floated from the ship. In the interviews already referred to, Harry Senior the fireman, referring to the same overturned boat, said: "The Captain had been able to reach this boat. They had pulled him on, but he slipped off again." Still another witness, the entrée cook of the *Titanic*, J. Maynard, who was on our boat, corroborates what I heard said at the time about the inability of the Captain to keep his hold on the boat. From several sources I have the information about the falling of the funnel, the splash of which swept from the upturned boat several who were first clinging thereto, and among the number possibly was the Captain. From the following account of Bride, it would appear he was swept off himself and regained his hold later. "I saw a boat of some kind near me and put all my strength into an effort to swim to it. It was hard work. I was all done when a hand reached out from the boat and pulled me aboard. It was our same collapsible. The same crew was on it. There was just room for me to roll on the edge. I lay there, not caring what happened." Fortunately for us all, the majority of us were not thus exhausted or desperate. On the contrary, these men on this upset boat had plenty of strength and the purpose to battle for their lives. There were no beacon torches on crag and cliff; no shouts in the pauses of the storm to tell them there was hope; nor deep-toned bell with its loudest peal sending cheerily, o'er the deep, comfort to these wretched souls in their extremity. There were, however, lights forward, and on the port side to be seen all the time until the *Carpathia* appeared. These lights were only those of the *Titanic*'s other lifeboats, and thus it was, as they gazed with eager anxious eyes that

"Fresh hope did give them strength and strength deliverance."[1]

The suffering on the boat from cold was intense. My neighbor in front, whom I had pulled aboard, must also have been suffering from exhaustion, but it was astern of us whence came later

1. Maturin's *Bertram*.

the reports about fellow boatmates who gave up the struggle and fell off from exhaustion, or died, unable to stand the exposure and strain. Among the number, we are told by Bride and Whiteley, was the senior Marconi operator, Phillips, but their statement that it was Phillips' lifeless body which we transferred first to a lifeboat and thence to the *Carpathia* is a mistake, for the body referred to both Lightoller and myself know to have been that of a member of the crew, as described later. Bride himself suffered severely. "Somebody sat on my legs," he says. "They were wedged in between slats and were being wrenched." When he reached the *Carpathia* he was taken to the hospital and on our arrival in New York was carried ashore with his "feet badly crushed and frostbitten."

The combination of cold and the awful scenes of suffering and death which he witnessed from our upturned boat deeply affected another first cabin survivor, an Englishman, Mr. R. H. Barkworth, whose tender heart is creditable to his character.

Another survivor of our upturned boat, James McGann, a fireman, interviewed by the New York *Tribune* on April 20th, says that he was one of the thirty of us, mostly firemen, clinging to it as she left the ship. As to the suffering endured that night he says: "All our legs were frostbitten and we were all in the hospital for a day at least."

"Hagan" also adds his testimony as to the sufferings endured by our boatmates. He says: "One man on the upturned boat rolled off, into the water, at the stern, dead with fright and cold. Another died in the lifeboat." Here he refers to the lifeless body which we transferred, and finally put aboard the *Carpathia*, but which was not Phillips'.

Lightoller testified: "I think there were three or four who died during the night aboard our boat. The Marconi junior operator told me that the senior operator was on this boat and died, presumably from cold."

But the uncommunicative little member of the crew beside me did not seem to suffer much. He was like a number of others who were possessed of hats or caps—his was an outing cap; while those who sank under water had lost them. The upper part of his body appeared to be comparatively dry; so I believe he and some others escaped being drawn under with the *Titanic* by clinging to the Engelhardt boat from the outset when it parted company with the ship and was washed from the deck by the "giant wave." He seemed so dry and comfortable while I felt so damp in my waterlogged clothing, my teeth chattering and my hair wet with the icy water, that I ventured to request the loan of his dry cap to warm my head for a short while. "And what wad oi do?" was his curt reply, "Ah, never mind," said I, as I thought it would make no difference a hundred years hence. Poor chap, it would seem that all his possessions were lost when his kit went down with the ship. Not far from me and on the starboard side was a more loquacious member of the crew. I was not near enough, however, to him to indulge in any imaginary warmth from the fumes of the O-be-joyful spirits which he gave unmistakable evidence of having indulged in before leaving the ship. Most of the conversation, as well as excitement, came from behind me, astern. The names of other survivors who, besides those mentioned, escaped on the same nearly submerged life craft with me are recorded in the history of Boat B in Chapter V, which contains the results of my research work in regard thereto.

After we paddled away free from the wreckage and swimmers in the water that surrounded us, our undivided attention until the dawn of the next day was concentrated upon scanning the horizon in every direction for the lights of a ship that might rescue us before the sea grew rougher, for the abnormal conditions of wind and weather that prevailed that night were the causes of the salvation, as well as the destruction, of those aboard this ill-fated vessel. The absolute calm of the sea, while it militated against the detection of the iceberg in our path, at the same time made it possible for all of the lifeboats lowered from the davits to make their long and dangerous descent to the water without being smashed against the sides of the ship, or swamped by the waves breaking against them, for, notwithstanding newspaper reports to the contrary, there appears no authentic testimony of any survivor showing that any loaded boat in the act of being lowered was capsized or suffered injury. On the other hand, we have the positive statements accounting for each individual boat-load, showing that every one of them was thus lowered in safety. But it was this very calm of the sea, as has been said, which encompassed the destruction of the ship. The beatings of the waves against the iceberg's sides usually give audible warning miles away to the approaching vessel, while the white foam at the base, due to the same cause, is also discernible. But in our case the beautiful star-lit night and cloudless sky, combined with the glassy sea, further facilitated the iceberg's approach without detection, for no background was afforded against which to silhouette the deadly outline of this black appearing Protean monster which only looks white when the sun is shining upon it.

All experienced navigators of the northern seas, as I am informed on the highest authority, knowing the dangers attending such conditions, invariably take extra precautions to avoid disaster. The *Titanic's* officers were no novices, and were well trained in the knowledge of this and all other dangers of the sea. From the Captain down, they were the pick of the best that the White Star Line had in its employ. Our Captain, Edward J. Smith, was the one always selected to "try out" each new ship of the Line, and was regarded, with his thirty-eight years of service in the company, as both safe and competent. Did he take any precautions for safety, in view of the existing dangerous conditions? Alas! no! as appears from the testimony in regard thereto, taken before the Investigating Committee and Board in America and in England which we review in another chapter. And yet, warnings had been received on the *Titanic's* bridge from six different neighboring ships, one in fact definitely locating the latitude and longitude where the iceberg was encountered, and that too at a point of time calculated by one of the *Titanic's* officers. Who can satisfactorily explain this heedlessness of danger?

It was shortly after we had emerged from the horrible scene of men swimming in the water that I was glad to notice the presence among us on the upturned boat of the same officer with whom all my work that night and all my experience was connected in helping to load and lower the boats on the *Titanic's* Boat Deck and Deck "A". I identified him at once by his voice and his appearance, but his name was not learned until I met him again later in my cabin on board the *Carpathia*—Charles H. Lightoller. For what he did on the ship that night whereby six or more boatloads of women and children were saved and discipline maintained aboard ship, as well as on the Engelhardt upturned boat, he is entitled to honor and the thanks of his own countrymen and of us Americans as well. As soon as he was recognized, the loquacious member of the crew astern, already referred to, volunteered in our behalf and called out to him "We will all obey what the officer orders." The result was at once noticeable. The presence of a leader among us was now felt, and lent us purpose and courage. The excitement at the stern was demonstrated by the frequent suggestion of, "Now boys, all together"; and then in unison we shouted, "Boat ahoy! Boat ahoy!" This was kept up for some time until it was seen to be a mere waste of strength. So it seemed to me, and I decided to husband mine and make provision for what the future, or the morrow, might require. After a while Lightoller, myself and others managed with success to discourage these continuous shouts regarded as a vain hope of attracting attention.

When the presence of the Marconi boy at the stern was made known, Lightoller called out, from his position in the bow, questions which all of us heard, as to the names of the steamships with which he had been in communication for assistance. We on the boat recall the names mentioned by Bride—the *Baltic, Olympic* and *Carpathia*. It was then that the *Carpathia*'s name was heard by us for the first time, and it was to catch sight of this sturdy little Cunarder that we strained our eyes in the direction whence she finally appeared.

We had correctly judged that most of the lights seen by us belonged to our own *Titanic*'s lifeboats, but Lightoller and all of us were badly fooled by the green-colored lights and rockets directly ahead of us, which loomed up especially bright at intervals. This, as will be noticed in a future chapter, was Third Officer Boxhall's Emergency Boat No. 2. We were assured that these were the lights of a ship and were all glad to believe it. There could be no mistake about it and our craft was navigated toward it as fast as its propelling conditions made possible; but it did not take long for us to realize that this light, whatever it was, was receding instead of approaching us.

Some of our boatmates on the *Titanic*'s decks had seen the same white light to which I have already made reference in Chapter II, and the argument was now advanced that it must have been a sailing ship, for a steamer would have soon come to our rescue; but a sailing ship would be prevented by wind, or lack of facilities in coming to our aid. I imagined that it was the lights of such a ship that we again saw on our port side astern in the direction where, when dawn broke, we saw the icebergs far away on the horizon.

Some time before dawn a call came from the stern of the boat, "There is a steamer coming behind us." At the same time a warning cry was given that we should not all look back at once lest the equilibrium of our precarious craft might be disturbed. Lightoller took in the situation and called out, "All you men stand steady and I will be the one to look astern." He looked, but there was no responsive chord that tickled our ears with hope.

The incident just described happened when we were all standing up, facing forward in column, two abreast. Some time before this, for some undefined reason, Lightoller had asked the question, "How many are there of us on this boat?" and someone answered "thirty, sir." All testimony on the subject establishes this number. I may cite Lightoller, who testified: "I should roughly estimate about thirty. She was packed standing from stem to stern at daylight. We took all on board that we could. I did not see any effort made by others to get aboard. There were a great number of people in the water but not near us. They were some distance away from us."

Personally, I could not look around to count, but I know that forward of me there were eight and counting myself and the man abreast would make two more. As every bit of room on the Engelhardt bottom was occupied and as the weight aboard nearly submerged it, I believe that more than half our boatload was behind me. There is a circumstance that I recall which further establishes how closely packed we were. When standing up

I held on once or twice to the life-preserver on the back of my boatmate in front in order to balance myself. At the same time and in the same way the man in my rear held on to me. This procedure, being objectionable to those concerned, was promptly discontinued.

It was at quite an early stage that I had seen far in the distance the unmistakable mast lights of a steamer about four or five points away on the port side, as our course was directed toward the green-colored lights of the imaginary ship which we hoped was coming to our rescue, but which, in fact, was the already-mentioned *Titanic* lifeboat of Officer Boxhall. I recall our anxiety, as we had no lights, that this imaginary ship might not see us and might run over our craft and swamp us. But my eyes were fixed for hours that night on the lights of that steamer, far away in the distance, which afterwards proved to be those of the *Carpathia*. To my great disappointment, they seemed to make no progress towards us to our rescue. This we were told later was due to meeting an iceberg as she was proceeding full speed toward the scene of the *Titanic*'s wreck. She had come to a stop in sight of the lights of our lifeboats (or such as had them). The first boat to come to her sides was Boxhall's with its green lights. Finally dawn appeared and there on the port side of our upset boat where we had been looking with anxious eyes, glory be to God, we saw the steamer *Carpathia* about four or five miles away, with other *Titanic* lifeboats rowing towards her. But on our starboard side, much to our surprise, for we had seen no lights on that quarter, were four of the *Titanic*'s lifeboats strung together in line. These were respectively Numbers 14, 10, 12 and 4, according to testimony submitted in our next chapter.

Meantime, the water had grown rougher, and, as previously described, was washing over the keel and we had to make shift to preserve the equilibrium. Right glad were all of us on our up-turned boat when in that awful hour the break of day brought this glorious sight to our eyes. Lightoller put his whistle to his cold lips and blew a shrill blast, attracting the attention of the boats about half a mile away. "Come over and take us off," he cried. "Aye, aye, sir," was the ready response as two of the boats cast off from the others and rowed directly towards us. Just before the bows of the two boats reached us, Lightoller ordered us not to scramble, but each to take his turn, so that the transfer might be made in safety. When my turn came, in order not to endanger the lives of the others, or plunge them into the sea, I went carefully, hands first, into the rescuing lifeboat. Lightoller remained to the last, lifting a lifeless body into the boat beside me. I worked over the body for some time, rubbing the temples and the wrists, but when I turned the neck it was perfectly stiff. Recognizing that *rigor mortis* had set in, I knew the man was dead. He was dressed like a member of the crew, and I recall that he wore gray woolen socks. His hair was dark. Our lifeboat was so crowded that I had to rest on this dead body until we reached the *Carpathia*, where he was taken aboard and buried. My efforts to obtain his name have been exhaustive, but futile. Lightoller was uncertain as to which one he was of two men he had in mind; but we both know that it was not the body of Phillips, the senior Marconi operator. In the lifeboat to which we were transferred were said to be sixty-five or seventy of us. The number was beyond the limit of safety. The boat sank low in the water, and the sea now became rougher. Lightoller assumed the command and steered at the stern. I was glad to recognize young Thayer amidships. There was a French woman in the bow near us actively ill but brave and considerate. She was very kind in loaning an extra steamer rug to Barkworth, by my side, who shared it with a member of the crew (a fireman perhaps) and myself. That steamer rug was a great comfort as we drew it over our heads and huddled close together to obtain some warmth. For a short time another *Titanic* lifeboat was towed by ours. My lifebelt was wet and uncomfortable and I threw it overboard. Fortunately there was no further need of it for the use intended. I regret I did not preserve it as a relic. When we were first transferred and only two of the lifeboats came to our rescue, some took it hard that the other two did not also come to our relief, when we saw how few these others had aboard; but the officer in command of them, whom we afterwards knew as Fifth Officer Lowe, had cleverly rigged up a sail on his boat and, towing another astern, made his way to the *Carpathia* a long time ahead of us, but picked up on his way other unfortunates in another Engelhardt boat, Boat A, which had shipped considerable water.

My research, particularly the testimony taken before the Senate Committee, establishes the identity of the *Titanic* lifeboats to which, at daydawn, we of the upset boat were transferred. There were Boats No. 12 and No. 4. The former was the one that Lightoller, Barkworth, Thayer, Jr., and myself were in. Frederick Clench, able seaman, was in charge of this boat, and his testimony, as follows, is interesting:

"I looked along the water's edge and saw some men on a raft. Then I heard two whistles blown. I sang out, 'Aye, aye, I am coming over,' and we pulled over and found it was not a raft exactly, but an overturned boat, and Mr. Lightoller was there on that boat and I thought the wireless operator, too. We took them on board our boat and shared the amount of room. They were all standing on the bottom, wet through apparently. Mr. Lightoller took charge of us. Then we started ahead for the *Carpathia*. We had to row a tidy distance to the *Carpathia* because there were boats ahead of us and we had a boat in tow, with others besides all the people we had aboard. We were pretty well full up before, but the additional ones taken on made about seventy in our boat."

This corresponds with Lightoller's testimony on the same point. He says:

"I counted sixty-five heads, not including myself, and none that were in the bottom of the boat. I roughly estimated about seventy-five in the boat, which was dangerously full, and it was all I could do to nurse her up to the sea."

From Steward Cunningham's testimony I found a corroboration of my estimate of our distance, at daydawn, from the *Carpathia*. This he says "was about four or five miles."

Another seaman, Samuel S. Hemming, who was in Boat No. 4, commanded by Quartermaster Perkis, also gave his testimony as follows:

"As day broke we heard some hollering going on and we saw some men standing on what we thought was ice about half a mile away, but we found them on the bottom of an upturned boat. Two boats cast off and we pulled to them and took them in our two boats. There were no women or children on this boat, and I heard there was one dead body. Second Officer Lightoller was on the overturned boat. He did not get into our boat. Only about four or five got into ours and the balance of them went into the other boat."

It seemed to me an interminable time before we reached the *Carpathia*. Ranged along her sides were others of the *Titanic's* lifeboats which had been rowed to the Cunarder and had been emptied of their loads of survivors. In one of these boats on the port side, standing up, I noticed my friend, Third Officer H. J. Pitman, with whom I had made my trip eastward on the Atlantic on board the *Oceanic*. All along the sides of the *Carpathia* were strung rope ladders. There were no persons about me needing my assistance, so I mounted the ladder, and, for the purpose of testing my strength, I ran up as fast as I could and experienced no difficulty or feeling of exhaustion. I entered the first hatchway I came to and felt like falling down on my knees and kissing the deck in gratitude for the preservation of my life. I made my way to the second-cabin dispensary, where I was handed a hot drink. I then went to the deck above and was met with a warm reception in the dining saloon. Nothing could exceed the kindness of the ladies, who did everything possible for my comfort. All my wet clothing, overcoat and shoes, were sent down to the bake-oven to be dried. Being thus in lack of clothing, I lay down on the lounge in the dining saloon corner to the right of the entrance under rugs and blankets, waiting for a complete outfit of dry clothing.

I am particularly grateful to a number of kind people on the *Carpathia* who helped replenish my wardrobe, but especially to Mr. Louis M. Ogden, a family connection and old friend. To Mrs. Ogden and to Mr. and Mrs. Spedden, who were on the *Titanic*, and to their boy's trained nurse, I am also most grateful. They gave me hot cordials and hot coffee which soon warmed me up and dispersed the cold. Among the *Carpathia's* passengers, bound for the Mediterranean, I discovered a number of friends of Mrs. Gracie's and mine—Miss K. Steele, sister of Charles Steele, of New York, Mr. and Mrs. Charles H. Marshall and Miss Marshall, of New York. Leaning over the rail of the port side I saw anxiously gazing down upon us many familiar faces of fellow survivors, and, among them, friends and acquaintances to whom I waved my hand as I stood up in the bow of my boat. This boat No. 12 was the last to reach the *Carpathia* and her passengers transferred about 8:30 a.m.

CHAPTER VI

The Port Side:
Women and Children First

FOREWORD

The previous chapters, describing my personal experience on board the *Titanic* and remarkable escape from death in the icy waters of the middle Atlantic, were written some months ago. In the interim I have received the pamphlets, printed in convenient form, containing the hearings of both the American and British Courts of Inquiry, and have given them considerable study.

These official sources of information have added materially to my store of knowledge concerning the shipwreck, and corroborate to a marked degree the description from my personal viewpoint, all the salient points of which were written before our arrival in New York, and on the S. S. *Carpathia*, under circumstances which will be related in a future chapter.

During the same interval, by correspondence with survivors and by reading all available printed matter in books, magazine articles and newspapers, I have become still more conversant with the story of this, the greatest of maritime disasters, which caused more excitement in our country than any other single event that has occurred in its history within a generation.

The adopted standard by which I propose to measure the truth of all statements in this book is the evidence obtained from these Courts of Inquiry, after it has been subjected to careful and impartial analysis. All accounts of the disaster, from newspapers and individual sources, for which no basis can be found after submission to this refining process, will find no place or mention herein. In the discussion of points of historical interest or of individual conduct, where such are matters of public record, I shall endeavor to present them fairly before the reader, who can pass thereon his or her own opinion after a study of the testimony bearing on both sides of any controversy. In connection with such discussion where the reflections cast upon individuals in the sworn testimony of witnesses have already gained publicity, I claim immunity from any real or imaginary animadversions which may be provoked by my impartial reference thereto.

I have already recorded my personal observation of how strictly the rule of human nature, "Women and Children First," was enforced on the port side of the great steamship, whence no man escaped alive who made his station on this quarter and bade good-bye to wife, mother or sister.

I have done my best, during the limited time allowed, to exhaust all the above-defined sources of information, in an effort to preserve as complete a list as possible of those comrades of mine who, from first to last, on this port side of the ship, helped to preserve order and discipline, upholding the courage of women and children, until all the boats had left the *Titanic*, and who then sank with the ship when she went down.

I shall now present the record and story of each lifeboat, on both port and starboard sides of the ship, giving so far as I have been able to obtain them the names of persons loaded aboard each boat, passengers and crew; those picked up out of the water; the stowaways found concealed beneath the thwarts, and those men who, without orders, jumped from the deck into boats being lowered, injuring the occupants and endangering the lives of women and children. At the same time will be described the conditions existing when each boat was loaded and lowered, and whatever incidents occurred in the transfer of passengers to the rescuing steamer *Carpathia*.

The general testimony of record, covering the conduct which was exhibited on the port side of the ship, is contained in the careful statements of that splendid officer, Charles H. Lightoller, before the United States Senate Committee (Am. Inq., p. 88):

Senator Smith: From what you have said, you discriminated entirely in the interest of the passengers—first women and children—in filling these lifeboats?

Mr. Lightoller: Yes, sir.

Senator Smith: Why did you do that? Because of the captain's orders, or because of the rule of the sea?

Mr. Lightoller: The rule of human nature.

And also in his testimony before the British Inquiry (p. 71):

"I asked the captain on the Boat Deck, 'Shall I get women and children in the boats?' The captain replied, 'Yes, and lower away.' I was carrying out his orders. I am speaking of the port side of the ship. I was running the port side only. All the boats on this side were lowered except the last, which was stowed on top of the officers' quarters. This was the surf boat—the Engelhardt boat (A). We had not time to launch it nor yet to open it."

(Br. Inq.) "I had no difficulty in filling the boat. The people were perfectly ready and quiet. There was no jostling or pushing or crowding whatever. The men all refrained from asserting their strength and from crowding back the women and children. They could not have stood quieter if they had been in church."

And referring to the last boats that left the ship (Br. Inq., p. 83):

"When we were lowering the women, there were any amount of Americans standing near who gave me every assistance they could."

The crow's nest on the foremast was just about level with the water when the bridge was submerged. The people left on the ship, or that part which was not submerged, did not make any demonstration. There was not a sign of any lamentation.

On the port side on deck I can say, as far as my own observations went, from my own endeavor and that of others to obtain women, there were none left on the deck.

My testimony on the same point before the United States Senate Committee (Am. Inq., p. 992) was as follows:

"I want to say that there was nothing but the most heroic conduct on the part of all men and women at that time where I was at the bow on the port side. There was no man who asked to get in a boat with the single exception that I have already mentioned.

(Referring to Col. Astor's request to go aboard to protect his wife. Am. Inq., p. 991.) No women even sobbed or wrung their hands, and everything appeared perfectly orderly. Lightoller was splendid in his conduct with the crew, and the crew did their duty. It seemed to me it was a little bit more difficult than it should have been to launch the boats alongside the ship. I do not know the cause of that. I know I had to use my muscle as best I could in trying to push those boats so as to get them over the gunwale. I refer to these in a general way as to its being difficult in trying to lift them and push them over. (As was the case with the Engelhardt "D.") The crew, at first, sort of resented my working with them, but they were very glad when I worked with them later on. Every opportunity I got to help, I helped."

How these statements are corroborated by the testimony of others is recorded in the detailed description of each boat that left the ship on the port side as follows:

BOAT NO. 6[1]

No male passengers

Passengers: Miss Bowerman, Mrs. J. J. Brown, Mrs. Candee, Mrs. Cavendish and her maid (Miss Barber), Mrs. Meyer, Miss Norton, Mrs. Rothschild, Mrs. L. P. Smith, Mrs. Stone and her maid (Miss Icard).

Ordered in to supply lack of crew: Major A. G. Peuchen.

Said good-bye to wives and sank with ship: Messrs. Cavendish, Meyer, Rothschild and L. P. Smith.

Crew: Hitchins, Q. M. (in charge). Seaman Fleet. (One fireman transferred from No. 16 to row.) Also a boy with injured arm whom Captain Smith had ordered in.

Total: 28. (Br. Inq.)

---

1. British Report (p. 38) puts this boat first to leave port side at 12:55. Lightoller's testimony shows it could not have been the first.

Incidents

Lightoller's testimony (Am. Inq., p. 79):

I was calling for seamen and one of the seamen jumped out of the boat and started to lower away. The boat was half way down when a woman called out that there was only one man in it. I had only two seamen and could not part with them, and was in rather a fix to know what to do when a passenger called out: "If you like, I will go." This was a first-class passenger, Major Peuchen, of Toronto. I said: "Are you a seaman?" and he said: "I am a yachtsman." I said: "If you are sailor enough to get out on that fall—that is a difficult thing to get to over the ship's side, eight feet away, and means a long swing, on a dark night—if you are sailor enough to get out there, you can go down"; and he proved he was, by going down.

F. Fleet, L. O. (Am. Inq., 363) and (Br. Inq.):

Witness says there were twenty-three women, Major Peuchen and Seamen Hitchens and himself. As he left the deck he heard Mr. Lightoller shouting: "Any more women?" No. 6 and one other cut adrift after reaching the *Carpathia*.

Major Arthur Godfrey Peuchen, Manufacturing Chemist, Toronto, Canada, and Major of Toronto's crack regiment, The Queen's Own Rifles (Am. Inq., p. 334), testified:

I was standing on the Boat Deck, port side, near the second officer and the captain. One of them said: "We must get these masts and sails out of these boats; you might give us a hand." I jumped in, and with a knife cut the lashings of the mast and sail and moved the mast out of the boat. Only women were allowed in, and the men had to stand back. This was the order, and the second officer stood there and carried it out to the limit. He allowed no men, except sailors who were manning the boat. I did not see one single male passenger get in or attempt to get in.

I never saw such perfect order. The discipline was perfect. I did not see a cowardly act by any man.

When I first came on this upper deck there were about 100 stokers coming up with their dunnage bags and they seemed to crowd this whole deck in front of the boats. One of the officers, I don't know which one, a very powerful man, came along and drove these men right off this deck like a lot of sheep. They did not put up any resistance. I admired him for it. Later, there were counted 20 women, one quartermaster, one sailor and one stowaway, before I was ordered in.

In getting into the boat I went aft and said to the quartermaster: "What do you want me to do?" "Get down and put that plug in," he answered. I made a dive down for the plug. The ladies were all sitting pretty well aft and I could not see at all. It was dark down there. I felt with my hands and then said it would be better for him to do it and me do his work. I said, "Now, you get down and put in the plug and I will undo the shackles," that is, take the blocks off, so he dropped the blocks and got down to fix the plug, and then he came back to assist me saying, "Hurry up." He said: "This boat is going to founder." I thought he meant our lifeboat was going to founder, but he meant the large boat, and that we were to hurry up and get away from it, so we got the rudder in and he told me to go forward and take an oar. I did so, and got an oar on the port side. Sailor Fleet was on my left on the starboard side. The quartermaster told us to row as hard as we could to get away from the suction. We got a short distance away when an Italian, a stowaway, made his appearance. He had a broken wrist or arm, and was of no use to row. He was stowed away under the boat where we could not see him.

Toward morning we tied up to another boat (No. 16) for fifteen minutes. We said to those in the other boat: "Surely you can spare us one man if you have so many." One man, a fireman, was accordingly transferred, who assisted in rowing on the starboard side. The women helped with the oars, and very pluckily too.[1]

1. "An English girl (Miss Norton) and I rowed for four hours and a half."
—Mrs. Meyer in New York *Times*, April 14th, 1912.

We were to the weather of the *Carpathia*, and so she stayed there until we all came down on her. I looked at my watch and it was something after eight o'clock.

Mrs. Candee's account of her experience is as follows:

She last saw Mr. Kent in the companionway between Decks A and B. He took charge of an ivory miniature of her mother, etc., which afterwards were found on his body when brought into Halifax. He appeared at the time to hesitate accepting her valuables, seeming to have a premonition of his fate.

She witnessed the same incident described by Major Peuchen, when a group of firemen came up on deck and were ordered by the officer to return below. She, however, gives praise to these men. They obeyed like soldiers, and without a murmur or a protest, though they knew better than anyone else on the ship that they were going straight to their death. No boats had been lowered when these firemen first appeared upon the Boat Deck, and it would have been an easy matter for them to have "rushed" the boats.

Her stateroom steward also gave an exhibition of courage. After he had tied on her life-preserver and had locked her room as a precaution against looters, which she believed was done all through the deck, she said to this brave man: "It is time for you to look out for yourself," to which the steward replied, "Oh, plenty of time for that, Madam, plenty of time for that." He was lost.

As she got into boat No. 6, it being dark and not seeing where she stepped, her foot encountered the oars lying lengthwise in the boat and her ankle was thus twisted and broken.

Just before her boat was lowered away a man's voice said: "Captain, we have no seaman." Captain Smith then seized a boy by the arm and said: "Here's one." The boy went into the boat as ordered by the captain, but afterwards he was found to be disabled. She does not think he was an Italian.

Her impression is that there were other boats in the water which had been lowered before hers. There was a French woman about fifty years of age in the boat who was constantly calling for her son. Mrs. Candee sat near her. After arrival on the *Carpathia* this French woman became hysterical.

Notwithstanding Hitchens' statements, she says that there was absolutely no upset feeling on the woman's part at any time, even when the boat, as it was being lowered, on several occasions hung at a dangerous angle—sometimes bow up and sometimes stern up. The lowering process seemed to be done by jerks. She herself called out to the men lowering the boat and gave instructions: otherwise they would have been swamped.

The Italian boy who was in the boat was not a stowaway, he was ordered in by the captain as already related. Neither did he refuse to row. When he tried to do so, it was futile, because of an injury to his arm or wrist.

Through the courtesy of another fellow passenger, Mrs. J. J. Brown, of Denver, Colorado, I am able to give her experiences in boat No. 6, told in a delightful, graphic manner; so much so that I would like to insert it all did not space prevent:

In telling of the people she conversed with, that Sunday evening, she refers to an exceedingly intellectual and much-traveled acquaintance, Mrs. Bucknell, whose husband had founded the Bucknell University of Philadelphia; also to another passenger from the same city, Dr. Brewe, who had done much in scientific research. During her conversation with Mrs. Bucknell, the latter reiterated a statement previously made on the tender at Cherbourg while waiting for the *Titanic*. She said she feared boarding the ship because she had evil forebodings that something might happen. Mrs. Brown laughed at her premonitions and shortly afterwards sought her quarters.

Instead of retiring to slumber, Mrs. Brown was absorbed in reading and gave little thought to the crash at her window overhead which threw her to the floor. Picking herself up she proceeded to see what the steamer had struck; but thinking nothing serious had occurred, though realizing that the engines had stopped immediately after the crash and the boat was at a standstill, she picked up her book and began reading again. Finally she saw her curtains moving while she was reading, but no one was visible. She again looked out and saw a man whose face was blanched, his eyes protruding, wearing the look of a haunted creature. He was gasping for breath and in an undertone gasped, "Get your life-preserver." He was one of the buyers for Gimbel Bros., of Paris and New York.

She got down her life-preserver, snatched up her furs and hurriedly mounted the stairs to A Deck, where she found passengers putting on lifebelts like hers. Mrs. Bucknell approached and whispered, "Didn't I tell you something was going to happen?" She found the lifeboats lowered from the falls and made flush with the deck. Madame de Villiers appeared from below in a nightdress and evening slippers, with no stockings. She wore a long woolen motorcoat. Touching Mrs. Brown's arm, in a terrified voice she said she was going below for her money and valuables. After much persuasion Mrs. Brown prevailed upon her not to do so, but to get into the boat. She hesitated and became very much excited, but was finally prevailed upon to enter the lifeboat. Mrs. Brown was walking away, eager to see what was being done elsewhere. Suddenly she saw a shadow and a few seconds later someone seized her, saying: "You are going, too," and she was dropped fully four feet into the lowering lifeboat. There was but one man in charge of the boat. As it was lowered by jerks by an officer above, she discovered that a great gush of water was spouting through the porthole from D Deck, and the lifeboat was in grave danger of being submerged. She immediately grasped an oar and held the lifeboat away from the ship.

When the sea was reached, smooth as glass, she looked up and saw the benign, resigned countenance, the venerable white hair and the Chesterfieldian bearing of the beloved Captain Smith with whom she had crossed twice before, and only three months previous on the *Olympic*. He peered down upon those in the boat, like a solicitous father, and directed them to row to the light in the distance—all boats keeping together.

Because of the fewness of men in the boat she found it necessary for someone to bend to the oars. She placed her oar in an oarlock and asked a young woman nearby to hold one while she placed the other on the further side. To Mrs. Brown's surprise the young lady (who must have been Miss Norton, spoken of elsewhere), immediately began to row like a galley slave, every stroke counting. Together they managed to pull away from the steamer.

By this time E and C Decks were completely submerged. Those ladies who had husbands, sons or fathers on the doomed steamer buried their heads on the shoulders of those near them and moaned and groaned. Mrs. Brown's eyes were glued on the fast-disappearing ship. Suddenly there was a rift in the water, the sea opened up and the surface foamed like giant arms and spread around the ship and the vessel disappeared from sight, and not a sound was heard.

Then follows Mrs. Brown's account of the conduct of the quartermaster in the boat which will be found under the heading presently given, and it will be noticed that her statements correspond with those of all others in the boat.

The dawn disclosed the awful situation. There were fields of ice on which, like points on the landscape, rested innumerable pyramids of ice. Seemingly a half hour later, the sun, like a ball of molten lead, appeared in the background. The hand of nature portrayed a scenic effect beyond the ken of the human mind. The heretofore smooth sea became choppy and retarded their progress. All the while the people in boat No. 6 saw the other small lifeboats being hauled aboard the *Carpathia*. By the time their boat reached the *Carpathia* a heavy sea was running, and, No. 6 boat being among the last to approach, it was found difficult to get close to the ship. Three or four unsuccessful attempts were made. Each time they were dashed against the keel, and bounded off like a rubber ball. A rope was then thrown down, which was spliced in four at the bottom, and a Jacob's ladder was made. Catching hold, they were hoisted up, where a dozen of the crew and officers and doctors were waiting. They were caught and handled as tenderly as though they were children.

Hitchens' Conduct

Major Peuchen (Am. Inq., p. 334) continued:

There was an officers' call, sort of a whistle, calling us to come back to the boat. The quartermaster told us to stop rowing. We all thought we ought to go back to the ship, but the quartermaster said "No, we are not going back to the boat; it is our lives now, not theirs." It was the women who rebelled against this action. I asked him to assist us in rowing and let some of the women steer the boat, as it was a perfectly calm night and no skill was required. He refused, and told me he was in command of that boat and that I was to row.

He imagined he saw a light. I have done a great deal of yachting in my life. I have owned a yacht for six years. I saw a reflection. He thought it was a boat of some kind: probably it might be a buoy, and he called out to the next boat asking them if they knew any buoys were around there. This struck me as being perfectly absurd.

I heard what seemed to be one, two, three rumbling sounds; then the lights of the ship went out. Then the terrible cries and calls for help—moaning and crying. It affected all the women in our boat whose husbands were among those in the water. This went on for some time, gradually getting fainter and fainter. At first it was horrible to listen to. We must have been five-eighths of a mile away when this took place. There were only two of us rowing a very heavy boat with a good many people in it, and I do not think we covered very much ground. Some of the women in the boat urged the quartermaster to return. He said there was no use going back—that there were only a "lot of stiffs there." The women resented it very much.

Seaman Fleet (Am. Inq., p. 363):

All the women asked us to pull to the place where the *Titanic* went down, but the quartermaster, who was at the tiller all the time, would not allow it. They asked him, but he would not hear of it.

Mrs. Candee continues:

Hitchens was cowardly and almost crazed with fear all the time. After we left the ship he thought he heard the captain say: "Come alongside," and was for turning back until reminded by the passengers that the Captain's final orders were: "Keep boats together and row away from the ship." She heard this order given.

After that he constantly reminded us who were at the oars that if we did not make better speed with our rowing we would all be sucked under the water by the foundering of the ship. This he repeated whenever our muscles flagged.

Directly the *Titanic* had foundered a discussion arose as to whether we should return. Hitchens said our boat would immediately be swamped if we went into the confusion. The reason for this was that our boat was not manned with enough oars.

Then after the sinking of the *Titanic* Hitchens reminded us frequently that we were hundreds of miles from land, without water, without food, without protection against cold, and if a storm should come up that we would be helpless. Therefore, we faced death by starvation or by drowning. He said we did not even know the direction in which we were rowing. I corrected him by pointing to the north star immediately over our bow.

When our boat came alongside No. 16, Hitchens immediately ordered the boats lashed together. He resigned the helm and settled down to rest. When the *Carpathia* hove in sight he ordered that we drift. Addressing the people in both boats Mrs. Candee said: "Where those lights are lies our salvation; shall we not go towards them?" The reply was a murmur of approval and immediate recourse to the oars.

Hitchens was requested to assist in the toilsome rowing. Women tried to taunt and provoke him into activity. When it was suggested that he permit the injured boy to take the tiller and that Hitchens should row, he declined, and in every case he refused labor. He spoke with such uncivility to one of the ladies that a man's voice was heard in rebuke: "You are speaking to a lady," to which he replied: "I know whom I am speaking to, and I am commanding this boat."

When asked if the *Carpathia* would come and pick us up he replied: "No, she is not going to pick us up; she is to pick up bodies." This when said to wives and mothers of the dead men was needlessly brutal.

When we neared the *Carpathia* he refused to go round on the smooth side because it necessitated keeping longer in the rough sea, so we made a difficult landing.

In Mrs. Brown's account of her experience she relates the following about the conduct of the quartermaster in charge of the boat in which she was:

He, Quartermaster Hitchens, was at the rudder and standing much higher than we were, shivering like an aspen. As they rowed away from the ship he burst out in a frightened voice and warned them of the fate that awaited them, saying that the task in rowing away from the sinking ship was futile, as she was so large that in sinking she would draw everything for miles around down with her suction, and, if they escaped that, the boilers would burst and rip up the bottom of the sea, tearing the icebergs asunder and completely submerging them. They were truly doomed either way. He dwelt upon the dire fate awaiting them, describing the accident that happened to the S. S. *New York* when the *Titanic* left the docks at Southampton.

After the ship had sunk and none of the calamities that were predicted by the terrified quartermaster were experienced, he was asked to return and pick up those in the water. Again the people in the boat were admonished and told how the frantic drowning victims would grapple the side of the boat and capsize it. He not yielding to the entreaties, those at the oars pulled away vigorously towards a faintly glimmering light on the horizon. After three hours of pulling the light grew fainter, and then completely disappeared. Then this quartermaster, who stood on his pinnacle trembling, with an attitude like some one preaching to the multitude, fanning the air with his hands, recommenced his tirade of awful forebodings, telling those in the boat that they were likely to drift for days, all the while reminding them that they were surrounded by icebergs, as he pointed to a pyramid of ice looming up in the distance, possibly seventy feet high. He forcibly impressed upon them that there was no water in the casks in the lifeboats, and no bread, no compass and no chart. No one answered him. All seemed to be stricken dumb. One of the ladies in the boat had had the presence of mind to procure her silver brandy flask. As she held it in her hand the silver glittered and he being attracted to it implored her to give it to him, saying that he was frozen. She refused the brandy, but removed her steamer blanket and placed it around his shoulders, while another lady wrapped a second blanket around his waist and limbs, he looking "as snug as a bug in a rug."

The quartermaster was then asked to relieve one or the other of those struggling at the oars, as someone else could manage the rudder while he rowed. He flatly refused and continued to lampoon them, shouting: "Here, you fellow on the starboard side, your oar is not being put in the water at the right angle." No one made any protest to his outbursts, as he broke the monotony, but they continued to pull at the oars with no goal in sight. Presently he raised his voice and shouted to another lifeboat to pull near and lash alongside, commanding some of the other ladies to take the light and signal to the other lifeboats. His command was immediately obeyed. He also gave another command to drop the oars and lay to. Some time later, after more shouts, a lifeboat hove to and obeyed his orders to throw a rope, and was tied alongside. On the cross-seat of that boat stood a man in white pajamas, looking like a snow man in that icy region. His teeth were chattering and he appeared quite numb. Seeing his predicament, Mrs. Brown told him he had better get to rowing and keep his blood in circulation. But the suggestion met with a forcible protest from the quartermaster in charge. Mrs. Brown and her companions at the oars, after their exercise, felt the blasts from the ice-fields and demanded that they should be allowed to row to keep warm.

Over into their boat jumped a half-frozen stoker, black and

covered with dust. As he was dressed in thin jumpers, she picked up a large sable stole which she had dropped into the boat and wrapped it around his limbs from his waist down and tied the tails around his ankles. She handed him an oar and told the pajama man to cut loose. A howl arose from the quartermaster in charge. He moved to prevent it, and Mrs. Brown told him if he did he would be thrown overboard. Someone laid a hand on her shoulder to stay her threats, but she knew it would not be necessary to push him over, for had she only moved in the quartermaster's direction, he would have tumbled into the sea, so paralyzed was he with fright. By this time he had worked himself up to a pitch of sheer despair, fearing that a scramble of any kind would remove the plug from the bottom of the boat. He then became very impertinent, and our fur-enveloped stoker in as broad a cockney as one hears in the Haymarket shouted: "Oi sy, don't you know you are talkin' to a lidy?" For the time being the seaman was silenced and we resumed our task at the oars. Two other ladies came to the rescue.

While glancing around watching the edge of the horizon, the beautifully modulated voice of the young Englishwoman at the oar (Miss Norton) exclaimed, "There is a flash of lightning." "It is a falling star," replied our pessimistic seaman. As it became bright he was then convinced that it was a ship. However, the distance, as we rowed, seemed interminable. We saw the ship was anchored. Again the declaration was made that we, regardless of what our quartermaster said, would row toward her, and the young Englishwoman from the Thames got to work, accompanying her strokes with cheerful words to the wilted occupants of the boat.

Mrs. Brown finishes the quartermaster in her final account of him. On entering the dining-room on the *Carpathia*, she saw him in one corner—this brave and heroic seaman! A cluster of people were around him as he wildly gesticulated, trying to impress upon them what difficulty he had in maintaining discipline among the occupants of his boat, but on seeing Mrs. Brown and a few others of the boat nearby he did not tarry long, but made a hasty retreat.

R. Hitchens, Q. M. (Am. Inq., p. 451. Br. Inq.) explains his conduct:

I was put in charge of No. 6 by the Second Officer, Mr. Ligh-toller. We lowered away from the ship. I told them in the boat somebody would have to pull. There was no use stopping alongside the ship, which was gradually going by the head. We were in a dangerous place, so I told them to man the oars—ladies and all. "All of you do your best." I relieved one of the young ladies with an oar and told her to take the tiller. She immediately let the boat come athwart, and the ladies in the boat got very nervous; so I took the tiller back again and told them to manage the best way they could. The lady I refer to, Mrs. Meyer, was rather vexed with me in the boat and I spoke rather straight to her. She accused me of wrapping myself up in the blankets in the boat, using bad language and drinking all the whisky, which I deny, sir. I was standing to attention, exposed, steering the boat all night, which is a very cold billet. I would rather be pulling the boat than be steering, but I saw no one there to steer, so I thought, being in charge of the boat, it was the best way to steer myself, especially when I saw the ladies get very nervous.

I do not remember that the women urged me to go toward the *Titanic*. I did not row toward the scene of the *Titanic* because the suction of the ship would draw the boat, with all its occupants, under water. I did not know which way to go back to the *Titanic*. I was looking at all the other boats. We were looking at each other's lights. After the lights disappeared and went out, we did hear cries of distress—a lot of crying, moaning and screaming, for two or three minutes. We made fast to another boat—that of the master-at-arms. It was No. 16. I had thirty-eight women in my boat. I counted them, sir. One seaman, Fleet; the Canadian Major, who testified here yesterday, myself and the Italian boy.

We got down to the *Carpathia* and I saw every lady and everybody out of the boat, and I saw them carefully hoisted on board the *Carpathia*, and I was the last man to leave the boat.

BOAT NO. 8[1]
No male passengers in this boat

Passengers: Mrs. Bucknell and her maid (Albina Bazzani); Miss Cherry, Mrs. Kenyon, Miss Leader, Mrs. Pears, Mrs. Penasco and her maid (Mlle. Olivia); Countess Rothes and her maid (Miss Maloney); Mrs. Swift, Mrs. Taussig, Miss Taussig, Mrs. White and her maid (Amelia Bessetti); Mrs. Wick, Miss Wick, Miss Young and Mrs. Straus' maid (Ellen Bird).

Women: 24.

Said good-bye to wives and sank with the ship: Messrs. Kenyon, Pears, Penasco, Taussig and Wick.

Crew: Seaman T. Jones, Stewards Crawford and Hart, and a cook.

Total: 28.

Incidents

T. Jones, seaman (Am. Inq., p. 570):

The captain asked me if the plug was in the boat and I answered, "Yes, sir." "All right," he said, "any more ladies?" He shouted twice again, "Any more ladies?"

I pulled for the light, but I found that I could not get to it; so I stood by for a while. I wanted to return to the ship, but the ladies were frightened. In all, I had thirty-five ladies and three stewards, Crawford, Hart and another. There were no men who offered to get in the boat. I did not see any children, and very few women when we left the ship. There was one old lady there and an old gentleman, her husband. She wanted him to enter the boat with her but he backed away. She never said anything; if she did, we could not hear it, because the steam was blowing so and making such a noise.[2]

---

1. British Report (p. 38) puts this boat second on port side at 1:10. Notwithstanding Seaman Fleet's testimony (Am. Inq., p. 363), I think she must have preceded No. 6.

2. By the testimony of the witness and Steward Crawford it appears that Mr. and Mrs. Straus approached this boat and their maid got in, but Mr. Straus would not follow his wife and she refused to leave him.

Senator Newlands: Can you give me the names of any passengers on this boat?

Witness: One lady—she had a lot to say and I put her to steering the boat.

Senator Newlands: What was her name?

Witness: Lady Rothes; she was a countess, or something.

A. Crawford, steward (Am. Inq., pp. Ill, 827, 842):

After we struck I went out and saw the iceberg, a large black object, much higher than B Deck, passing along the starboard side. We filled No. 8 with women. Captain Smith and a steward lowered the forward falls. Captain Smith told me to get in. He gave orders to row for the light and to land the people there and come back to the ship. The Countess Rothes was at the tiller all night. There were two lights not further than ten miles— stationary masthead lights. Everybody saw them—all the ladies in the boat. They asked if we were drawing nearer to the steamer, but we could not seem to make any headway, and near daybreak we saw another steamer coming up, which proved to be the *Carpathia*, and then we turned around and came back. We were the furthest boat away. I am sure it was a steamer, because a sailing vessel would not have had two masthead lights.

Mrs. J. Stuart White (Am. Inq., p. 1008):

Senator Smith: Did you see anything after the accident bearing on the discipline of the officers or crew, or their conduct which you desire to speak of?

Mrs. White: Before we cut loose from the ship these stewards took out cigarettes and lighted them. On an occasion like that! That is one thing I saw. All of these men escaped under the pretense of being oarsmen. The man who rowed near me took his oar and rowed all over the boat in every direction. I said to him: "Why don't you put the oar in the oarlock?" He said: "Do you put it in that hole?" I said: "Certainly." He said: "I never had an oar in my hand before." I spoke to the other man and he said: "I have never had an oar in my hand before, but I think I can row." These were the men we were put to sea with, that night—with all those magnificent fellows left on board who would have been such a protection to us—those were the kind of men with whom we were put to sea that night! There were twenty-two women and four men in my boat. None of the men seemed to understand the management of a boat except one who was at the end of our boat and gave the orders. The officer who put us in the boat gave strict orders to make for the light opposite, land passengers and then get back just as soon as possible. That was the light everybody saw in the distance. I saw it distinctly. It was ten miles away, but we rowed, and rowed, and rowed, and then we all decided that it was impossible for us to get to it, and the thing to do was to go back and see what we could do for the others. We had only twenty-two in our boat. We turned and went back and lingered around for a long time. We could not locate the other boats except by hearing them. The only way to look was by my electric light. I had an electric cane with an electric light in it. The lamp in the boat was worth absolutely nothing. There was no excitement whatever on the ship. Nobody seemed frightened. Nobody was panic-stricken. There was a lot of pathos when husbands and wives kissed each other good-bye.

We were the second boat (No. 8) that got away from the ship and we saw nothing that happened after that. We were not near enough. We heard the yells of the passengers as they went down, but we saw none of the harrowing part of it. The women in our boat all rowed—every one of them. Miss Young rowed every minute. The men (the stewards) did not know the first thing about it and could not row. Mrs. Swift rowed all the way to the *Carpathia*. Countess Rothes stood at the tiller. Where would we have been if it had not been for the women, with such men as were put in charge of the boat? Our head seaman was giving orders and these men knew nothing about a boat. They would say: "If you don't stop talking through that hole in your face there will be one less in the boat." We were in the hands of men of that kind. I settled two or three fights between them and quieted them down. Imagine getting right out there and taking out a pipe and smoking it, which was most dangerous. We had woolen rugs all around us. There was another thing which I thought a disgraceful point. The men were asked when they got in if they could row. Imagine asking men who are supposed to be at the head of lifeboats if they can row!

Senator Smith: There were no male passengers in your boat?

Mrs. White: Not one. I never saw a finer body of men in my life than the men passengers on this ship—athletes and men of sense—and if they had been permitted to enter these lifeboats with their families, the boats would have been properly manned and many more lives saved, instead of allowing stewards to get in the boats and save their lives under the pretense that they could row when they knew nothing about it.

BOAT NO. 10[1]
No male passengers in this boat

Passengers: First cabin, Miss Andrews, Miss Longley, Mrs. Hogeboom. Second cabin, Mrs. Parrish, Mrs. Shelley. 41 women, 7 children.

Crew: Seamen: Buley (in charge), Evans; Fireman Rice; Stewards Burke and one other.

Stowaway: 1 Japanese.

Jumped from A Deck into boat being lowered: 1 Armenian.

Total: 55.

Incidents

Edward J. Buley, A. B. (Am. Inq., p. 604):

Chief Officer Wilde said: "See if you can find another seaman to give you a hand, and jump in." I found Evans, my mate, the able-bodied seaman, and we both got in the boat.

---

1. British Report (p. 38) says third at 1:20. I think No. 6 went later, though Buley (Am. Inq., p. 604) claims No. 10 as the last lifeboat lowered.

*Much of Seaman Buley's and of Steward Burke's testimony is a
repetition of that of Seaman Evans, so I cite the latter only:*

F. O. Evans, A. B. (Am. Inq., p. 675):

I went up (on the Boat Deck) with the remainder of the crew
and uncovered all of the port boats. Then to the starboard side
and lowered the boats there with the assistance of the Boatswain
of the ship, A. Nichol. I went next (after No. 12) to No. 10. Mr.
Murdoch was standing there. I lowered the boat with the assistance of a steward. The chief officer said: "Get into that boat." I
got into the bows. A young ship's baker (J. Joughin) was getting
the children and chucking them into the boat. Mr. Murdoch and
the baker made the women jump across into the boat about two
feet and a half. "He threw them on to the women and he was
catching children by their dresses and chucking them in." One
woman in a black dress slipped and fell. She seemed nervous and
did not like to jump at first. When she did jump she did not go far
enough, but fell between the ship and the boat. She was pulled in
by some men on the deck below, went up to the Boat Deck again,
took another jump, and landed safely in the boat. There were
none of the children hurt. The only accident was with this
woman. The only man passenger was a foreigner, up forward.
He, as the boat was being lowered, jumped from A Deck into the
boat—deliberately jumped across and saved himself.

When we got to the water it was impossible to get to the tripper underneath the thwart on account of women being packed
so tight. We had to lift the fall up off the hook by hand to release
the spring to get the block and fall away from it. We pushed off
from the ship and rowed away about 200 yards. We tied up to
three other boats. We gave the man our painter and made fast to
No. 12. We stopped there about an hour, and Officer Lowe
came over with his boat No. 14 and said: "You seamen will have
to distribute these passengers among these boats. Tie them
together and come into my boat to go over to the wreckage and
pick up anyone that is alive there."

Witness testified that the larger lifeboats would hold sixty people.

Senator Smith: Do you wish to be understood that each life-boat like Nos. 12 and 14 and 10 could be filled to its fullest capacity and lowered to the water with safety?

Mr. Evans: Yes, because we did it then, sir.

Senator Smith: That is a pretty good answer.

Mr. Evans: It was my first experience in seeing a boat loaded like that, sir.

The stern of the ship, after plunging forward, remained floating in a perpendicular position about four or five minutes.

W. Burke, dining-room steward (Am. Inq., p. 822):

I went to my station and found that my boat, No. 1, had gone. Then to the port side and assisted with No. 8 boat and saw her lowered. Then I passed to No. 10. The officer said, "Get right in there," and pushed me toward the boat, and I got in. When there were no women to be had around the deck the officer gave the order for the boat to be lowered.

After the two seamen (Buley and Evans) were transferred to boat No. 14, some of the women forward said to me: "There are two men down here in the bottom of the boat." I got hold of them and pulled one out. He apparently was a Japanese and could not speak English. I put him at an oar. The other appeared to be an Italian. I tried to speak to him but he said: "Armenian." I also put him at an oar. I afterwards made fast to an officer's boat—I think it was Mr. Lightoller's (i. e., No. 12).

Mrs. Imanita Shelley's affidavit (Am. Inq., p. 1146):

Mrs. Shelley with her mother, Mrs. L. D. Parrish, were second-cabin passengers. Mrs. Shelley had been sick and it was with difficulty that she reached the deck, where she was assisted to a chair. After some time a sailor ran to her and implored her to get in the lifeboat that was then being launched—one of the last on the ship. Pushing her mother toward the sailor, Mrs. Shelley made for the davits where the boat hung.

There was a space of between four or five feet between the edge of the deck and the suspended boat. The sailor picked up Mrs. Parrish and threw her bodily into the boat. Mrs. Shelley jumped and landed safely. There were a fireman and a ship's baker among the crew at the time of launching. The boat was filled with women and children, as many as could get in without overcrowding. There was trouble with the tackle and the ropes had to be cut.

Just as they reached the water, a crazed Italian jumped from the deck into the lifeboat, landing on Mrs. Parrish, severely bruising her right side and leg.

Orders had been given to keep in sight of the ship's boat which had been sent out ahead to look for help. Throughout the entire period, from the time of the collision and taking to the boats, the ship's crew behaved in an ideal manner. Not a man tried to get into a boat unless ordered to, and many were seen to strip off their clothing and wrap it around the women and children, who came up half-clad from their beds. Mrs. Shelley says that no crew could have behaved in a more perfect manner.

J. Joughin, head baker (Br. Inq.):

Chief Officer Wilde shouted to the stewards to keep the men passengers back, but there was no necessity for the order as they were keeping back. The order was splendid. The stewards, firemen and sailors got in line and passed the ladies in; and then we had difficulty to find ladies to go into the boat. No distinction at all as to class was made. I saw a number of third-class women with their bags, which they would not let go.

The boat was let down and the women were forcibly drawn into it. The boat was a yard and a half from the ship's side. There was a slight list and we had to drop them in. The officer ordered two sailors and a steward to get in.

BOAT NO. 12[1]

No male passenger in this boat

Passengers: Miss Phillips.

Bade good-bye to his daughter and sank with the ship: Mr. Phillips.

Women and children: 40.

Crew: Seamen Poigndestre (in charge), F. Clench. Later, Lucas and two firemen were transferred from boat "D."

Jumped from deck below as boat was lowered: 1 Frenchman.

Total: 43.

Transfers were made to this boat *first* from Engelhardt "D" and *second*, from Engelhardt upset boat "B," so that it reached the *Carpathia*'s side with seventy, or more.

Incidents

F. Clench, A. B. (Am. Inq., p. 636):

The second officer and myself stood on the gunwale and helped load women and children. The chief officer passed them along to us and we filled three boats, No. 12 first. In each there were about forty or fifty people. After finishing No. 16 boat, I went back to No. 12. "How many men (crew) have you in this boat?" the chief officer said, and I said, "Only one, sir." He looked up and said: "Jump into that boat," and that made a complement of two seamen. An able seaman was in charge of this boat. (Poigndestre.) We had instructions to keep our eye on No. 14 and keep together.

There was only one male passenger in our boat, and that was a Frenchman who jumped in and we could not find him. He got under the thwart, mixed up with the women, just as we dropped into the water before the boat was lowered and without our knowledge. Officer Lowe transferred some of his people into

1. British Report (p. 38) says this was the fourth boat lowered on port side at 1:25 a.m.

our boat and others, making close on to sixty, and pretty full up. When Mr. Lowe was gone I heard shouts. I looked around and saw a boat in the way that appeared to be like a funnel; we thought it was the top of a funnel. (It was Engelhardt overturned boat "B.") There were about twenty on this, and we took off approximately ten, making seventy in my boat.

John Poigndestre, A. B. (Br. Inq., p. 82):

Lightoller ordered us to lay off and stand by close to the ship. Boat "D" and three lifeboats made fast to No. 12. Stood off about 100 yards after ship sank. Not enough sailors to help pick up swimmers. No light. Transfer of about a dozen woman passengers from No. 14 to No. 12. About 150 yards off when *Titanic* sank. No compass.

BOAT NO. 14[1]

No male passenger in this boat

Passengers: Mrs. Compton, Miss Compton, Mrs. Minahan, Miss Minahan, Mrs. Collyer, Miss Collyer.

Picked up out of sea: W. F. Hoyt (who died), Steward J. Stewart, and a plucky Japanese.

Women: 50.

Volunteer when crew was short: C. Williams.

Crew: Fifth Officer Lowe, Seaman Scarrot, 2 firemen, Stewards Crowe and Morris.

Stowaway: 1 Italian.

Bade good-bye and sank with ship: Dr. Minahan, Mr. Compton, Mr. Collyer.

Total: 60.

---

1. British Report (p. 38) says this was the fifth boat on the port side, lowered at 1:30.

Incidents

H. G. Lowe, Fifth Officer (Am. Inq., 116):

Nos. 12, 14 and 16 were down about the same time. I told Mr. Moody that three boats had gone away and that an officer ought to go with them. He said: "You go." There was difficulty in lowering when I got near the water. I dropped her about five feet, because I was not going to take the chance of being dropped down upon by somebody. While I was on the Boat Deck, two men tried to jump into the boat. I chased them out.

We filled boats 14 and 16 with women and children. Moody filled No. 16 and I filled No. 14. Lightoller was there part of the time. They were all women and children, barring one passenger, who was an Italian, and he sneaked in dressed like a woman. He had a shawl over his head. There was another passenger, a chap by the name of C. Williams, whom I took for rowing. He gave me his name and address (referring to book), "C. Williams, Racket Champion of the World, 2 Drury Road, Harrow-on-the-Hill, Middlesex, England."

As I was being lowered, I expected every moment that my boat would be doubled up under my feet. I had overcrowded her, but I knew that I had to take a certain amount of risk. I thought if one additional body was to fall into that boat, that slight additional weight might part the hooks, or carry away something; so as we were coming down past the open decks, I saw a lot of Latin people all along the ship's rails. They were glaring more or less like wild beasts, ready to spring. That is why I yelled out to "look out," and let go, bang! right along the ship's side. There was a space I should say of about three feet between the side of the boat and the ship's side, and as I went down I fired these shots without any intention of hurting anybody and with the positive knowledge that I did not hurt anybody. I fired, I think, three times.

Later, 150 yards away, I herded five boats together. I was in No. 14; then I had 10, 12, collapsible "D" and one other boat

(No. 4), and made them tie up. I waited until the yells and shrieks had subsided for the people to thin out, and then I deemed it safe for me to go amongst the wreckage; so I transferred all my passengers, somewhere about fifty-three, from my boat and equally distributed them among my other four boats. Then I asked for volunteers to go with me to the wreck, and it was at this time that I found the Italian. He came aft and had a shawl over his head, and I suppose he had skirts. Anyhow, I pulled the shawl off his face and saw he was a man. He was in a great hurry to get into the other boat and I got hold of him and pitched him in.

Senator Smith: Pitched him in?

Mr. Lowe: Yes; because he was not worth being handled better.

Senator Smith: You pitched him in among the women?

Mr. Lowe: No, sir; in the forepart of the lifeboat in which I transferred my passengers.

Senator Smith: Did you use some pretty emphatic language when you did this?

Mr. Lowe: No, sir: I did not say a word to him.

Then I went off and rowed to the wreckage and around the wreckage and picked up four people alive. I do not know who these live persons were. They never came near me afterwards either to say this or that or the other. But one died, Mr. W. F. Hoyt, of New York. After we got him in the boat we took his collar off so as to give him more chance to breathe, but unfortunately, he died. He was too far gone when we picked him up. I then left the wreck. I went right around, and, strange to say, I did not see a single female body around the wreckage. I did not have a light in my boat. Then I could see the *Carpathia* coming up and I thought: "Well, I am the fastest boat of the lot," as I was sailing, you see. I was going through the water four or five knots, bowling along very nicely.

By and by, I noticed a collapsible boat, Engelhardt "D." It looked rather sorry, so I thought: "Well, I will go down and pick her up and make sure of her." This was Quartermaster Bright's boat. Mrs. H. B. Harris, of New York, was in it. She had a broken arm. I had taken this first collapsible ("D") in tow and I noticed that there was another collapsible ("A") in a worse plight than this one that I had in tow. I got to her just in time and took off, I suppose, about twenty men and one lady. I left three male bodies in it. I may have been a bit hard-hearted in doing this. I thought: "I am not here to worry about bodies; I am here to save life and not bother about bodies." The people on the raft told me these had been dead for some time. I do not know whether any one endeavored to find anything on their persons that would identify them, because they were all up to their ankles in water when I took them off.

Joseph Scarrot, A. B. (Br. Inq., pp. 29, 30): I myself took charge of No. 14 as the only sailorman there. The Chief Officer ordered women and children to be taken in. Some men came and tried to rush the boat. They were foreigners and could not understand the orders I gave them, but I managed to keep them away. I had to use some persuasion with a boat tiller. One man jumped in twice and I had to throw him out the third time. I got all the women and children into the boat. There were fifty-four women and four children—one of them a baby in arms. There were myself, two firemen, three or four stewards and Mr. Lowe, who got into the boat. I told him the trouble I had with the men and he brought out his revolver and fired two shots and said: "If there is any more trouble I will fire at them." The shots fired were fired between the boat and the ship's side. The after fall got twisted and we dropped the boat by the releasing gear and got clear of the ship. There were four men rowing. There was a man in the boat who we thought was a sailor, but he was not. He was a window cleaner. The *Titanic* was then about fifty yards off, and we lay there with the other boats. Mr. Lowe was at the helm. We went in the direction of the cries and came among hundreds of dead bodies and lifebelts. We got one man, who died shortly after he got into the boat. One of the stewards tried to restore him, but without avail. There was another man who was calling for help, but among the bodies and wreckage it was too late for us to reach him. It took half an hour to get to that man. Cannot say exactly, but think we got about twenty off of the Engelhardt boat ("A").

E. J. Buley, A. B. (Am. Inq., p. 605):

(After his transfer from No. 10 to No. 14.) Then, with Lowe in his boat No. 14, I went back to where the *Titanic* sank and picked up the remaining live bodies. We got four; all the others were dead. We turned over several to see if they were alive. It looked as if none of them were drowned. They looked as if frozen. The life-belts they had on were that much (indicating) out of the water, and their heads lay back with their faces on the water. They were head and shoulders out of water, with their heads thrown back. In the morning, after we had picked up all that were alive, there was a collapsible boat ("A") swamped, which we saw with a lot of people up to their knees in water. We sailed over to them. We then picked up another boat ("D") and took her in tow. I think we were about the seventh or eighth boat alongside the *Carpathia*.

F. O. Evans, A. B. (Am. Inq., p. 677):

So from No. 10 we got into his (Lowe's) boat, No. 14, and went straight over towards the wreckage with eight or nine men and picked up four persons alive, one of whom died on the way to the *Carpathia*. Another picked up was named J. Stewart, a steward. You could not hardly count the number of dead bodies. I was afraid to look over the sides because it might break my nerves down. We saw no other people in the water or heard their cries, other than these four picked up. The officer said: "Hoist a sail forward." I did so and made sail in the direction of the collapsible boat "A" about a mile and a half away, which had been swamped. There were in it one woman and about ten or eleven men. Then we picked up another collapsible boat ("D") and took her in tow to the *Carpathia*. There were then about twenty-five people in our boat No. 14, including the one who died.

One of the ladies there passed over a flask of whisky to the people who were all wet through. She asked if anybody needed the spirits, and these people were all soaking wet and nearly perished and they passed it around among these men and women.

It took about twenty minutes after we sighted the *Carpathia* to get alongside of her. We saw five or six icebergs—some of them tremendous, about the height of the *Titanic*—and field ice. After we got on the *Carpathia* we saw, at a rough estimate, a twenty-five mile floe, sir, flat like the floor.

F. Crowe, steward (Am. Inq., p. 615):

I assisted in handing the women and children into boat No. 12, and was asked if I could take an oar. I said: "Yes," and was told to man the boat, I believe, by Mr. Murdoch. After getting the women and children in we lowered down to within four or five feet of the water, and then the block and tackle got twisted in some way, causing us to have to cut the ropes to allow the boat to get into the water. This officer, Lowe, told us to do this. He was in the boat with us. I stood by the lever—the lever releasing the blocks from the hooks in the boat. He told me to wait, to get away and cut the line to raise the lever, thereby causing the hooks to open and allow the boat to drop in the water.

There was some shooting that occurred at the time the boat was lowered. There were various men passengers, probably Italians or some foreign nationality other than English or American, who attempted to "rush" the boats. The officers threatened to shoot any man who put his foot into the boat. An officer fired a revolver, but either downward or upward, not shooting at any one of the passengers at all and not injuring anybody. He fired perfectly clear upward and downward and stopped the rush. There was no disorder after that. One woman cried, but that was all. There was no panic or anything in the boat.

After getting into the water I pushed out to the other boats. In No. 14 there were fifty-seven women and children and about six men, including one officer, and I may have been seven. I am not quite sure. I know how many, because when we got out a distance the officer asked me how many people were in the boat.

When the boat was released and fell I think she must have sprung a leak. A lady stated that there was some water coming up over her ankles. Two men and this lady assisted in bailing it out with bails that were kept in the boat for that purpose. We transferred our people to other boats so as to return to the wreck and see if we could pick up anybody else. Returning to the wreck, we heard various cries and endeavored to get among them, and we were successful in doing so, and picked up one body that was floating around in the water. It was that of a man and he expired shortly afterwards. Going further into the wreckage we came across a steward (J. Stewart) and got him into the boat. He was very cold and his hands were kind of stiff. He recovered by the time that we got back to the *Carpathia*.

A Japanese or Chinese young fellow that we picked up on top of some wreckage, which may have been a sideboard or table that was floating around, also survived.[1] We stopped (in the wreckage) until daybreak, and we saw in the distance an Engelhardt collapsible boat ("A") with a crew of men in it. We went over to the boat and found twenty men and one woman; also three dead bodies, which we left. Returning under sail we took another collapsible boat in tow (boat "D") containing fully sixty people, women and children.

I did not see the iceberg that struck the ship. When it came daylight and we could see, there were two or three bergs around, and one man pointed out that that must have been the berg, and another man pointed out another berg. Really, I do not think anybody knew which one struck the ship.

Mrs. Charlotte Collyer, third-class passenger,
in The Semi-Monthly *Magazine, May, 1912:*

A little further on we saw a floating door that must have been torn loose when the ship went down. Lying upon it, face downward, was a small Japanese. He had lashed himself with a rope to his frail raft, using the broken hinges to make the knots

1. Undoubtedly reference is here made to the same Japanese described in an account attributed to a second-class passenger, Mrs. Collyer, and which follows Crowe's testimony.

secure. As far as we could see, he was dead. The sea washed over him every time the door bobbed up and down, and he was frozen stiff. He did not answer when he was hailed, and the officer hesitated about trying to save him.

"What's the use?" said Mr. Lowe. "He's dead, likely, and if he isn't there's others better worth saving than a Jap!"

He had actually turned our boat around, but he changed his mind and went back. The Japanese was hauled on board, and one of the women rubbed his chest, while others chafed his hands and feet. In less time than it takes to tell, he opened his eyes. He spoke to us in his own tongue; then, seeing that we did not understand, he struggled to his feet, stretched his arms above his head, stamped his feet and in five minutes or so had almost recovered his strength. One of the sailors near to him was so tired that he could hardly pull his oar. The Japanese bustled over, pushed him from his seat, took his oar and worked like a hero until we were finally picked up. I saw Mr. Lowe watching him in open-mouthed surprise.

"By Jove!" muttered the officer, "I'm ashamed of what I said about the little blighter. I'd save the likes o' him six times over if I got the chance."

Miss Minahan's affidavit (Am. Inq., p. 1109):

After the *Titanic* went down the cries were horrible. Some of the women implored Officer Lowe of No. 10 to divide his passengers among the three other boats and go back to rescue them. His first answer to these requests was: "You ought to be d—— glad you are here and have got your own life." After some time he was persuaded to do as he was asked. As I came up to him to be transferred to the other boat, he said: "Jump, G—d d—n you, jump." I had shown no hesitancy and was waiting until my turn. He had been so blasphemous during the hours we were in his boat that the women in my end of the boat all thought he was under the influence of liquor. (Testimony elsewhere shows that Officer Lowe is a teetotaler.) Then he took all the men who had rowed No. 14, together with the men from other boats, and went back to the scene of the wreck. We were left with a steward and a stoker to row our boat, which was crowded. The steward did his best, but the stoker refused at first to row, but finally helped two men who were the only ones pulling on that side. It was just four o'clock when we sighted the *Carpathia*, and we were three hours getting to her. On the *Carpathia* we were treated with every kindness and given every comfort possible.

The above affidavit being of record shows Officer Lowe in an unfortunate, bad light. There is no doubt of it that he was intemperate in his language only. In all other respects he was a first-class officer, as proven by what he accomplished. But I am glad that I have the account of another lady passenger in the same boat, which is a tribute to what he did. I met Officer Lowe in Washington the time that both of us were summoned before the U. S. Court of Inquiry, and I am quite sure that the only point against him is that he was a little hasty in speech in the accomplishment of his work.

Miss Compton, who lost her brother, I had the pleasure of meeting on the *Carpathia*. She is still a sufferer from injuries received in the wreck, and yet has been very kind in sending me an account of her experience, from which I cite the following:

As she stood on the rail to step into boat No. 14 it was impossible to see whether she would step into the boat or into the water. She was pushed into the boat with such violence that she found herself on her hands and knees, but fortunately landed on a coil of rope. This seemed to be the general experience of the women. All the passengers entered the lifeboat at the same point and were told to move along to make place for those who followed. This was difficult, as the thwarts were so high that it was difficult to climb over them, encumbered as the ladies were with lifebelts. It was a case of throwing one's self over rather than climbing over.

Miss Compton from her place in the stern of the lifeboat

overheard the conversation between Officer Lowe and another officer, which the former gave in his testimony.

Just before the boat was lowered a man jumped in. He was immediately hauled out. Mr. Lowe then pulled his revolver and said: "If anyone else tries that this is what he will get." He then fired his revolver in the air.

She mentions the same difficulties, elsewhere recorded, about the difficulties in lowering the boat, first the stern very high, and then the bow; also how the ropes were cut and No. 14 struck the water hard. At this time the count showed 58 in the boat, and a later one made the number 60. A child near her answered in neither of the counts.

"Mr. Lowe's manly bearing," she says, "gave us all confidence. As I look back now he seems to me to personify the best traditions of the British sailor. He asked us all to try and find a lantern, but none was to be found. Mr. Lowe had with him, however, an electric light which he flashed from time to time. Almost at once the boat began to leak and in a few moments the women in the forward part of the boat were standing in water. There was nothing to bail with and I believe the men used their hats.

"Officer Lowe insisted on having the mast put up. He crawled forward and in a few moments the mast was raised and ready. He said this was necessary as no doubt with dawn there would be a breeze. He returned to his place and asked the stewards and firemen, who were acting as crew, if they had any matches, and insisted on having them passed to him. He then asked if they had any tobacco and said: 'Keep it in your pockets, for tobacco makes you thirsty.' Mr. Lowe wished to remain near the ship that he might have a chance to help someone after she sank. Some of the women protested and he replied: 'I don't like to leave her, but if you feel that way about it we will pull away a little distance.'"

Miss Compton's account corroborates other information about boat No. 14, which we have elsewhere. She was among the number transferred to Engelhardt boat "D." "I now found myself," she said, "in the stern of a collapsible boat. In spite of Mr. Lowe's warning the four small boats began to separate, each going its own way. Soon it seemed as though our boat was the only one on the sea. We went through a great deal of wreckage. The men who were supposed to be rowing—one was a fireman—made no effort to keep away from it. They were all the time looking towards the horizon. With daylight we saw the *Carpathia*, and not so very long afterwards Officer Lowe, sailing towards us, for, as he had predicted, quite a strong breeze had sprung up. We caught the rope which he threw us from the stern of his boat. Someone in ours succeeded in catching it and we were taken in tow to the *Carpathia*."

BOAT NO. 16[1]

No male passenger

Passengers: Fifty women and children—second and third-class.
Crew: Master-at-arms Bailey in charge. Seaman Archer, Steward Andrews, Stewardess Leather, and two others.
Total: 56.

Incidents

E. Archer, A. B. (Am. Inq., p. 645):

I assisted in getting Nos. 12, 14 and 16 out—getting the falls and everything ready and passengers into No. 14. Then I went to No. 16. I saw that the plug was in tight. I never saw any man get in, only my mate. I heard the officer give orders to lower the boat and to allow nobody in it, having fifty passengers and only my mate and myself. The master-at-arms came down after us; he was the coxswain and took charge. When we were loading the boat there was no effort on the part of others to crowd into it; no confusion at all. No individual men, or others were repelled from getting in; everything was quiet and steady. One of the lady passengers

1. British Report (p. 38) gives this as the sixth boat lowered from the port side at 1:35 a.m.

suggested going back to see if there were any people in the water we could get, but I never heard any more of it after that. There was one lady in the boat, a stewardess (Mrs. Leather) who tried to assist in rowing. I told her it was not necessary, but she said she would like to do it to keep herself warm. There was one fireman found in the boat after we got clear. I do not know how he came there. He was transferred to another boat (No. 6) to help row.

C. E. Andrews, steward (Am. Inq., p. 623):

Besides these six men I should think there were about fifty passengers.

There was no effort on the part of the steerage men to get into our boat. I was told by the officer to allow none in it. When the officer started to fill the boat with passengers and the men to man it, there were no individuals who tried to get in, or that he permitted to get in. There was no confusion whatever. The officer asked me if I could take an oar. I said I could.

BOAT NO. 2[1]

Only one old man, third-class, a foreigner in this boat.

Passengers: Miss Allen (now Mrs. J. B. Mennell), Mrs. Appleton, Mrs. Cornell, Mrs. Douglas and maid (Miss Le Roy), Miss Madill, Mrs. Robert and maid (Amelia Kenchen). One old man, third-class, foreigner, and family: Brahim Youssef, Hanne Youssef, and children Marian and Georges. The rest second and third-class.

Bade good-bye to wife and sank with ship: Mr. Douglas.

Crew: Fourth Officer Boxhall, Seamen Osman and Steward Johnston, cook.

Total: 25.

---

1. British Report (p. 38) gives this as the seventh boat lowered on the port side at 1:45 a.m.

Incidents

J. G. Boxhall, Fourth Officer (Am. Inq., p. 240, and Br. Inq.):

I was sent away in Emergency boat 2, the last boat but one on the port side. There was one of the lifeboats (No. 4) lowered away a few minutes after I left. That was the next lifeboat to me aft. Engelhardt boat "D" was being got ready. There was no anxiety of people to get into these boats. There were four men in this boat—a sailorman (Osman), a steward (Johnston), a cook and myself, and one male passenger who did not speak English—a middle-aged man with a black beard. He had his wife there and some children. When the order was given to lower the boat, which seemed to be pretty full, it was about twenty minutes to half an hour before the ship sank. Someone shouted through a megaphone: "Some of the boats come back and come around to the starboard side." All rowed except this male passenger. I handled one oar and a lady assisted me. She asked to do it. I got around to the starboard side intending to go alongside. I reckoned I could take about three more people off the ship with safety; and when about 22 yards off there was a little suction, as the boat seemed to be drawn closer, and I thought it would be dangerous to go nearer the ship. I suggested going back (after ship sank) to the sailorman in the boat, but decided it was unwise to do so. There was a lady there, Mrs. Douglas, whom I asked to steer the boat according to my orders. She assisted me greatly in it. They told me on board the *Carpathia* afterwards that it was about ten minutes after four when we went alongside.

After we left the *Titanic* I showed green lights most of the time. When within two or three ship lengths of the *Carpathia*, it was just breaking daylight, and I saw her engines were stopped. She had stopped within half a mile or a quarter of a mile of an iceberg. There were several other bergs, and I could see field ice as far as I could see. The bergs looked white in the sun, though when I first saw them at daylight they looked black. This was the first time I had seen field ice on the Grand Banks. I estimate about 25 in my boat.

F. Osman, A. B. (Am. Inq., p. 538):

All of us went up and cleared away the boats. After that we loaded all the boats there were. I went away in No. 2, the fourth from the last to leave the ship. Boxhall was in command. Murdoch directed the loading. All passengers were women and children, except one man, a third-class passenger, his wife and two children. After I got in the boat the officer found a bunch of rockets which was put in the boat by mistake for a box of biscuits. The officer fired some off, and the *Carpathia* came to us first and picked us up half an hour before anybody else. Not until morning did we see an iceberg about 100 feet out of the water with one big point sticking on one side of it, apparently dark, like dirty ice, 100 yards away. I knew that was the one we struck. It looked as if there was a piece broken off.

There was no panic at all. There was no suction whatever. When we were in the boat I shoved off from the ship and I said to the officer: "See if you can get alongside to see if you can get some more hands—squeeze some more hands in"; so the women started to get nervous after I said that, and the officer said: "All right." The women disagreed to that. We pulled around to the starboard side of the ship and found that we could not get to the starboard side because it was listing too far. We pulled astern again that way, and after we lay astern we lay on our oars and saw the ship go down. It seemed to me as if all the engines and everything that was in the after part slid down into the forward part. We did not go back to the place where the ship had sunk because the women were all nervous, and we pulled around as far as we could get from it so that the women would not see and cause a panic. We got as close as we would dare to. We could not have taken any more hands into the boat. It was impossible. We might have gotten one in; that is all. There was no panic amongst the steerage pasengers when we started manning the boats. I saw several people come up from the steerage and go straight up to the Boat Deck, and the men stood back while the women and children got into the boats—steerage passengers as well as others.

Senator Burton: So in your judgment it was safer to have gone on the boat than to have stayed on the *Titanic?*
Witness: Oh, yes, sir.
Senator Burton: That was when you left?
Witness: Yes, sir.
Senator Burton: What did you think when the first boat was launched?
Witness: I did not think she was going down then.

J. Johnston, steward (Br. Inq.):

Crew: Boxhall and four men, including perhaps McCullough. (None such on list.) Boxhall said: "Shall we go back in the direction of cries of distress?" which were a half or three-quarters of a mile off. Ladies said: "No." Officer Boxhall signaled the *Carpathia* with lamp. Soon after launching the swish of the water was heard against the icebergs. In the morning *Carpathia* on the edge of ice-field about 200 yards off.

Mrs. Walter D. Douglas's affidavit (Am. Inq., p. 1100):

Mr. Boxhall had difficulty in getting the boat loose and called for a knife. We finally were launched. Mrs. Appleton and a man from the steerage faced me. Mrs. Appleton's sister, Mrs. Cornell, was back of me and on the side of her the officer. I think there were eighteen or twenty in the boat. There were many who did not speak English. The rowing was very difficult, for no one knew how. We tried to steer under Mr. Boxhall's orders, and he put an old lantern, with very little oil in it, on a pole, which I held up for some time. Mrs. Appleton and some other women had been rowing, and did row all the time. Mr. Boxhall had put into the Emergency boat a tin box of green lights like rockets. These he sent off at intervals, and very quickly we saw the lights of the *Carpathia*, whose captain said he saw our green lights ten miles away and steered directly towards us, so we were the first boat to arrive at the *Carpathia*. When we pulled alongside, Mr. Boxhall called out: "Slow down your engines and take us aboard. I have only one seaman."

Mrs. J. B. Mennell (née Allen):

My aunt, Mrs. Roberts' maid, came to the door and asked if she could speak to me. I went into the corridor and she said: "Miss Allen, the baggage room is full of water." I replied she needn't worry, that the water-tight compartments would be shut and it would be all right for her to go back to her cabin. She went back and returned to us immediately to say her cabin, which was forward on Deck E, was flooded.

We were on the Boat Deck some minutes before being ordered into the lifeboat. Neither my aunt, Mrs. Roberts, my cousin, Miss Madill, nor myself ever saw or heard the band. As we stood there we saw a line of men file by and get into the boat—some sixteen or eighteen stokers. An officer[1] came along and shouted to them: "Get out, you damned cowards; I'd like to see everyone of you overboard." They all got out and the officer said: "Women and children into this boat," and we got in and were lowered.

With the exception of two very harrowing leave-takings, we saw nothing but perfect order and quiet on board the *Titanic*. We were rowed round the stern to the starboard side and away from the ship, as our boat was a small one and Boxhall feared the suction. Mrs. Cornell helped to row all the time.

As the *Titanic* plunged deeper and deeper we could see her stern rising higher and higher until her lights began to go out. As the last lights on the stern went out we saw her plunge distinctively, bow first and intact. Then the screams began and seemed to last eternally. We rowed back, after the *Titanic* was under water, toward the place where she had gone down, but we saw no one in the water, nor were we near enough to any other

1. Probably the same officer, Murdoch, described by Major Peuchen, p. 95, this chapter.

lifeboats to see them. When Boxhall lit his first light the screams grew louder and then died down.

We could hear the lapping of the water on the icebergs, but saw none, even when Boxhall lit his green lights, which he did at regular intervals, till we sighted the *Carpathia*. Our boat was the first one picked up by the *Carpathia*. I happened to be the first one up the ladder, as the others seemed afraid to start up, and when the officer who received me asked where the *Titanic* was, I told him she had gone down.

Capt. A. H. Rostron, of the Carpathia *(Am. Inq., p. 22):*

We picked up the first boat, which was in charge of an officer who I saw was not under full control of his boat. He sang out that he had only one seaman in the boat, so I had to maneuver the ship to get as close to the boat as possible, as I knew well it would be difficult to do the pulling. By the time we had the first boat's people it was breaking day, and then I could see the remaining boats all around within an area of about four miles. I also saw icebergs all around me. There were about twenty icebergs that would be anywhere from about 150 to 200 feet high, and numerous smaller bergs; also numerous ones we call "growlers" anywhere from 10 to 12 feet high and 10 to 15 feet long, above the water.

BOAT NO. 4[1]

No man passenger in this boat

Passengers: Mrs. Astor and maid (Miss Bidois), Miss Bowen, Mrs. Carter and maid (Miss Serepeca), Mrs. Clark, Mrs. Cummings, Miss Eustis, Mrs. Ryerson and children, Miss S. R., Miss

1. British Report (p. 38) says this was the eighth and last *lifeboat* that left the ship and lowered at 1:55 a.m.

E. and Master J. B. and maid (Chandowson), Mrs. Stephenson, Mrs. Thayer and maid, Mrs. Widener and maid.

Women and children: 36. (Br. Rpt.)

Crew: Perkis, Q. M., in charge. Seamen: McCarthy, Hemmings,[1] Lyons[2]; Storekeeper Foley and Assistant Storekeeper Prentice[1]; Firemen: Smith and Dillon[1]; Greasers: Granger and Scott[1]; Stewards: Cunningham,[1] Siebert.[2]

Bade good-bye to wives and sank with ship: Messrs. Astor, Clark, Cummings, Ryerson, Thayer, Widener and his son Harry.

Stowaway: 1 Frenchman.

Total: 40. (Br. Rpt.)

Incidents

C. H. Lightoller, Second Officer (Am. Inq., p. 81):

Previous to putting out Engelhardt Boat "D," Lightoller says, referring to boat No. 4: "We had previously lowered a boat from A Deck, one deck down below. That was through my fault. It was the first boat I had lowered. I was intending to put the passengers in from A Deck. On lowering the boat I found that the windows were closed; so I sent someone down to open the windows and carried on with the other boats, but decided it was not worth while lowering them down—that I could manage just as well from the Boat Deck. When I came forward from the other boats I loaded that boat from A Deck by getting the women out through the windows. My idea in filling the boats there was because there was a wire hawser running along the side of the ship for coaling purposes and it was handy to tie the boat in to hold it so that nobody could drop between the side of the boat and the ship. No. 4 was the fifth boat or the sixth lowered on the port side."[3]

---

1. Picked up from sea.

2. Picked up from sea but died in boat.

3. I agree with this statement though other testimony and the British Report decide against us. The difference may be reconciled by the fact that the loading of this boat began early, but the final lowering was delayed.

W. J. Perkis, Quartermaster (Am. Inq., p. 581):

I lowered No. 4 into the water and left that boat and walked aft; and I came back and a man that was in the boat, one of the seamen, sang out to me: "We need another hand down here," so I slid down the lifeline there from the davit into the boat. I took charge of the boat after I got in, with two sailormen besides myself. There were forty-two, including all hands. We picked up eight people afterwards swimming with life-preservers when about a ship's length away from the ship. No. 4 was the last big boat on the port side to leave the ship. Two that were picked up died in the boat—a seaman (Lyons) and a steward (Siebert). All the others were passengers. After we picked up the men I could not hear any more cries anywhere. The discipline on board the ship was excellent. Every man knew his station and took it. There was no excitement whatever among the officers or crew, the firemen or stewards. They conducted themselves the same as they would if it were a minor, everyday occurrence.

Senator Perkins (addressing Perkis, Symon and Hogg):

All three of you seem to be pretty capable young men and have had a great deal of experience at sea, and yet you have never been wrecked?

Mr. Perkis: Yes, sir.

Senator Perkins: Is there any other one of you who has been in a shipwreck?

Mr. Hogg: I have been in a collision, Senator, but with no loss of life.

Senator Perkins: Unless you have something more to state that you think will throw light on this subject, that will be all, and we thank you for what you have said.

Mr. Hogg: That is all I have to say except this: I think the women ought to have a gold medal on their breasts. God bless them. I will always raise my hat to a woman after what I saw.

Senator Perkins: What countrywomen were they?

Mr. Hogg: They were American women I had in mind. They were all Americans.

Senator Perkins: Did they man the oars? Did they take the oars and pull?

Mr. Hogg: Yes, sir; I took an oar all the time myself and also steered. Then I got one lady to steer; then another to assist me with an oar. She rowed to keep herself warm.

Senator Perkins: One of you stated that his boat picked up eight people, and the other that he did not pick up any. Could you not have picked up just as well as this other man?

Mr. Hogg: I wanted to assist in picking up people, but I had an order from somebody in the boat (No. 7)—I do not know who it was—not to take in any more; that we had done our best.

Senator Perkins: I merely ask the question because of the natural thought that if one boat picked up eight persons the other boat may have been able to do so.—You did not get any orders, Mr. Symon (boat No. 1), not to pick up any more people?

Mr. Symon: No, sir; there were no more around about where I was.

Senator Perkins: As I understand, one of the boats had more packed into it than the other. As I understand it, Mr. Symon pulled away from the ship and then when he came back there they picked up all the people that were around?

Mr. Symon made no reply.

S. S. Hemming, A. B. (Am. Inq.):

Everything was black over the starboard side. I could not see any boats. I went over to the port side and saw a boat off the port quarter and I went along the port side and got up the after boat davits and slid down the fall and swam to the boat about 200 yards. When I reached the boat I tried to get hold of the grab-line on the bows. I pulled my head above the gunwale, and I said: "Give us a hand, Jack." Foley was in the boat; I saw him standing up. He said: "Is that you, Sam?" I said: "Yes" to him and the women and children pulled me in the boat.

After the ship sank we pulled back and picked up seven of the crew including a seaman, Lyons, a fireman, Dillon, and two stewards, Cunningham and Siebert. We made for the light of another lifeboat and kept in company with her. Then day broke and we saw two more lifeboats. We pulled toward them and we all made fast by the painter. Then we helped with boat No. 12 to take off the people on an overturned boat ("B"). From this boat ("B") we took about four or five, and the balance went into the other boat. There were about twenty altogether on this boat ("B").

A. Cunningham, steward (Am. Inq., p. 794):

I first learned of the very serious character of the collision from my own knowledge when I saw the water on the post-office deck. I waited on the ship until all the boats had gone, and then threw myself into the water. This was about 2 o'clock. I was in the water about half an hour before the ship sank. I swam clear of the ship about three-quarters of a mile. I was afraid of the suction. My mate, Siebert, left the ship with me. I heard a lifeboat and called to it and went toward it. I found Quartermaster Perkis in charge. Hemmings, the sailor, Foley (storekeeper) and a fireman (Dillon) were in this boat. I never saw any male passengers in the boat. We picked up Prentice, assistant storekeeper. I think No. 4 was the nearest to the scene of the accident because it picked up more persons in the water. About 7:30 we got aboard the Carpathia. When we sighted her she might have been four or five miles away.

R. P. Dillon, trimmer (Br. Inq.):

I went down with the ship and sank about two fathoms. Swam about twenty minutes in the water and was picked up by No. 4. About 1,000 others in the water in my estimation. Saw no women. Recovered consciousness and found Sailor Lyons and another lying on top of me dead.

Thomas Granger, greaser (Br. Inq.):

I went to the port side of the Boat Deck aft, climbed down a rope and got into a boat near the ship's side, No. 4, which had come back because there were not enough men to pull her. She was full of women and children. F. Scott, greaser, also went down the falls and got into this boat. Perkis, quartermaster, and Hemmings then in it. Afterwards picked up Dillon and another man (Prentice) out of the water.

F. Scott, greaser (Br. Inq.):

We went on deck on starboard side first as she had listed over to the port side, but we saw no boats. When I came up the engineers came up just after me on the Boat Deck. I saw only eight of them out of thirty-six on the deck. Then we went to the port side and saw boats. An officer fired a shot and I heard him say that if any man tried to get in that boat he would shoot him like a dog. At this time all the boats had gone from the starboard side. I saw one of the boats, No. 4, returning to the ship's side and I climbed on the davits and tried to get down the falls but fell in the water and was picked up. It was nearly two o'clock when I got on the davits and down the fall.

Mrs. E. B. Ryerson's affidavit (Am. Inq., p. 1107):

We were ordered down to A Deck, which was partly enclosed. We saw people getting into boats, but waited our turn. My boy, Jack, was with me. An officer at the window said: "That boy cannot go." My husband said: "Of course that boy goes with his mother; he is only thirteen"; so they let him pass. I turned and kissed my husband and as we left he and the other men I knew, Mr. Thayer, Mr. Widener and others, were standing together very quietly. There were two men and an officer inside and a sailor outside to help us. I fell on top of the women who were already in the boat and scrambled to the bow with my eldest daughter. Miss Bowen and my boy were in the stern, and my second daughter was in the middle of the boat with my maid. Mrs. Thayer, Mrs. Widener, Mrs. Astor and Miss Eustis were the only ones I knew in our boat.

Presently an officer called out from the upper deck: "How many women are there in that boat?" Someone answered: "Twenty-four." "That's enough; lower away."

The ropes seemed to stick at one end. Someone called for a knife, but it was not needed until we got into the water as it was but a short distance; and then I realized for the first time how far the ship had sunk. The deck we left was only about twenty feet from the sea. I could see all the portholes open and the water washing in, and the decks still lighted. Then they called out: "How many seamen have you?" and they answered: "One." "That is not enough," said the officer, "I will send you another"; and he sent a sailor down the rope. In a few minutes several other men, not sailors, came down the ropes over the davits and dropped into our boat. The order was given to pull away, and then they rowed off. Someone shouted something about a gangway, and no one seemed to know what to do. Barrels and chairs were being thrown overboard. As the bow of the ship went down the lights went out. The stern stood up for several minutes black against the stars and then the boat plunged down. Then began the cries for help of people drowning all around us, which seemed to go on forever. Someone called out: "Pull for your lives or you will be sucked under," and everyone that could rowed like mad. I could see my younger daughter and Mrs. Thayer and Mrs. Astor rowing, but there seemed to be no suction. Then we turned and picked up some of those in the water. Some of the women protested, but others persisted, and we dragged in six or seven men. The men rescued were stewards, stokers, sailors, etc., and were so chilled and frozen already that they could hardly move. Two of them died in the stern later and many of them were raving and moaning and delirious most of the time. We had no lights or compass. There were several babies in the boat.

Officer Lowe called out to tie together, and as soon as we could make out the other boats in the dark five were tied together. We could dimly see an overturned boat with about twenty men standing on it, back to back. As the sailors in our boat said we could still carry from eight to ten people, we called for another boat to volunteer and go and rescue them, so we cut loose our painters and between us got all the men off. Then when the sun rose we saw the *Carpathia* standing up about five miles away, and for the first time saw the icebergs all around us. We got on board about 8 o'clock.

Mrs. Thayer's affidavit:

The after part of the ship then reared in the air, with the stern upwards, until it assumed an almost vertical position. It seemed to remain stationary in this position for many seconds (perhaps twenty), then suddenly dove straight down out of sight. It was 2:20 a.m. when the *Titanic* disappeared, according to a wrist watch worn by one of the passengers in my boat.

We pulled back to where the vessel had sunk and on our way picked up six men who were swimming—two of whom were drunk and gave us much trouble all the time. The six men we picked up were hauled into the boat by the women. Two of these men died in the boat.

The boat we were in started to take in water; I do not know how. We had to bail. I was standing in ice cold water up to the top of my boots all the time, and rowing continuously for nearly five hours. We took off about fifteen more people who were standing on a capsized boat. In all, our boat had by that time sixty-five or sixty-six people. There was no room to sit down in our boat, so we all stood, except some sitting along the side.

I think the steerage passengers had as good a chance as any of the rest to be saved.

The boat I was in was picked up by the *Carpathia* at 7 a.m. on Monday, we having rowed three miles to her, as we could not wait for her to come up on account of our boat taking in so much water that we would not have stayed afloat much longer.

I never saw greater courage or efficiency than was displayed by the officers of the ship. They were calm, polite and perfectly splendid. They also worked hard. The bedroom stewards also behaved extremely well.

Mrs. Stephenson's and Miss Eustis's story kindly handed me for publication in my book contains the following:

"We were in the companionway of A Deck when order came for *women and children to Boat Deck and men to starboard side.* Miss Eustis and I took each other's hands, not to be separated in the crowd, and all went on deck, we following close to Mrs. Thayer and her maid and going up narrow iron stairs to the forward Boat Deck which, on the *Titanic*, was the captain's bridge.

"At the top of the stairs we found Captain Smith looking much worried and anxiously waiting to get down after we got up. The ship listed heavily to port just then. As we leaned against the walls of the officers' quarters rockets were being fired over our heads, which was most alarming, as we fully realized if the *Titanic* had used her wireless to ill effect and was sending rockets it must be serious. Shortly after that the order came from the head dining room steward (Dodd) to go down to A Deck, when Mrs. Thayer remarked, 'Tell us where to go and we will follow. You ordered us up here and now you are taking us back,' and he said, 'Follow me.'

"On reaching the A Deck we could see, for the decks were lighted by electricity, that a boat was lowered parallel to the windows; these were opened and a steamer chair put under the rail for us to step on. The ship had listed badly by that time and the boat hung far out from the side, so that some of the men said, 'No woman could step across that space.' A call was made for a ladder on one of the lower decks, but before it ever got there we were all in the boat. Whether they had drawn the boat over with boathooks nearer the side I do not know, but the space was easily jumped with the help of two men in the boat.

"I remember seeing Colonel Astor, who called 'Good-bye' and said he would follow in another boat, asking the number of our boat, which they said was 'No. 4.' In going through the window I was obliged to throw back the steamer rug, for, with my fur coat and huge cork life-preserver, I was very clumsy. Later we found the stewards or crew had thrown the steamer rugs into the boat, and they did good service, Miss Eustis' around a baby thinly clad, and mine for a poor member of the crew pulled in from the sea.

"Our boat I think took off every woman on the deck at that time and was the last on the port side to be lowered.

"When we reached the sea we found the ship badly listed, her nose well in so that there was water on the D Deck, which we could plainly see as the boat was lighted and the ports on D Deck were square instead of round. No lights could be found in our boat and the men had great difficulty in casting off the blocks as they did not know how they worked. My fear here was great, as she seemed to be going faster and faster and I dreaded lest we should be drawn in before we could cast off.

"When we finally were ready to move the order was called from the deck to go to the stern hatch and take off some men. There was no hatch open and we could see no men, but our crew obeyed orders, much to our alarm, for they were throwing wreckage over and we could hear a cracking noise resembling china breaking. We implored the men to pull away from the ship, but they refused, and we pulled three men into the boat who had dropped off the ship and were swimming towards us. One man was drunk and had a bottle of brandy in his pocket which the quartermaster promptly threw overboard and the drunken man was thrown into the bottom of the boat and a blanket thrown over him. After these three men were hauled in, they told how fast the ship was sinking and we all implored them to pull for our lives to get out from the suction when she should go down. The lights on the ship burned till just before she went. When the call came that she was going I covered my face and heard some one call, 'She's broken.' After what seemed a long time I turned my head only to see the stern almost perpendicular in the air so that the full outline of the blades of the propeller showed above the water. She then gave her final plunge and the air was filled with cries. We rowed back and pulled in five more men from the sea. Their suffering from the icy water was intense and two men who had been pulled into the stern afterwards died, but we kept their bodies with us until we reached the *Carpathia*, where they were taken aboard and Monday afternoon given a decent burial with three others.

"After rescuing our men we found several lifeboats near us and an order was given to tie together, which we obeyed. It did not seem as if we were together long when one boat said they could rescue more could they get rid of some of the women and children aboard and some of them were put into our boat. Soon after cries of 'Ship ahoy' and a long low moan came to us and an officer in command of one of the boats ordered us to follow him. We felt that we were already too crowded to go, but our men, with quartermaster and boatswain in command, followed the officer and we pulled over to what proved to be an overturned boat crowded with men. We had to approach it very cautiously, fearing our wash would sweep them off. We could take only a few and they had to come very cautiously. The other boat (No. 12) took most of them and we then rowed away."

This rescue, which Mrs. Stephenson so well describes, occurred at dawn. Her story now returns to the prior period of night time.

"The sea was smooth and the night brilliant with more stars than I had ever seen.

"Occasionally a green light showed which proved to be on the Emergency boat, and our men all recognized it as such. We all prayed for dawn, and there was no conversation, everyone being so awed by the disaster and bitterly cold.

"With the dawn came the wind, and before long quite a sea was running. Just before daylight on the horizon we saw what we felt sure must be the lights of a ship. The quartermaster was a long time in admitting that we were right, urging that it was

the moon, but we insisted and they then said it might be the
Carpathia as they had been told before leaving the *Titanic* that
she was coming to us. For a long time after daylight we were in
great wreckage from the *Titanic*, principally steamer chairs and
a few white pilasters.

"We felt we could never reach the *Carpathia* when we found
she had stopped, and afterwards when we asked why she didn't
come closer we were told that some of the early boats which put
off from the starboard side reached her a little after four, while
it was after six when we drew under the side of the open hatch.

"It had been a long trying row in the heavy sea and impossible
to keep bow on to reach the ship. We stood in great danger of
being swamped many times and Captain Rostron, who watched
us come up, said he doubted if we could have lived an hour longer in that high sea. Our boat had considerable water in the centre, due to the leakage and also the water brought in by the eight
men from their clothing. They had bailed her constantly in order
to relieve the weight. Two of the women near us were dying seasick, but the babies slept most of the night in their mothers'
arms. The boatswain's chair was slung down the side and there
were also rope ladders. Only few, however, of the men were able
to go up the ladders. Mail bags were dropped down in which the
babies and little children were placed and hoisted up. We were
told to throw off our life-preservers and then placed in a boatswain's chair and hoisted to the open hatch where ready arms
pulled us in; warm blankets waited those in need and brandy
was offered to everybody. We were shown at once to the saloon,
where hot coffee and sandwiches were being served."

ENGELHARDT BOAT "D"[1]

No male passenger in this boat

Passengers: Mrs. J. M. Brown, Mrs. Harris, Mrs. Frederick
Hoyt, the Navratil children.

1. British Report (p. 38) puts this as the last boat lowered at 2:05.

Picked up from the sea: Frederick Hoyt.

Bade good-bye to wife and sank with ship: Mr. Harris.

Crew: Bright, Q. M., in charge; Seaman Lucas; Steward Hardy.

Stowaway: One steerage foreigner, Joseph Dugemin.

Jumped from deck below as boat was lowered: H. B. Steffanson (Swede), and H. Woolner (Englishman).

Total: 44. British Report (p. 38): Crew 2, men passengers 2, women and children 40.

Incidents

C. H. Lightoller, Second Officer (Am. Inq., p. 81):

In the case of the last boat I got out, the very last of all to leave the ship, I had the utmost difficulty in finding women. After all the other boats were put out we came forward to put out the Engelhardt collapsible boats. In the meantime the forward Emergency boat (No. 2) had been put out by one of the other officers, so we rounded up the tackles and got the collapsible boat to put that over. Then I called for women and could not get any. Somebody said: "There are no women." This was on the Boat Deck where all the women were supposed to be because the boats were there. There were between fifteen and twenty people put into this boat—one seaman and another seaman, or steward. This was the very last boat lowered in the tackles. I noticed plenty of Americans standing near me, who gave me every assistance they could, regardless of nationality.

And before the British Court of Inquiry the same officer testified:

Someone shouted: "There are no more women." Some of the men began climbing in. Then someone said: "There are some more women," and when they came forward the men got out of the boat again. I saw no men in her, but I believe a couple of Chinese stowed away in her.

When that boat went away there were no women whatever. I did not consider it advisable to wait, but to try to get at once away from the ship. I did not want the boat to be "rushed." Splendid order was maintained. No attempt was made to "rush" that boat by the men. When this boat was being loaded I could see the water coming up the stairway. There was splendid order on the boat until the last. As far as I know there were no male passengers in the boats I saw off except the one man I ordered in, Major Peuchen.

A. J. Bright, Q. M. (Am. Inq., p. 831):

Quartermaster Rowe, Mr. Boxhall and myself fired the distress signals, six rockets I think in all, at intervals. After we had finished firing the distress signals, there were two boats left (Engelhardt collapsibles "C" and "D"). All the lifeboats were away before the collapsible boats were lowered. They had to be, because the collapsible boats were on the deck and the other boats had to be lowered before they could be used. The same tackle with which the lifeboats and the Emergency boats were lowered was employed after they had gone in lowering the collapsible boats.

Witness says that both he and Rowe assisted in getting out the starboard collapsible boat "C" and then he went to the port side and filled up the other boat "D" with passengers, about twenty-five in all. There was a third-class passenger, a man, in the boat, who was on his way to Albion, N.Y. (The passenger list shows this man to have been Joseph Dugemin.)

We were told to pull clear and get out of the suction. When boat "D" was lowered the forecastle head was just going under water; that would be about twenty feet lower than the bridge, and the ship had then sunk about fifty feet—all of that, because when boat "D" was lowered the foremost fall was lower down and the after one seemed to hang and he called out to hang on to the foremost fall and to see what was the matter and let go the after fall. Boat "D" was fifty to a hundred yards away when the ship sank.[1] They had a lantern in the boat but no oil to light it. After leaving the boat, witness heard something but not an explosion. It was like a rattling of chains more than anything else.

After "D" got away Mr. Lowe came alongside in another boat, No. 14, and told them to stick together and asked for the number in "D" boat. Steward Hardy counted and told him. Lowe then put about ten or a dozen men from some other boat into witness's boat because it was not filled up. One seaman was taken out. This would make thirty-seven in "D" boat. Just at daylight they saw one of the collapsible boats, "A," that was awash—just flush with the water. Officer Lowe came and took boat "D" in tow, because it had very few men to pull, and towed it to boat "A" and took twelve men and one woman off and put them into his boat No. 14. They were standing in water just about to their ankles when No. 14 and "D" came up to them. They turned the swamped boat adrift with two (three) dead bodies. They were then towed under sail by Mr. Lowe's boat to the *Carpathia*, about four miles away.

William Lucas, A. B. (Br. Inq.):

Got into Engelhardt "D." The water was then right up under the bridge. Had not gone more than 100 yards when there was an explosion and 150 yards when the *Titanic* sank. Had to get some of the women to take oars. There was no rudder in the boat. Changed oars from one side to the other to get her away. Saw a faint red light abaft the *Titanic*'s beam about nine miles away—the headlight also. The witness was transferred to No. 12.

J. Hardy, Chief Steward, second-class (Am. Inq., p. 587):

We launched this boat filled with passengers. Mr. Lightoller and myself loaded it. I went away in it with the quartermaster

---

1. The interval of time can then be approximated as nearly a half hour, that we remained on the ship after the lifeboats left.

(Bright) and two firemen. There were Syrians in the bottom of the boat, third-class passengers, chattering the whole night in their strange language. There were about twenty-five women and children. We lowered away and got to the water; the ship then had a heavy list to port. We got clear of the ship and rowed out some distance from her. Mr. Lowe told us to tie up with other boats, that we would be better seen and could keep better together. He, having a full complement of passengers in his boat, transferred about ten to ours, making thirty-five in our boat. When we left the ship, where we were lowered, there were no women and children there in sight at all. There was nobody to lower the boat. No men passengers when we were ready to lower it. They had gone; where, I could not say. We were not more than forty feet from the water when we were lowered. We picked up the husband (Frederick W. Hoyt) of a wife that we had loaded in the boat. The gentleman took to the water and climbed in the boat after we had lowered it. He sat there wringing wet alongside me, helping to row.

I had great respect and great regret for Officer Murdoch. I was walking along the deck forward with him and he said: "I believe she is gone, Hardy." This was a good half hour before my boat was lowered.

Senator Fletcher: Where were all these passengers; these 1,600 people?

Mr. Hardy: They must have been between decks or on the deck below or on the other side of the ship. I cannot conceive where they were.

In his letter to me, Mr. Frederick M. Hoyt relates his experience as follows:

"I knew Captain Smith for over fifteen years. Our conversation that night amounted to little or nothing. I simply sympathized with him on the accident; but at that time, as I then never expected to be saved, I did not want to bother him with questions, as I knew he had all he wanted to think of. He did suggest that I go down to A Deck and see if there were not a boat alongside. This I did, and to my surprise saw the boat "D" still hanging on the davits (there having been some delay in lowering her), and it occurred to me that if I swam out and waited for her to shove off they would pick me up, which was what happened."

Hugh Woolner, first-class passenger (Am. Inq., p. 887):

Then I said to Steffanson, "Let us go down on to A Deck." And we went down again, but there was nobody there. I looked on both sides of the deck and saw no people. It was absolutely deserted, and the electric lights along the ceiling of A Deck were beginning to turn red, just a glow, a red sort of glow. So I said to Steffanson, "This is getting to be rather a tight corner; let us go out through the door at the end." And as we went out *the sea came in onto the deck at our feet.* Then we hopped up onto the gunwale, preparing to jump into the sea, because if we had waited a minute longer we should have been boxed in against the ceiling. And as we looked out we saw this collapsible boat, the last boat on the port side, being lowered right in front of our faces.

Senator Smith: How far out?

Mr. Woolner: It was about nine feet out.

Senator Smith: Nine feet away from the side of A Deck?

Mr. Woolner: Yes.

Senator Smith: You saw a collapsible boat being lowered?

Mr. Woolner: Being lowered; yes.

Senator Smith: Was it filled with people?

Mr. Woolner: It was full up to the bow, and I said to Steffanson, "There is nobody in the bows. Let us make a jump for it. You go first." And he jumped out and tumbled in head over heels into the boat, and I jumped too and hit the gunwale with my chest, which had on the life-preserver, of course, and I sort of tumbled off the gunwale and caught the gunwale with my fingers and slipped off backwards.

Senator Smith: Into the water?

Mr. Woolner: As my legs dropped down I felt that they were in the sea.

Senator Smith: You are quite sure you jumped nine feet to get that boat?

Mr. Woolner: That is my estimate. By that time you see we were jumping slightly downward.

Senator Smith: Did you jump out or down?

Mr. Woolner: Both.

Senator Smith: Both out and down?

Mr. Woolner: Slightly down and out.

Senator Smith: It could not have been very far down if the water was on A Deck; it must have been out.

Mr. Woolner: Chiefly out; but it was sufficiently down for us to see just over the edge of the gunwale of the boat.

Senator Smith: You pulled yourself up out of the water?

Mr. Woolner: Yes; and then I hooked my right heel over the gunwale, and by this time Steffanson was standing up and he caught hold of me and lifted me in.

One lady (Mrs. Harris) had a broken elbow bone. She was in a white woolen jacket. At dawn Officer Lowe transferred five or six from his boat No. 14 to ours, which brought us down very close to the water. At daylight we saw a great many icebergs of different colors, as the sun struck them. Some looked white, some looked blue, some looked mauve and others were dark gray. There was one double-toothed one that looked to be of good size; it must have been about one hundred feet high.

The *Carpathia* seemed to come up slowly, and then she stopped. We looked out and saw there was a boat alongside and then we realized she was waiting for us to come up to her instead of her coming to us, as we hoped. Then Mr. Lowe towed us with his boat, No. 14, under sail. After taking a group of people off of boat "A"—a dozen of them—including one woman, we sailed to the *Carpathia*. There was a child in the boat—one of those little children whose parents everybody was looking for (the Navatil children).

• • •

The last of the Titanic's boats which were never launched, but floated off, were the two Engelhardt collapsibles "A" and "B" on the roof of the officer's house. In my personal account I have already given the story of boat "B", the upset one on which Second Officer Lightoller, Jack Thayer, myself and others escaped. Since I wrote the account of my personal experience I have had access to other sources of information, including some already referred to; and though at the expense of some repetition, I think it may be of interest to include the record of this boat in the present chapter, as follows:

ENGELHARDT BOAT "B"

[The Upset Boat]

Passengers: A. H. Barkworth, Archibald Gracie, John B. Thayer, Jr., first cabin.

Crew: Second Officer Lightoller, Junior Marconi Operator Bride, Firemen: McGann, Senior; Chief Baker Joughin; Cooks: Collins, Maynard; Steward Whiteley, "J. Hagan." Seaman J. Mc-Gough (possibly). Two men died on boat. Body of one transferred to No. 12 and finally to *Carpathia*. He was a fireman probably, but Cunard Co. preserved no record of him or his burial.

Incidents

C. H. Lightoller, Second Officer (Am. Inq., pp. 87, 91, 786):

I was on top of the officers' quarters and there was nothing more to be done. The ship then took a dive and I turned face forward and also took a dive from on top, practically amidships a little to the starboard, where I had got to. I was driven back against the blower, which is a large thing that shape (indicating) which faces forward to the wind and which then goes down to the stoke hole; but there is a grating there and it was against this grating that I was sucked by the water, and held there under water. There was a terrific blast of air and water and I was blown out clear. I came up above the water, which barely threw me away at all, because I went down again against these fiddley gratings immediately abreast of the funnel over the stoke hole to which this fiddley leads. Colonel Gracie, I believe, was sucked down in identically the same manner on the fiddley gratings, caused by the water rushing down below as the ship was going down.

I next found myself alongside of that overturned boat. This was before the *Titanic* sank. The funnel then fell down and if there was anybody on that side of the Engelhardt boat it fell on them. The ship was not then submerged by considerable. The stern was completely out of the water. I have heard some controversy as to the boilers exploding owing to coming in contact with salt water, by men who are capable of giving an opinion, but there seems to be an open question as to whether cold water actually does cause boilers to explode.

I hardly had any opportunity to swim. It was the action of the funnel falling that threw us out a considerable distance away from the ship. We had no oars or other effective means for propelling the overturned boat. We had little bits of wood, but they were practically ineffective.

On our boat, as I have said before, were Colonel Gracie and young Thayer. I think they were the only two passengers. There were no women on our overturned boat. These were all taken out of the water and they were firemen and others of the crew— roughly about thirty. I take that from my own estimate and from the estimate of someone who was looking down from the bridge of the *Carpathia*.

And from the same officer's testimony before the British Court as follows:

An order was given to cut the lashings of the other Engelhardt boats. It was then too late as the water was rushing up to the

Boat Deck and there was not time to get them to the falls. He
then went across to the officers' quarters on the starboard side to
see what he could do. Then the vessel seemed to take a bit of a
dive. He swam off and cleared the ship. The water was so intensely cold that he first tried to get out of it into the crow's nest,
close at hand. Next he was pushed up against the blower on the
forepart of the funnel, the water rushing down this blower, holding him against the grating for a while. Then there seemed to be
a rush of air and he was blown away from the grating. He was
dragged below the surface, but not for many moments. He came
up near the Engelhardt boat "B" which was not launched, but
had been thrown into the water. The forward funnel then fell
down. Some little time after this he saw half a dozen men standing on the collapsible boat, and got on to it. The whole of the
third funnel was still visible, the vessel gradually raising her stern
out of the water. The ship did not break in two, and could not be
broken in two. She actually attained the perpendicular before
sinking. His impression was that no lights were then burning in
the after part not submerged. It is true that the after part of the
vessel settled level with the water. He watched the ship keenly all
the time. After she reached an angle of 60 degrees there was a
rumbling sound which he attributed to the boilers leaving their
beds and crashing down. Finally she attained an absolute perpendicular position and then went slowly down. He heard no explosion whatever, but noticed about that time that the water
became much warmer. There were about those on the Engelhardt
boat "B," several people struggling in the water who came on it.
Nearly twenty-eight or thirty were taken off in the morning at
daybreak. In this rescuing boat (No. 12), after the transfer, there
were seventy-five. It was the last boat to the *Carpathia*. The next
morning (Monday) he saw some icebergs from fifty to sixty to
two hundred feet high, but the nearest was about ten miles away.

After the boats had left the side of the ship he heard orders
given by the commander through the megaphone. He heard him
say: "Bring that boat alongside." Witness presumed allusion was
made to bringing of boats to the gangway doors. Witness could
not gather whether the orders were being obeyed. Said he had

not been on the Engelhardt boat more than half an hour before a swell was distinctly visible. In the morning there was quite a breeze. It was when he was at No. 6 boat that he noticed the list. Though the ship struck on the starboard side, it was not an extraordinary thing that there should be a list to port. It does not necessarily follow that there should be a list to the side where the water was coming in.

Harold Bride, junior Marconi operator in his Report of April 27th to W. B. Cross, Traffic Manager, Marconi Co. (Am. Inq., p. 1053), says:

Just at this moment the captain said: "You cannot do any more; save yourselves." Leaving the captain we climbed on top of the house comprising the officers' quarters and our own. Here I saw the last of Mr. Phillips, for he disappeared, walking aft. I now assisted in pushing off the collapsible boat on to the Boat Deck. Just as the boat fell, I noticed Captain Smith dive from the bridge into the sea. Then followed a general scramble out on to the Boat Deck, but no sooner had we got there than the sea washed over. I managed to catch hold of the boat we had previously fixed up and was swept overboard with her. I then experienced the most exciting three or four hours anyone can reasonably wish for, and was, in due course with the rest of the survivors, picked up by the *Carpathia*. As you probably heard, I got on the collapsible boat the second time, which was, as I had left it, upturned. I called Phillips but got no response. I learned later from several sources that he was on this boat and expired even before we were picked up by the *Titanic*'s lifeboat (No. 12). I am told that fright and exposure were the causes of his death. So far as I can find out, he was taken on board the *Carpathia* and buried at sea from her, though for some reason the bodies of those who died were not identified before burial from the *Carpathia*, and so I cannot vouch for the truth of this.

He also gave testimony before the American
Inquiry (pp. 110, 161):

This boat was over the officers' cabin at the side of the forward funnel. It was pushed over on to the Boat Deck. It went over the starboard side and I went over with it. It was washed off and over the side of the ship by a wave into the water bottom side upward. I was inside the boat and under it, as it fell bottom side upward. I could not tell how long. It seemed a lifetime to me really. I got on top of the boat eventually. There was a big crowd on top when I got on. I should say that I remained under the boat three-quarters of an hour, or a half hour. I then got away from it as quickly as I could. I freed myself from it and cleared out of it but I do not know why, but swam back to it about three-quarters of an hour to an hour afterwards. I was upside down myself—I mean I was on my back.

It is estimated that there were between thirty and forty on the boat; no women. When it was pushed over on the Boat Deck we all scrambled down on to the Boat Deck again and were going to launch it properly when it was washed over before we had time to launch it. I happened to be nearest to it and I grabbed it and went down with it. There was a passenger on this boat; I could not see whether he was first, second or third class. I heard him say at the time that he was a passenger. I could not say whether it was Colonel Gracie. There were others who struggled to get on; dozens of them in the water. I should judge they were all part of the boat's crew.

I am twenty-two years old. Phillips was about twenty-four or twenty-five. My salary from the Marconi Co. is four pounds a month.

As to the attack made upon Mr. Phillips to take away his life-belt I should say the man was dressed like a stoker. We forced him away. I held him and Mr. Phillips hit him.

J. Collins, cook (Am. Inq., p. 628):

This was my first voyage. I ran back to the upper deck to the port side with another steward and a woman and two children. The steward had one of the children in his arms and the woman was crying. I took the child from the woman and made for one of the boats. Then the word came around from the starboard side that there was a collapsible boat getting launched on that side and that all women and children were to make for it, so the other steward and I and the two children and the woman came around to the starboard side. We saw the collapsible boat taken off the saloon deck, and then the sailors and the firemen who were forward saw the ship's bow in the water and that she was sinking by her bow. They shouted out for us to go aft. We were just turning round to make for the stern when a wave washed us off the deck—washed us clear of it, and the child was washed out of my arms. I was kept down for at least two or three minutes under water.

Senator Bourne: Two or three minutes?

Mr. Collins: Yes; I am sure.

Senator Bourne: Were you unconscious?

Mr. Collins: No; not at all. It did not affect me much—the salt water.

Senator Bourne: But you were under water? You cannot stay under water two or three minutes.

Mr. Collins: Well, it seemed so to me. I could not exactly state how long. When I came to the surface I saw this boat that had been taken off. I saw a man on it. They had been working on it taking it off the saloon deck, and when the wave washed it off the deck, they clung to it. Then I made for it when I came to the surface, swimming for it. I was only four or five yards off of it. I am sure there were more than fifteen or sixteen who were then on it. They did not help me to get on. They were all watching the ship. All I had to do was to give a spring and I got on to it. We were drifting about for two hours in the water.

Senator Bourne: When you came up from the water on this

collapsible boat, did you see any evidence of the ship as she sank then?

Mr. Collins: I did, sir; I saw her stern end.

Senator Bourne: Where were you on the boat at the time you were washed off the ship?

Mr. Collins: Amidships, sir.

Senator Bourne: You say you saw the stern end after you got on the collapsible boat?

Mr. Collins: Yes, sir.

Senator Bourne: Did you see the bow?

Mr. Collins: No, sir.

Senator Bourne: How far were you from the stern end of the ship when you came up and got on to the collapsible boat?

Mr. Collins: I could not just exactly state how far I was away from the *Titanic* when I came up. I was not far, because her lights were out then. Her lights went out when the water got almost to amidships on her.

Senator Bourne: As I understand it, you were amidships of the bow as the ship sank?

Mr. Collins: Yes, sir.

Senator Bourne: You were washed off by a wave? You were under water as you think for two or three minutes and then swam five or six yards to the collapsible boat and got aboard the boat? The stern (of ship) was still afloat?

Mr. Collins: The stern was still afloat.

Senator Bourne: The lights were burning?

Mr. Collins: I came to the surface, sir, and I happened to look around and I saw the lights and nothing more, and looked in front of me and saw the collapsible boat and I made for it.

Senator Bourne: How do you account for this wave that washed you off amidships?

Mr. Collins: By the suction which took place when the bow went down in the water. There were probably fifteen on the boat when I got on. There was some lifeboat that had a green light on it and we thought it was a ship, after the *Titanic* had sunk, and we commenced to shout. All we saw was the green light. We were drifting about two hours, and then we saw the topmast lights of the *Carpathia*. Then came daylight and we saw our own lifeboats and we were very close to them. When we spied them we shouted to them and they came over to us and they lifted a whole lot of us that were on the collapsible boat.

J. Joughin, head baker (Br. Inq.):

I got on to the starboard side of the poop; found myself in the water. I do not believe my head went under the water at all. I thought I saw some wreckage. Swam towards it and found collapsible boat ("B") with Lightoller and about twenty-five men on it. There was no room for me. I tried to get on, but was pushed off, but I hung around. I got around to the opposite side and cook Maynard, who recognized me, helped me and held on to me.

The experience of my fellow passenger on this boat, John B. Thayer, Jr., is embodied in accounts written by him on April 20th and 23rd, just after landing from the Carpathia: the first given to the press as the only statement he had made, the second in a very pathetic letter written to Judge Charles L. Long, of Springfield, Mass., whose son, Milton C. Long, was a companion of young Thayer all that evening, April 14th, until at the very last both jumped into the sea and Long was lost, as described:

"Thinking that father and mother had managed to get off in a boat we, Long and myself, went to the starboard side of the Boat Deck where the boats were getting away quickly. Some were already off in the distance. We thought of getting into one of them, the last boat on the forward part of the starboard side, but there seemed to be such a crowd around that I thought it unwise to make any attempt to get into it. I thought it would never reach the water right side up, but it did.

"Here I noticed nobody that I knew except Mr. Lingrey, whom I had met for the first time that evening. I lost sight of him in a few minutes. Long and I then stood by the rail just a little aft of the captain's bridge. There was such a big list to port that it seemed as if the ship would turn on her side.

"About this time the people began jumping from the stern. I thought of jumping myself, but was afraid of being stunned on hitting the water. Three times I made up my mind to jump out and slide down the davit ropes and try to swim to the boats that were lying off from the ship, but each time Long got hold of me and told me to wait a while. I got a sight on a rope between the davits and a star and noticed that the ship was gradually sinking. About this time she straightened up on an even keel again, and started to go down fairly fast at an angle of about thirty degrees. As she started to sink we left the davits and went back and stood by the rail aft, even with the second funnel. Long and myself stood by each other and jumped on the rail. We did not give each other any messages for home because neither of us thought we would ever get back. Long put his legs over the rail, while I straddled it. Hanging over the side and holding on to the rail with his hands he looked up at me and said: 'You are coming, boy, aren't you?' I replied: 'Go ahead, I'll be with you in a minute.' He let go and slid down the side and I never saw him again. Almost immediately after he jumped I jumped. All this last part took a very short time, and when we jumped we were about ten yards above the water. Long was perfectly calm all the time and kept his nerve to the very end."

How he sank and finally reached the upset boat is quoted accurately from the newspaper report from this same source given in my personal narrative. He continues as follows:

"As often as we saw other boats in the distance we would yell, 'Ship ahoy!' but they could not distinguish our cries from any of the others, so we all gave it up, thinking it useless. It was very cold, and the water washed over the upset boat almost all the time. Towards dawn the wind sprung up, roughening the water and making it difficult to keep the boat balanced. The wireless man raised our hopes a great deal by telling us that the *Carpathia* would be up in about three hours. About 3:30 or 4 o'clock some men at the bow of our boat sighted her mast lights. I could not see them as I was sitting down with a man kneeling on my leg. He finally got up, and I stood up. We had the Second Officer, Mr. Lightoller, on board. He had an officer's whistle and whistled for the boats in the distance to come up and take us off. Two of them came up. The first took half and the other took the balance, including myself. In the transfer we had difficulty in balancing our boat as the men would lean too far over, but we were all taken aboard the already crowded boats and taken to the *Carpathia* in safety."

One of these boats was No. 4, in which his mother was.

CHAPTER VII

Starboard Side: Women First, but Men when There Were No Women

I know of the conditions existing on the port side of the ship from personal knowledge, as set forth in the first five chapters describing my personal experience, while the previous Chapter VI is derived from an exhaustive study of official and of other authoritative information relating to the same side from experiences of others. I have devoted an equal amount of study to the history of what happened on the starboard side of the ship, and the tabulated statements in this chapter are the outcome of my research into the experiences of my fellow passengers on this side of the ship where I was located only during the last half hour before the ship foundered, after all passengers on the port side had been ordered to the starboard in consequence of the great list to port, and after the departure of the last boat "D," that left the ship on the port side. During this last half hour, though it seemed shorter, my attention was confined to the work of the crew, assisting them in their vain efforts to launch the Engelhardt boat "B" thrown down from the roof of the officers' house. All the starboard boats had left the ship before I came there.

Many misunderstandings arose in the public mind because of ignorance of the size of the ship and inability to understand that the same conditions did not prevail at every point and that the same scenes were not witnessed by every one of us. Consider the great length of the ship, 852 feet; its breadth of beam, 92.6 feet; and its many decks, eleven in number; counting the roof of the officers' house as the top deck, then the Boat Deck, and Decks A, B, C, D, E, F, G, and, in the hold, two more. Bearing this in mind I illustrated to my New York friends, in answer to their questions, how impossible it would be for a person standing at the corner of 50th Street and Fifth Avenue to know just what was going on at 52nd Street on the same Avenue, or what was going on at the corner of 52nd Street and Madison Avenue. Therefore, when one survivor's viewpoint differs from that of another, the explanation is easily found.

Consideration must also be taken of the fact that the accident occurred near midnight, and though it was a bright, starlit night, and the ship's electric lights shone almost to the last, it was possible to recognize only one's intimates at close quarters.

My research shows that there was no general order from the ship's officers on the starboard side for "Women and children first." On the other hand, I have the statements of Dr. Washington Dodge, John B. Thayer, Jr., and Mrs. Stephenson, also the same of a member of the crew testifying before the British Court of Inquiry, from which it appears that some sort of a command was issued ordering the women to the port side and the men to the starboard, indicating that no men would be allowed in the port boats, and only in the starboard side boats after the women had entered them first. If such were the orders, they were carried out to the letter. Another point of difference, especially conspicuous to myself, is the fact that on the starboard side there appears to have been an absence of women at the points where the boats were loaded, while on the port side all the boats loaded, from the first up to the last, found women at hand and ready to enter them. It was only at the time of the loading of the last boat "D," that my friend, Clinch Smith, and I ran up and down the port side shouting: "Are there any more women?" This too is the testimony of Officer Lightoller, in charge of loading boats on the port side.

BOAT NO. 7[1]

No disorder in loading or lowering this boat.

Passengers: Mesdames Bishop, Earnshaw, Gibson, Greenfield, Potter, Snyder and Misses Gibson and Hays, Messrs. Bishop, Chevré, Daniel, Greenfield, McGough, Maréchal, Seward, Sloper, Snyder, Tucker.

Transferred from Boat No. 5: Mrs. Dodge and her boy; Messrs. Calderhead and Flynn.

Crew: Seamen: Hogg (in charge), Jewell, Weller.
Total: 28.

Incidents

Archie Jewell, L. O. (Br. Inq.):

Was awakened by the crash and ran at once on deck where he saw a lot of ice. All went below again to get clothes on. The boat-swain called all hands on deck. Went to No. 7 boat. The ship had stopped. All hands cleared the boats, cleared away the falls and got them all right. Mr. Murdoch gave the order to lower boat No. 7 to the rail with women and children in the boat. Three or four Frenchmen, passengers, got into the boat. No. 7 was lowered from the Boat Deck. The orders were to stand by the gangway. This boat was the first on the starboard side lowered into the water. All the boats were down by the time it was pulled away from the ship because it was thought she was settling down.

Witness saw the ship go down by the head very slowly. The other lifeboats were further off, his being the nearest. No. 7 was then pulled further off and about half an hour later, or about an hour and a half after this boat was lowered, and when it was about 200 yards away, the ship took the final dip. He saw the stern straight up in the air with the lights still burning. After a few moments she then sank very quickly and he heard two or

1. First to leave ship starboard side at 12:45 (Br. Rpt., p. 38).

three explosions just as the stern went up in the air. No. 7 picked up no dead bodies. At daylight they saw a lot of icebergs all around, and reached the *Carpathia* about 9 o'clock. This boat had no compass and no light. (The above, given in detail, represents the general testimony of the next witness.)

G. A. Hogg, A. B. (Am. Inq., p. 577):

He had forty-two when the boat was shoved from the ship's side. He asked a lady if she could steer who said she could. He pulled around in search of other people. One man said: "We have done our best; there are no more people around." He said: "Very good, we will get away now." There was not a ripple on the water; it was as smooth as glass.

Mrs. H. W. Bishop, first-class passenger (Am. Inq., p. 998):

The Captain told Colonel Astor something in an undertone. He came back and told six of us who were standing with his wife that we had better put on our lifebelts. I had gotten down two flights of stairs to tell my husband, who had returned to the stateroom for the moment, before I heard the Captain announce that the lifebelts should be put on. We came back upstairs and found very few people on deck. There was very little confusion— only the older women were a little frightened. On the starboard side of the Boat Deck there were only two people—a young French bride and groom. By that time an old man had come upstairs and found Mr. and Mrs. Harder, of New York. He brought us all together and told us to be sure and stay together—that he would be back in a moment. We never saw him again.

About five minutes later the boats were lowered and we were pushed in. This was No. 7 lifeboat. My husband was pushed in with me and we were lowered with twenty-eight people in the boat. We counted off after we reached the water. There were only about twelve women and the rest were men—three crew and thirteen male passengers; several unmarried men—three or four of them foreigners. Somewhat later five people were put into our boat from another one, making thirty-three in ours. Then we rowed still further away as the women were nervous about suction. We had no compass and no light. We arrived at the *Carpathia* five or ten minutes after five. The conduct of the crew, as far as I could see, was absolutely beyond criticism. One of the crew in the boat was Jack Edmonds,(?) and there was another man, a Lookout (Hogg), of whom we all thought a great deal. He lost his brother.

D. H. Bishop, first-class passenger (Am. Inq., p. 1000):

There was an officer stationed at the side of the lifeboat. As witness's wife got in, he fell into the boat. The French aviator Maréchal was in the boat; also Mr. Greenfield and his mother. There was little confusion on the deck while the boat was being loaded; no rush to boats at all. Witness agrees with his wife in the matter of the counting of twenty-eight, but he knows that there were some who were missed. There was a woman with her baby transferred from another lifeboat. Witness knows of his own knowledge that No. 7 was the first boat lowered from the starboard side. They heard no order from any one for the men to stand back or "women first," or "women and children first." Witness also says that at the time his lifeboat was lowered that that order had not been given on the starboard side.

J. R. McGough's affidavit (Am. Inq., p. 1143):

After procuring life-preservers we went back to the top deck and discovered that orders had been given to launch the lifeboats, which were already being launched. Women and children were called for to board the boats first. Both women and men hesitated and did not feel inclined to get into the small boats. He had his back turned, looking in an opposite direction, and was caught by the shoulder by one of the officers who gave him a push saying: "Here, you are a big fellow; get into that boat."

Our boat was launched with twenty-eight people in all. Five were transferred from one of the others. There were several of us who wanted drinking water. It was unknown to us that there was a tank of water and crackers also in our boat until we reached the *Carpathia*. There was no light in our boat.

Mrs. Thomas Potter, Jr. Letter:

There was no panic. Everyone seemed more stunned than anything else. . . . We watched for upwards of two hours the gradual sinking of the ship—first one row of light and then another disappearing at shorter and shorter intervals, with the bow well bent in the water, as though ready for a dive. After the lights went out, some ten minutes before the end, she was like some great living thing who made a last superhuman effort to right herself and then, failing, dove bow forward to the unfathomable depths below.

We did not row except to get away from the suction of the sinking ship, but remained lashed to another boat until the *Carpathia* came in sight just before dawn.

BOAT NO. 5[1]

No disorder in loading or lowering this boat.

Passengers: Mesdames Cassebeer, Chambers, Crosby, Dodge and her boy, Frauenthal, Goldenberg, Harder, Kimball, Stehli, Stengel, Taylor, Warren, and Misses Crosby, Newson, Ostby and Frolicher Stehli.

Messrs. Beckwith, Behr, Calderhead, Chambers, Flynn, Goldenberg, Harder, Kimball, Stehli, Taylor.

1. Second boat lowered on the starboard side at 12:55 (Br. Rpt., p. 38).

Bade good-bye to wives and daughters and sank with ship:
Captain Crosby, Mr. Ostby and Mr. Warren.

Jumped from deck into boat being lowered: German Doctor
Frauenthal and brother Isaac, P. Maugé.

Crew: Third Officer Pitman. Seaman: Olliver, Q. M.; Fireman Shiers; Stewards, Etches, Guy. Stewardess——

Total: 41.

Incidents

H. J. Pitman, Third Officer (Am. Inq., p. 277, and Br. Inq.):

I lowered No. 5 boat to the level with the rail of the Boat Deck.
A man in a dressing gown said that we had better get her loaded
with women and children. I said: "I wait the commander's orders," to which he replied: "Very well," or something like that. It
then dawned on me that it might be Mr. Ismay, judging by the
description I had had given me. I went to the bridge and saw
Captain Smith and told him that I thought it was Mr. Ismay that
wanted me to get the boat away with women and children in it
and he said: "Go ahead; carry on." I came along and brought in
my boat. I stood in it and said: "Come along, ladies." There was
a big crowd. Mr. Ismay helped get them along. We got the boat
nearly full and I shouted out for any more ladies. None were to
be seen so I allowed a few men to get into it. Then I jumped on
the ship again. Mr. Murdoch said: "You go in charge of this boat
and hang around the after gangway." About thirty (Br. Inq.) to
forty women were in the boat, two children, half a dozen male
passengers, myself and four of the crew. There would not have
been so many men had there been any women around, but there
were none. Murdoch shook hands with me and said "Good-bye;
good luck," and I said: "Lower away." This boat was the second
one lowered on the starboard side. No light in the boat.

The ship turned right on end and went down perpendicularly.
She did not break in two. I heard a lot of people say that they
heard boiler explosions, but I have my doubts about that. I do
not see why the boilers would burst, because there was no steam

there. They should have been stopped about two hours and a half. The fires had not been fed so there was very little steam there. From the distance I was from the ship, if it had occurred, I think I would have known it. As soon as the ship disappeared I said: "Now, men, we will pull toward the wreck." Everyone in my boat said it was a mad idea because we had far better save what few I had in my boat than go back to the scene of the wreck and be swamped by the crowds that were there. My boat would have accommodated a few more—about sixty in all. I turned No. 5 boat around to go in the direction from which these cries came but was dissuaded from my purpose by the passengers. My idea of lashing Nos. 5 and 7 together was to keep together so that if anything hove in sight before daylight we could steady ourselves and cause a far bigger show than one boat only. I transferred two men and a woman and a child from my boat to No. 7 to even them up a bit.

H. S. Etches, steward (Am. Inq., p. 810):

Witness assisted Mr. Murdoch, Mr. Ismay, Mr. Pitman and Quartermaster Olliver and two stewards in the loading and launching of No. 7, the gentlemen being asked to keep back and the ladies in first. There were more ladies to go in No. 7 because No. 5 boat, which we went to next, took in over thirty-six ladies. In No. 7 boat I saw one child, a baby boy, with a small woolen cap. After getting all the women that were there they called out three times—Mr. Ismay twice—in a loud voice: "Are there any more women before this boat goes?" and there was no answer. Mr. Murdoch called out, and at that moment a female came up whom he did not recognize. Mr. Ismay said: "Come along; jump in." She said: "I am only a stewardess." He said: "Never mind—you are a woman; take your place." That was the last woman I saw get into boat No. 5. There were two firemen in the bow; Olliver, the sailor, and myself; and Officer Pitman ordered us into the boat and lowered under Murdoch's order.

Senator Smith: What other men got into that boat?

Mr. Etches: There was a stout gentleman, sir, stepped forward then. He had assisted to put his wife in the boat. He leaned forward and she stood up in the boat and put her arms around his neck and kissed him, and I heard her say: "I cannot leave you," and with that I turned my head. The next moment I saw him sitting beside her in the bottom of the boat, and some voice said: "Throw that man out of the boat," but at that moment they started lowering away and the man remained.

Senator Smith: Who was he?

Mr Etches: I do not know his name, sir, but he was a very stout gentleman. (Dr. H. W. Frauenthal.)

We laid off about 100 yards from the ship and waited. She seemed to be going down at the head and we pulled away about a quarter of a mile and laid on our oars until the *Titanic* sank. She seemed to rise once as though she was going to take a final dive, but sort of checked as though she had scooped the water up and had levelled herself. She then seemed to settle very, very quiet, until the last when she rose and seemed to stand twenty seconds, stern in that position (indicating) and then she went down with an awful grating, like a small boat running off a shingley beach. There was no inrush of water, or anything. Mr. Pitman then said to pull back to the scene of the wreck. The ladies started calling out. Two ladies sitting in front where I was pulling said: "Appeal to the officer not to go back. Why should we lose all of our lives in a useless attempt to save others from the ship?" We did not go back. When we left the ship No. 5 had forty-two, including the children and six crew and the officer. Two were transferred with a lady and a child into boat No. 7.

Senator Smith: Of your own knowledge do you know whether any general call was made for passengers to rouse themselves from their berths; and when it was, or whether there was any other signal given?

Mr. Etches: The second steward (Dodd), sir, was calling all around the ship. He was directing some men to storerooms for provisions for the lifeboats, and others he was telling to arouse

all the passengers and to tell them to be sure to take their life-
preservers with them.

There was no lamp in No. 5. On Monday morning we saw a
very large floe of flat ice and three or four bergs between in different places, and on the other bow there were two large bergs
in the distance. The field ice was about three quarters of a mile
at least from us between four and five o'clock in the morning. It
was well over on the port side of the *Titanic* in the position she
was going.

A. Olliver, Q. M. (Am. Inq., p. 526):

There were so many people in the boat when I got into it that
I could not get near the plug to put the plug in. I implored the
passengers to move so I could do it. When the boat was put in
the water I let the tripper go and water came into the boat. I then
forced my way to the plug and put it in; otherwise it would have
been swamped. There was no rush when I got into the boat. I
heard Mr. Pitman give an order to go back to the ship, but the
women passengers implored him not to go. We were then about
300 yards away. Nearly all objected.

A. Shiers, fireman (Br. Inq., p. 48):

He saw no women left. There were about forty men and
women in the boat. There was no confusion among the officers
and crew. We did not go back when the *Titanic* went down. The
women in the boat said: "Don't go back." They said: "If we go
back the boat will be swamped." No compass in boat.

Paul Maugé, Ritz kitchen clerk (Br. Inq.):

Witness was berthed in the third-class corridor. Was awakened and went up on deck. Went down again and woke up the

chef. Going through the second-class cabin he noticed that the assistants of the restaurant were there and not allowed to go on the Boat Deck. He saw the second or third boat on the starboard side let down into the water, and when it was about ten feet down from the Boat Deck he jumped into it. Before this he asked the chef to jump, but he was too fat and would not do so. (Laughter.) I asked him again when I got in the boat, but he refused. When his boat was passing one of the lower decks one of the crew of the *Titanic* tried to pull him out of the boat. He saw no passengers prevented from going up on deck. He thinks he was allowed to pass because he was dressed like a passenger.

Mrs. Catherine E. Crosby's affidavit (Am. Inq., p. 1144):

Deponent is the widow of Captain Edward Gifford Crosby and took passage with him and their daughter, Harriette R. Crosby.

At the time of the collision, Captain Crosby got up, dressed, went out, came back and said to her: "You will lie there and drown," and went out again. He said to their daughter: "The boat is badly damaged, but I think the water-tight compartments will hold her up."

Mrs. Crosby then got up and dressed, as did her daughter, and followed her husband on deck. She got into the first or second boat. About thirty-six persons got in with them.

There was no discrimination between men and women. Her husband became separated from her. She was suffering from cold while drifting around and one of the officers (Pitman) put a sail around her and over her head to keep her warm.

George A. Harder, first-class passenger (Am. Inq., p. 1028):

As we were being lowered, they lowered one side quicker than the other, but reached the water safely after a few scares. Someone said the plug was not in, and they could not get the boat detached from the tackle. Finally, a knife was found and the rope cut. We had about forty-two people in the boat—about thirty women, Officer Pitman, a sailor and three men of the crew. We rowed some distance from the ship—it may have been a quarter or an eighth of a mile. We were afraid of the suction. Passengers said: "Let us row a little further." They did so. Then this other boat, No. 7, came along. We tied alongside. They had twenty-nine in their boat, and we counted at the time thirty-six in ours, so we gave them four or five of our people in order to make it even.

After the ship went down we heard a lot of cries and a continuous yelling and moaning. I counted about ten icebergs in the morning. Our boat managed very well. It is true that the officer did want to go back to the ship, but all the passengers held out and said: "Do not do that; it would only be foolish; there would be so many around that it would only swamp the boat." There was no light in our boat.

C. E. H. Stengel, first-cabin passenger (Am. Inq., p. 975):

Senator Smith: Did you see any man attempt to enter these lifeboats who was forbidden to do so?

Mr. Stengel: I saw two. A certain physician[1] in New York, and his brother, jumped into the same boat my wife was in. Then the officer, or the man who was loading the boat said: "I will stop that. I will go down and get my gun." He left the deck momentarily and came right back again. I saw no attempt of anyone else to get into the lifeboats except these two gentlemen that jumped into the boat after it was started to lower.

Senator Bourne: When you were refused admission into the boat in which your wife was, were there a number of ladies and children there at the time?

Mr. Stengel: No, sir, there were not. These two gentlemen had put their wives in and were standing on the edge of the deck and when they started lowering away, they jumped in. I saw only two.

1. Dr. H. W. Frauenthal.

N. C. Chambers, first-class passenger (Am. Inq., 1041):

Witness referring to boat No. 5 as appearing sufficiently loaded says: "However, my wife said she was going in that boat and proceeded to jump in, calling to me to come. As I knew she would get out again had I not come, I finally jumped into the boat, although I did not consider it, from the looks of things, safe to put many more in. As I remember it, there were two more men, both called by their wives, who jumped in after I did. One of them, a German I believe, told me as I recollect it on the *Carpathia* that he had looked around and had seen no one else, and no one to ask whether he could get in, or not, and had jumped in. Witness describes the difficulty in finding whether the plug was in, or not, and recalls someone calling from above: "It's your own blooming business to see that the plug is in anyhow."

Mrs. C. E. H. Stengel, first-class passenger, writes as follows:

"As I stepped into the lifeboat an officer in charge said: 'No more; the boat is full.' My husband stepped back, obeying the order. As the boat was being lowered, four men deliberately jumped into it. One of them was a Hebrew doctor—another was his brother. This was done at the risk of the lives of all of us in the boat. The two companions of this man who did this were the ones who were later transferred to boat No. 7, to which we were tied. He weighed about 250 pounds and wore two life-preservers. These men who jumped in struck me and a little child. I was rendered unconscious and two of my ribs were very badly dislocated. With this exception there was absolutely no confusion and no disorder in the loading of our boat."

Mrs. F. M. Warren, first-class passenger's account:

. . . Following this we then went to our rooms, put on all our heavy wraps and went to the foot of the grand staircase on Deck

D, again interviewing passengers and crew as to the danger. While standing there Mr. Andrews, one of the designers of the vessel, rushed by, going up the stairs. He was asked if there was any danger but made no reply. But a passenger who was afterwards saved told me that his face had on it a look of terror. Immediately after this the report became general that water was in the squash courts, which were on the deck below where we were standing, and that the baggage had already been submerged.

At the time we reached the Boat Deck, starboard side, there were very few passengers there, apparently, but it was dark and we could not estimate the number. There was a deafening roar of escaping steam, of which we had not been conscious while inside.

The only people we remembered seeing, except a young woman by the name of Miss Ostby, who had become separated from her father and was with us, were Mr. Astor, his wife and servants, who were standing near one of the boats which was being cleared preparatory to being lowered. The Astors did not get into this boat. They all went back inside and I saw nothing of them again until Mrs. Astor was taken onto the *Carpathia*.

We discovered that the boat next to the one the Astors had been near had been lowered to the level of the deck, so went towards it and were told by the officers in charge to get in. At this moment both men and women came crowding toward the spot. I was the second person assisted in. I supposed that Mr. Warren had followed, but saw when I turned that he was standing back and assisting the women. People came in so rapidly in the darkness that it was impossible to distinguish them, and I did not see him again.

The boat was commanded by Officer Pitman and manned by four of the *Titanic*'s men. The lowering of the craft was accomplished with great difficulty. First one end and then the other was dropped at apparently dangerous angles, and we feared that we would swamp as soon as we struck the water.

Mr. Pitman's orders were to pull far enough away to avoid suction if the ship sank. The sea was like glass, so smooth that the stars were clearly reflected. We were pulled quite a distance away and then rested, watching the rockets in terrible anxiety and realizing that the vessel was rapidly sinking, bow first. She went lower and lower, until the lower lights were extinguished, and then suddenly rose by the stern and slipped from sight. We had no light on our boat and were left in intense darkness save from an occasional glimmer of light from other lifeboats and one steady green light on one of the ship's boats which the officers of the *Carpathia* afterwards said was of material assistance in aiding them to come direct to the spot.

With daylight the wind increased and the sea became choppy, and we saw icebergs in every direction; some lying low in the water and others tall, like ships, and some of us thought they were ships. I was on the second boat picked up.

From the time of the accident until I left the ship there was nothing which in any way resembled a panic. There seemed to be a sort of aimless confusion and an utter lack of organized effort.

BOAT NO. 3[1]

No disorder in loading or lowering this boat.

Passengers: Mesdames Cardeza and maid (Anna Hard), Davidson, Dick, Graham, Harper, Hays and maid (Miss Pericault), Spedden and maid (Helen Wilson) and son Douglas and his trained nurse, Miss Burns, and Misses Graham and Shutes.

Men: Messrs. Cardeza and man-servant (Lesneur), Dick, Harper and man-servant (Hamad Hassah) and Spedden.

Men who helped load women and children in this boat and sank with the ship: Messrs. Case, Davidson, Hays and Roebling.

Crew: Seamen: Moore (in charge), Forward Pascoe, Steward: McKay; Firemen: "5 or 6"; or "10 or 12."

Total: 40.[2]

1. Third boat lowered on starboard side, 1:00 (Br. Rpt., p. 38).

2. British Report (p. 38) says 15 crew, 10 men passengers, 25 women and children. Total 50.

Incidents

G. Moore, A. B. (Am. Inq., 559):

When we swung boat No. 3 out I was told by the first officer
to jump in the boat and pass the ladies in, and when there were
no more about we took in men passengers. We had thirty-two in
the boat, all told, and then lowered away. Two seamen were in
the boat. There were a few men passengers and some five or six
firemen. They got in after all the women and children. I took
charge of the boat at the tiller.

Mrs. Frederick O. Spedden, first-class passenger's account:

. . . Number 3 and Number 5 were both marked on our boat.
Our seaman told me that it was an old one taken from some
other ship,[1] and he didn't seem sure at the time which was the
correct number, which apparently was 3.

We tied up to a boat filled with women once, but the rope
broke and we got pretty well separated from all the other lifeboats for some time. We had in all about forty in our boat, including ten or twelve stokers in the bow with us who seemed to
exercise complete control over our coxswain, and urged him to
order the men to row away from the sinking *Titanic*, as they
were in mortal terror of the suction. Two oars were lost soon
after we started and they didn't want to take the time to go back
after them, in spite of some of the passengers telling them that
there was absolutely no danger from suction. All this accounts
for the fact of our being some distance off when the ship went
down. We couldn't persuade the coxswain to turn around till we
saw the lights of the *Carpathia* on the horizon. It was then that
we burned some paper, as we couldn't find our lantern. When
the dawn appeared and my small boy Douglas saw the bergs
around us and remarked: "Oh, Muddie, look at the beautiful

1. "All boats were new and none transferred from another ship," President
Ismay's testimony.

North Pole with no Santa Claus on it," we all couldn't refrain from smiling in spite of the tragedy of the situation.

No more accurately written or interesting account (one which I freely confess moves me to tears whenever re-read) has come to my notice than the following, which I have the consent of the author to insert in its entirety:

WHEN THE *TITANIC* WENT DOWN
By
Miss Elizabeth W. Shutes

Such a biting cold air poured into my stateroom that I could not sleep, and the air had so strange an odor,[1] as if it came from a clammy cave. I had noticed that same odor in the ice cave on the Eiger glacier. It all came back to me so vividly that I could not sleep, but lay in my berth until the cabin grew so very cold that I got up and turned on my electric stove. It threw a cheerful red glow around, and the room was soon comfortable; but I lay waiting. I have always loved both day and night on shipboard, and am never fearful of anything, but now I was nervous about the icy air.

Suddenly a queer quivering ran under me, apparently the whole length of the ship. Startled by the very strangeness of the shivering motion, I sprang to the floor. With too perfect a trust in that mighty vessel I again lay down. Some one knocked at my door, and the voice of a friend said: "Come quickly to my cabin; an iceberg has just passed our window; I know we have just struck one."

No confusion, no noise of any kind, one could believe no danger imminent. Our stewardess came and said she could learn nothing. Looking out into the companionway I saw heads appearing asking questions from half-closed doors. All sepulchrally still, no excitement. I sat down again. My friend was by this time dressed; still her daughter and I talked on, Margaret pretending to eat a sandwich. Her hand shook so that the bread kept parting company from the chicken. Then I saw she was frightened, and for the first time I was

1. Seaman Lee testifies to this odor.

too, but why get dressed, as no one had given the slightest hint of any possible danger? An officer's cap passed the door. I asked: "Is there an accident or danger of any kind?" "None, so far as I know," was his courteous answer, spoken quietly and most kindly. This same officer then entered a cabin a little distance down the companionway and, by this time distrustful of everything, I listened intently, and distinctly heard, "We can keep the water out for a while." Then, and not until then, did I realize the horror of an accident at sea. Now it was too late to dress; no time for a waist, but a coat and skirt were soon on; slippers were quicker than shoes; the stewardess put on our life-preservers, and we were just ready when Mr. Roebling came to tell us he would take us to our friend's mother, who was waiting above.

We passed by the palm room, where two short hours before we had listened to a beautiful concert, just as one might sit in one's own home. With never a realizing sense of being on the ocean, why should not one forget?—no motion, no noise of machinery, nothing suggestive of ship. Happy, laughing men and women constantly passing up and down those broad, strong staircases, and the music went on and the ship went on—nearer and nearer to its end. So short a life, so horrible a death for that great, great ship. What is a more stupendous work than a ship! The almost human pieces of machinery, yet a helpless child, powerless in its struggle with an almighty sea, and the great boat sank, fragile as a rowboat.

How different are these staircases now! No laughing throng, but on either side stand quietly, bravely, the stewards, all equipped with the white, ghostly life-preservers. Always the thing one tries not to see even crossing a ferry. Now only pale faces, each form strapped about with those white bars. So gruesome a scene. We passed on. The awful good-byes. The quiet look of hope in the brave men's eyes as the wives were put into the lifeboats. Nothing escaped one at this fearful moment. We left from the Sun Deck, seventy-five feet above the water. Mr. Case and Mr. Roebling, brave American men, saw us to the lifeboat, made no effort to save themselves, but stepped back on deck. Later they were left to an honored grave.

Our lifeboat, with thirty-six in it, began lowering to the sea. This was done amid the greatest confusion. Rough seamen all giving different orders. No officer aboard. As only one side of the ropes worked, the lifeboat at one time was in such a position that it seemed we must capsize in mid-air. At last the ropes worked together, and we drew nearer and nearer the black, oily water. The first touch of our lifeboat on that black sea came to me as a last good-bye to life, and so we put off—a tiny boat on a great sea—rowed away from what had been a safe home for five days. The first wish on the part of all was to stay near the *Titanic*. We all felt so much safer near the ship. Surely such a vessel could not sink. I thought the danger must be exaggerated, and we could all be taken aboard again. But surely the outline of that great, good ship was growing less. The bow of the boat was getting black. Light aft light was disappearing, and now those rough seamen put to their oars and we were told to hunt under seats, any place, any-where, for a lantern, a light of any kind. Every place was empty. There was no water—no stimulant of any kind. Not a biscuit—nothing to keep us alive had we drifted long. Had no good *Carpathia*, with its splendid Captain Rostron, its orderly crew, come to our rescue we must have all perished. Our men knew nothing about the position of the stars, hardly how to pull together. Two oars were soon overboard. The men's hands were too cold to hold on. We stopped while they beat their hands and arms, then started on again. A sea, calm as a pond, kept our boat steady, and now that mammoth ship is fast, fast disappearing. Only one tiny light is left—a powerless little spark, a lantern fastened to the mast. Fascinated, I watched that black outline until the end. Then across the water swept that awful wail, the cry of those drowning people. In my ears I heard: "She's gone, lads; row like hell or we'll get the devil of a swell." And the horror, the helpless hor-ror, the worst of all—need it have been?

To-day the question is being asked, "Would the *Titanic* disaster be so discussed had it not been for the great wealth gathered there?" It surely would be, for at a time like this wealth counts for nothing, but man's philanthropy, man's brains, man's heroism, count forever. So many men that stood for the making of a great nation, morally and politically, were swept away by the sinking of that big ship. That is why, day after day, the world goes on asking the why of it all. Had a kind Providence a guiding hand in this? Did our nation need so mighty a stroke to prove that man had grown too self-reliant, too sure of his own power over God's sea? God's part was the saving of the few souls on that calmest of oceans on that fearful night. Man's part was the pushing of the good ship, pushing against all reason, to save what?—a few hours and lose a thousand souls—to have the largest of ships arrive in port even a few hours sooner than anticipated. Risk all, but push, push on, on. The icebergs could be avoided. Surely man's experience ought to have lent aid, but just so surely it did not.

In years past a tendency to live more simply away from pomp and display led to the founding of our American nation. Now what are we demanding to-day? Those same needless luxuries. If they were not demanded they would not be supplied. Gymnasiums, swimming pools, tea rooms, had better give way to make space for the necessary number of lifeboats; lifeboats for the crew, also, who help pilot the good ship across the sea.

Sitting by me in the lifeboat were a mother and daughter (Mrs. Hays and Mrs. Davidson). The mother had left a husband on the *Titanic*, and the daughter a father and husband, and while we were near the other boats those two stricken women would call out a name and ask, "Are you there?" "No," would come back the awful answer, but these brave women never lost courage, forgot their own sorrow, telling me to sit close to them to keep warm. Now I began to wish for the warm velvet suit I left hanging in my cabin. I had thought of it for a minute, and then had quickly thrown on a lighter weight skirt. I knew the heavier one would make the life-preserver less useful. Had I only known how calm the ocean was that night, I would have felt that death was not so sure, and would have dressed for life rather than for the end. The life-preservers helped to keep us warm, but the night was bitter cold, and it grew colder and colder, and just before dawn, the coldest, darkest hour of all, no help seemed possible. As we put off from the *Titanic* never was a sky more brilliant, never have I seen so many falling stars. All tended to make those distress rockets that were sent up from the sinking ship look so small, so dull and futile. The brilliancy of the sky only intensified the blackness of the water, our utter loneliness on the sea. The other boats had drifted away from us; we must wait now for dawn and what the day was to bring us we dare not even hope. To see if I could not make the night seem shorter, I tried to imagine myself again in Japan. We had made two strange night departures there, and I was unafraid, and this Atlantic now was calmer than the Inland sea had been at that time. This helped a while, but my hands were freezing cold, and I had to give up pretending and think of the dawn that must soon come.

Two rough looking men had jumped into our boat as we were about to lower, and they kept striking matches, lighting cigars, until I feared we would have no matches left and might need them, so I asked them not to use any more, but they kept on. I do not know what they looked like. It was too dark to really distinguish features clearly, and when the dawn brought the light it brought something so wonderful with it no one looked at anything else or anyone else. Some one asked: "What time is it?" Matches were still left; one was struck. Four o'clock! Where had the hours of the night gone? Yes, dawn would soon be here; and it came, so surely, so strong with cheer. The stars slowly disappeared, and in their place came the faint pink glow of another day. Then I heard, "A light, a ship." I could not, would not, look while there was a bit of doubt, but kept my eyes away. All night long I had heard, "A light!" Each time it proved to be one of our other lifeboats, someone lighting a piece of paper, anything they could find to burn, and now I could not believe. Someone found a newspaper; it was lighted and held up. Then I looked and saw a ship. A ship bright with lights; strong and steady she waited, and we were to be saved. A straw hat was offered (Mrs. Davidson's); it would burn longer. That same ship that had come to save us might run us down. But no; she is still. The two, the ship and the dawn, came together, a living painting. White was the vessel, but whiter still were those horribly beautiful icebergs, and as we drew nearer and nearer that good ship we drew nearer to those mountains of ice. As far as the eye could reach they rose. Each one more fantastically chiselled than its neighbor. The floe glistened like a never-ending meadow covered with new-fallen snow. Those same white mountains, marvellous in their purity, had made of the just ended night one of the blackest the sea has ever known. And near them stood the ship which had come in such quick response to the *Titanic*'s call for help. The man who works over hours is always the worth-while kind, and the Marconi operator awaiting a belated message had heard the poor ship's call for help, and we few out of so many were saved.

From the *Carpathia* a rope forming a tiny swing was lowered into our lifeboat, and one by one we were drawn into safety. The lady pulled up just ahead of me was very large, and I felt myself being jerked fearfully, when I heard some one say: "Careful, fellers; she's a lightweight." I bumped and bumped against the side of the ship until I felt like a bag of meal. My hands were so cold I could hardly hold on to the rope, and I was fearful of letting go. Again I heard: "Steady, fellers; not so fast!" I felt I should let go and bounce out of the ropes; I hardly think that would have been possible, but I felt so at the time. At last I found myself at an opening of some kind and there a kind doctor wrapped me in a warm rug and led me to the dining room, where warm stimulants were given us immediately and everything possible was done for us all. Lifeboats kept coming in, and heart-rending was the sight as widow after widow was brought aboard. Each hoped some lifeboat ahead of hers might have brought her husband safely to this waiting vessel. But always no.

I was still so cold that I had to get a towel and tie it around my waist. Then I went back to the dining-room and found dear little Louis,[1] the French baby, lying alone; his cold, bare feet had become unwrapped. I put a hot water bottle against this very beautiful boy. He smiled his thanks.

Knowing how much better I felt after taking the hot stimulant, I tried to get others to take something; but often they just shook their heads and said, "Oh, I can't."

Towards night we remembered we had nothing—no comb, brush, nothing of any kind—so we went to the barber-shop. The barber always has everything, but now he had only a few toothbrushes left. I bought a cloth cap of doubtful style; and felt like a walking orphan asylum, but very glad to have anything to cover my head. There were also a few showy silk handkerchiefs left. On the corner of each was embroidered in scarlet, "From a friend." These we bought and we were now fitted out for our three remaining days at sea.

Patiently through the dismal, foggy days we lived, waiting for land and possible news of the lost. For the brave American man, a heart full of gratitude, too deep for words, sends out a thanksgiving. That such men are born, live and die for others is a cause for deep gratitude. What country could have shown such men as belong to our American manhood? Thank God for them and for their noble death.

---

1. One of the Navratil children whose pathetic story has been fully related in the newspapers.

EMERGENCY BOAT NO. 1[1]

No disorder in loading or lowering this boat.
   Passengers: Lady Duff Gordon and maid (Miss Francatelli).
   Men: Lord Duff Gordon and Messrs. Solomon and Stengel.
   Total: 5.
   Crew: Seamen: Symons (in charge), Horswell. Firemen: Collins, Hendrickson, Pusey, Shee, Taylor.
   Total: 7.
   Grand Total: 12.

Incidents

G. Symons, A. B. (Br. Inq.):

Witness assisted in putting passengers in Nos. 5 and 3 under Mr. Murdoch's orders, women and children first. He saw 5 and 3 lowered away and went to No. 1. Mr. Murdoch ordered another sailor and five firemen in. Witness saw two ladies running out of the Saloon Deck who asked if they could get in the boat. Murdoch said: "Jump in." The officer looked around for more, but none were in sight and he ordered to lower away, with the witness in charge. Before leaving the Boat Deck witness saw a white light a point and a half on the port bow about five miles away.

   Just after boat No. 1 got away, the water was up to C Deck just under where the ship's name is. Witness got about 200 yards away and ordered the crew to lay on their oars. The ship's stern was well up in the air. The foremost lights had disappeared and the only light left was the mast light. The stern was up out of the water at an angle of forty-five degrees; the propeller could just be seen. The boat was pulled away a little further to escape suction; then he stopped and watched.

   After the *Titanic* went down he heard the people shrieking for help, but was afraid to go back for fear of their swarming upon him, though there was plenty of room in the boat for eight or a

1. This was the fourth boat to leave the starboard side.

dozen more. He determined on this course himself as *"master of the situation."*[1] About a day before landing in New York a present of five pounds came as a surprise to the witness from Sir Cosmo Duff Gordon.

The President: You state that you were surprised that no one in the boat suggested that you should go back to the assistance of the drowning people?

Witness: Yes.

The President: Why were you surprised?

Witness: I fully expected someone to do so.

The President: It seemed reasonable that such a suggestion should be made?

Witness: Yes: I should say it would have been reasonable.

The President: You said in America to Senator Perkins that you had fourteen to twenty passengers in the boat?

Witness: I thought I had; I was in the dark.

The President: You were not in the dark when you gave that evidence.

Witness said he thought he was asked how many people there were in the boat, all told.

The Attorney-General: You meant that the 14 to 20 meant everybody?

Witness: Yes.

The Attorney-General: But you know you only had twelve all told?

Witness: Yes.

The President: You must have known perfectly well when you gave this evidence that the number in your boat was twelve. Why did you tell them in America that there were fourteen to twenty in the boat?

Witness: I do not know; it was a mistake I made then and the way they muddled us up.

The Attorney-General: It was a very plain question. Did you know the names of any passengers?

1. Italics are mine. —AUTHOR.

Witness: I knew Sir Cosmo Duff Gordon's name when we arrived in America.

The Attorney-General: Did you say anything in America about having received the five pounds?

Witness: No, sir; and I was not asked.

The Attorney-General: You were asked these very questions in America which we have been putting to you to-day about going back?

Witness: Yes, sir.

The Attorney-General: Why did you not say that you heard the cries, but in the exercise of your discretion as "master of the situation" you did not go back?

Witness: They took us in three at a time in America and they hurried us through the questions.

The Attorney-General: They asked you: "Did you make any effort to get there," and you said: "Yes; we went back and could not see anything." But you said nothing about your discretion. Why did you not tell them that part of the story? You realized that if you had gone back you might have rescued a good many people?

Witness: Yes.

The Attorney-General: The sea was calm, the night was calm and there could not have been a more favorable night for rescuing people?

Witness: Yes.

The testimony at the American Inquiry above referred to, because of which this witness was called to account, follows:

G. Symons, L. O. (Am. Inq., p. 573):

I was in command of boat No. 1.

Senator Perkins: How many passengers did you have on her?

Mr. Symons: From fourteen to twenty.

Senator Perkins: Were they passengers or crew?

Mr. Symons: There were seven men ordered in; two seamen and five firemen. They were ordered in by Mr. Murdoch.

Senator Perkins: How many did you have all told?

Mr. Symons: I would not say for certain; it was fourteen or twenty. Then we were ordered away.

Senator Perkins: You did not return to the ship again?

Mr. Symons: Yes; we came back after the ship was gone and saw nothing.

Senator Perkins: Did you rescue anyone that was in the water?

Mr. Symons: No, sir; we saw nothing when we came back.

Witness then testified that there was no confusion or excitement among the passengers. It was just the same as if it was an everyday affair. He never saw any rush whatever to get into either of the two boats. He heard the cries of the people in the water.

Senator Perkins: Did you say your boat could take more? Did you make any effort to get them?

Mr. Symons: Yes. We came back, but when we came back we did not see anybody or hear anybody.

He says that his boat could have accommodated easily ten more. He was in charge of her and was ordered away by Officer Murdoch. Did not pull back to the ship again until she went down.

Senator Perkins: And so you made no attempt to save any other people after you were ordered to pull away from the ship by someone?

Mr. Symons: I pulled off and came back after the ship had gone down.

Senator Perkins: And then there were no people there?

Mr. Symons: No, sir; I never saw any.

C. E. H. Stengel, first-class passenger (Am. Inq., p. 971):

There was a small boat they called an Emergency boat in which were three people, Sir Duff Gordon, his wife and Miss Francatelli. I asked to get into the boat. There was no one else around that I could see except the people working at the boats. The officer said: "Jump in." The railing was rather high. I jumped onto it and rolled into the boat. The officer said: "That's the funniest thing I have seen to-night," and laughed heartily. After getting down part of the way the boat began to tip and somebody "hollered" to stop lowering. A man named A. L. Soloman also asked to get in with us. There were five passengers, three stokers and two seamen in the boat.

Senator Smith: Do you know who gave instructions?

Mr. Stengel: I think between Sir Cosmo Duff Gordon and myself we decided which way to go. We followed a light that was to the bow of the ship. . . . Most of the boats rowed toward that light, and after the green lights began to burn I suggested that it was better to turn around and go towards them. They were from another lifeboat. When I got into the boat it was right up against the side of the ship. If it had not been, I would have gone right out into the water because I rolled. I did not step in it; I just simply rolled. There was one of the icebergs particularly that I noticed—a very large one which looked something like the Rock of Gibraltar.

The Duff Gordon Episode

Charles Hendricksen, leading fireman (Br. Inq.):

When the ship sank we picked up nobody. The passengers would not listen to our going back. Of the twelve in the boat, seven were of the crew. Symons, who was in charge, said nothing and we all kept our mouths shut. None of the crew objected to going back. It was a woman who objected, Lady Duff Gordon, who said we would be swamped. People screaming for help could be heard by everyone in our boat. I suggested going back. Heard no one else do so. Mr. Duff Gordon upheld his wife.

After we got on the *Carpathia* Gordon sent for them all and said he would make them a present. He was surprised to receive five pounds from him the day after docking in New York.

Hendricksen recalled.

Witness cross-examined by Sir Cosmo Duff Gordon's counsel.

What did you say about Sir Cosmo's alleged statement preventing you from going back?

Witness: It was up to us to go back.

Did anyone in the boat say anything to you about going back?

Witness: Lady Duff Gordon said something to the effect that
if we went back the boat would be swamped.

Who was it that first said anything about Sir Cosmo making a
presentation to the crew?

Witness: Fireman Collins came down and said so when we
were on board the *Carpathia*.

Before we left the *Carpathia* all the people rescued were pho-
tographed together. We members of the crew wrote our names
on Lady Duff Gordon's lifebelt. From the time we first left off
rowing until the time the vessel sank, Lady Duff Gordon was
violently seasick and lying on the oars.

A. E. Horswell, A. B. (Br. Inq.):

Witness said it would have been quite a safe and proper thing
to have gone back and that it was an inhuman thing not to do
so, but he had to obey the orders of the coxswain. Two days
after boarding the *Carpathia* some gentlemen sent for him and
he received a present.

J. Taylor, fireman (Br. Inq.):

Witness testifies that No. 1 boat stood by about 100 yards to
avoid suction and was 200 yards off when the *Titanic* sank. He
heard a suggestion made about going back and a lady passenger
talked of the boat's being swamped if they did so. Two gentlemen in the boat said it would be dangerous.

Did your boat ever get within reach of drowning people?

Witness: No.

How many more could the boat have taken in?

Witness: Twenty-five or thirty in addition to those already in it.

Did any of the crew object to going back?

Witness: No.

Did you ever hear of a boat's crew consisting of six sailors and one fireman?

Witness: No.

Lord Mersey: What was it that Sir Cosmo Duff Gordon said to you in the boat?

Witness: He said he would write to our homes and to our wives and let them know that we were safe.

Witness said he received five pounds when he was on board the *Carpathia*.

R. W. Pusey, fireman (Br. Inq.):

After the ship went down we heard cries for a quarter of an hour, or twenty minutes. Did not go back in the direction the *Titanic* had sunk. I heard one of the men say: "We have lost our kit," and then someone said: "Never mind, we will give you enough to get a new kit." I was surprised that no one suggested going back. I was surprised that I did not do so, but we were all half dazed. It does occur to me now that we might have gone back and rescued some of the stragglers. I heard Lady Duff Gordon say to Miss Francatelli: "You have lost your beautiful nightdress," and I said: "Never mind, you have saved your lives; but we have lost our kit"; and then Sir Cosmo offered to provide us with new ones.

Sir Cosmo Duff Gordon (Br. Inq.):

No. 7 was the first boat I went to. It was just being filled. There were only women and the boat was lowered away. No. 3 was partially filled with women, and as there were no more, they filled it up with men. My wife would not go without me. Some men on No. 3 tried to force her away, but she would not go. I heard an officer say: "Man No. 1 boat." I said to him: "May we get in that boat?" He said: "With pleasure; I wish you would." He handed the ladies in and then put two Americans in, and after that he said to two or three firemen that they had better get in. When the boat was lowered I thought the *Titanic* was in a very grave condition. At the time I thought that certainly all the women had gotten off. No notice at all was taken in our boat of these cries. No thought entered my mind about its being possible to go back and try to save some of these people. I made a promise of a present to the men in the boat.

There was a man sitting next to me and about half an hour after the *Titanic* sank a man said to me: "I suppose you have lost everything?" I said: "Yes." He said: "I suppose you can get more." I said: "Yes." He said: "Well, we have lost all our kit, for we shall not get anything out of the Company, and our pay ceases from to-night." I said: "Very well, I will give you five pounds each towards your kit."

Were the cries from the *Titanic* clear enough to hear the words, "My God, My God"?

No. You have taken that from the story in the American papers.

Mr. Stengel in his evidence in New York said, "Between Mr. Duff Gordon and myself we decided the direction of the boat."

That's not so; I did not speak to the coxswain in any way.

Lady Duff Gordon (Br. Inq.):

After the three boats had been gotten away my husband and I were left standing on the deck. Then my husband went up and said, might we not get into this boat, and the officer said very politely: "If you will do so I should be very pleased." Then somebody hitched me up at the back, lifted me up and pitched me into the boat. My husband and Miss Francatelli were also pitched into the boat; and then two Americans were also pitched in on top of us. Before the *Titanic* sank I heard terrible cries.

Q. Is it true in an article signed by what purports to be your signature that you heard the last cry which was that of a man shouting, "My God, My God"?

A. Absolutely untrue.

Address by Mr. A. Clement Edwards, M. P., Counsel for Dock Workers' Union (Br. Inq.):

Referring to the Duff Gordon incident he said that the evidence showed that in one of the boats there were only seven seamen and five passengers. If we admitted that, this boat had accommodation for twenty-eight more passengers.

The primary responsibility for this must necessarily be placed on the member of the crew who was in charge of the boat— Symons, no conduct of anyone else in the boat, however reprehensible, relieving that man from such responsibility.

Here was a boat only a short distance from the ship, so near that the cries of those struggling in the water could be heard. Symons had been told to stand by the ship, and that imposed upon him a specific duty. It was shown in Hendricksen's evidence that there was to the fullest knowledge of those in the boat a large number of people in the water, and that someone suggested that they should return and try to rescue them. Then it was proved that one of the ladies, who was shown to be Lady Duff Gordon, had said that the boat might be swamped if they went back, and Sir Cosmo Duff Gordon had admitted that this also represented his mental attitude at the time. He (Mr. Edwards) was going to say, and to say quite fearlessly, that a state of mind which could, while within the hearing of the screams of drowning people, think of so material a matter as the giving of money to replace kits was a state of mind which must have contemplated the fact that there was a possibility of rescuing some of these people, and the danger which might arise if this were attempted.

He was not going to say that there was a blunt, crude bargain, or a deal done with these men: "If you will not go back I will give you five pounds"; but he was going to suggest as a right and true inference that the money was mentioned at that time under these circumstances to give such a sense of ascendancy or supremacy to Sir Cosmo Duff Gordon in the boat that the view to which he gave expression that they should not go back would weigh more with the men than if he had given it as a piece of good advice. There were twenty-eight places on that boat and no one on board had a right to save his own life by avoiding any possible risk involved in filling the vacant places. To say the least of it, it was most reprehensible that there should have been any offer of money calculated to influence the minds of the men or to seduce them from their duty.

From the address of the Attorney-General,
Sir Rufus Isaacs, K. C., M. P. (Br. Inq.):

In regard to boat No. 1, I have to make some comment. This was the Emergency boat on the starboard side, which figured somewhat prominently in the inquiry on account of the evidence which was given in the first instance by Hendricksen, and which led to the calling of Sir Cosmo Duff Gordon. Any comment I have to make in regard to that boat is, I wish to say, not directed to Sir Cosmo or his wife. For my part, I would find it impossible to make any harsh or severe comment on the conduct of any woman who, in circumstances such as these, found herself on the water in a small boat on a dark night, and was afraid to go back because she thought there was a danger of being swamped. At any rate, I will make no comment about that, and the only reason I am directing attention to No. 1 boat is that it is quite plain that it was lowered with twelve persons in it instead of forty. I am unable to say why it was that that boat was so lowered with only five passengers and seven of the crew on board, but that circumstance, I contend, shows the importance of boat drill.

As far as he knew from the evidence, no order was given as to the lowering of this boat. He regretted to say that he was quite unable to offer any explanation of it, but he could not see why the boat was lowered under the circumstances. The point of this part of the inquiry was twofold—(1) the importance of a boat drill; (2) that you should have the men ready.

No doubt if there had been proper organization there would have been a greater possibility of saving more passengers. What struck one was that no one seemed to have known what his duty was or how many persons were to be placed in the boat before it was lowered. In all cases no boat had its complement of what could be carried on this particular night. The vessel was on her first passage, and if all her crew had been engaged on the next voyage no doubt things would have been better, but there was no satisfactory organization with regard to calling passengers and getting them on deck. Had these boats had their full complement it would have been another matter, but the worst of them was this boat No. 1, because the man, Symons, in charge did not exercise his duty. No doubt he was told to stand by, but he went quite a distance away. His evidence was unsatisfactory, and gave no proper account why he did not return. He only said that he "exercised his discretion," and that he was "master of the situation." There was, however, no explanation why he went away and why he did not go back except that he would be swamped. That was no explanation. I can see no justification for his not going back. From the evidence, there were no people on the starboard deck at the time. They must have been mistaken in making that statement, because, as they knew, four more boats were subsequently lowered with a number of women and children. The capacity of this boat was forty. No other boat went away with so small a proportion as compared with its capacity, and there was no other boat which went away with a larger number of the crew. I confess it is a thing which I do not understand why that boat was lowered when she was. Speaking generally, the only boats that took their full quantity were four. One had to see what explanation could be given of that. In this particular case it happened that the officers were afraid the boats would buckle. Then they said that no more women were available, and, thirdly, it was contemplated to go back. It struck one as very regrettable that the officers should have doubts in their minds on these points with regard to the capacity of the boats.

BOAT NO. 9[1]

No disorder when this boat was loaded and lowered.

Passengers: Mesdames Aubert and maid (Mlle. Segesser), Futrelle, Lines; Miss Lines, and second and third-class.

Men: Two or three.

Said good-bye to wife and sank with ship: Mr. Futrelle.

Crew: Seamen: Haines (in charge), Wynne, Q. M., McGough, Peters; Stewards Ward, Widgery and others.

Total: 56.

Incidents

A. Haines, boatswain's mate (Am. Inq., 755):

Officer Murdoch and witness filled boat 9 with ladies. None of the men passengers tried to get into the boats. Officer Murdoch told them to stand back. There was one woman who refused to get in because she was afraid. When there were no more women forthcoming the boat was full, when two or three men jumped into the bow. There were two sailors, three or four stewards, three or four firemen and two or three men passengers. No. 9 was lowered from the Boat Deck with sixty-three people in the boat and lowered all right. Officer Murdoch put the witness in charge and ordered him to row off and keep clear of the ship. When we saw it going down by the head he pulled further away for the safety of the people in the boat: about 100 yards away at first. Cries were heard after the ship went down. He consulted with the sailors about going back and concluded with so many in the boat it was unsafe to do so. There was no compass in the boat, but he had a little pocket lamp. On Monday morning he saw from thirty to fifty icebergs and a big field of ice miles long and large bergs and "growlers," the largest from eighty to one hundred feet high.

---

1. The fifth boat lowered on starboard side, 1:20 (Br. Rpt., p. 38).

W. Wynne, Q. M. (Br. Inq.):

Officer Murdoch ordered witness into boat No. 9. He assisted the ladies and took an oar. He says there were fifty-six all told in the boat, forty-two of whom were women. He saw the light of a steamer—a red light first, and then a white one—about seven or eight miles away. After an interval both lights disappeared. Ten or fifteen minutes afterwards he saw a white light again in the same direction. There was no lamp or compass in the boat.

W. Ward, steward (Am. Inq., 595):

Witness assisted in taking the canvas cover off of boat No. 9 and lowered it to the level of the Boat Deck.[1]

Officer Murdoch, Purser McElroy and Mr. Ismay were near this boat when being loaded. A sailor came along with a bag and threw it into the boat. He said he had been sent to take charge of it by the captain. The boatswain's mate, Haines, was there and ordered him out. He got out. Either Purser McElroy or Officer Murdoch said: "Pass the women and children that are here into that boat." There were several men standing around and they fell back. There were quite a quantity of women but he could not say how many were helped into the boat. There were no children. One old lady made a great fuss and absolutely refused to enter the boat. She went back to the companionway and forced her way in and would not get into the boat. One woman, a French lady, fell and hurt herself a little. Purser McElroy ordered two more men into the boat to assist the women. When No. 9 was being lowered the first listing of the ship was noticeable.

From the rail to the boat was quite a distance to step down to the bottom of it, and in the dark the women could not see where they were stepping. Purser McElroy told witness to get into the boat to assist the women. Women were called for, but none came

---

1. Brice, A. B. (Am. Inq., p. 648) and Wheate, assistant second steward (Br. Inq.), say No. 9 was filled from A Deck with women and children only.

along and none were seen on deck at the time. Three or four men were then taken into the boat until the officers thought there were sufficient to lower away with safety.

No. 9 was lowered into the water before No. 11. There was some difficulty in unlashing the oars because for some time no one had a knife. There were four men who rowed all night, but there were some of them in the boat who had never been to sea before and did not know the first thing about an oar, or the bow from the stern. Haines gave orders to pull away. When 200 yards off, rowing was stopped for about an hour. Haines was afraid of suction and we pulled away to about a quarter of a mile from the ship. The ship went down very gradually for a while by the head. We could just see the ports as she dipped. She gave a kind of a sudden lurch forward. He heard a couple of re-ports like a volley of musketry; not like an explosion at all. His boat was too full and it would have been madness to have gone back. He thinks No. 9 was the fourth or fifth boat picked up by the *Carpathia*. There was quite a big lot of field ice and several large icebergs in amongst the field; also two or three separated from the main body of the field.

J. Widgery, bath steward (Am. Inq., 602):

Witness says that all passengers were out of their cabins on deck before he went up.

When he got to the Boat Deck No. 7 was about to be lowered, but the purser sent him to No. 9. The canvas had been taken off and he helped lower the boat. Purser McElroy ordered him into the boat to help the boatswain's mate pass in women. Women were called for. An elderly lady came along. She was frightened. The boatswain's mate and himself assisted her, but she pulled away and went back to the door (of the companionway) and downstairs. Just before they left the ship the officer gave the order to Haines to keep about 100 yards off. The boat was full as it started to lower away. When they got to the water he was the only one that had a knife to cut loose the oars. He says that the balance of his testimony would be the same as that of Mr. Ward, the previous witness.

BOAT NO. 11[1]

No disorder when this boat was loaded and lowered.

Passengers: Women: Mrs. Schabert and two others of first cabin; all the rest second and third class. Fifty-eight women and children in all.

Men: Mr. Mock, first cabin, and two others.

Crew: Seamen: Humphreys (in charge), Brice; Stewards: Wheate, MacKay, McMicken, Thessinger, Wheelton; Fireman——; Stewardess: Mrs. Robinson.

Total: 70.

Incidents

W. Brice, A. B. (Am. Inq., 648):

This boat was filled from A Deck. An officer said: "Is there a sailor in the boat?" There was no answer. I jumped out and went down the fall into the bow. Nobody was in the stern. I went aft and shipped the rudder. By that time the boat had been filled with women and children. We had a bit of difficulty in keeping the boat clear of a big body of water coming from the ship's side. The after-block got jammed, but I think that must have been on account of the trip not being pushed right down to disconnect the block from the boat. We managed to keep the boat clear from this body of water. It was the pump discharge. There were only two seamen in the boat, a fireman, about six stewards and fifty-one passengers. There were no women and children who tried to get into the boat and were unable to do so. There was no rush and no panic whatever. Everything was done in perfect order and discipline.

Mr. Humphreys, A. B., was in charge of No. 11. There was no

1. Sixth boat lowered on starboard side, 1:25 (Br. Rpt., p. 38).

light or lantern in our boat. I cut the lashing from the oil bottle and cut rope and made torches. The ship sank bow down first almost perpendicularly. She became a black mass before she made the final plunge when boat was about a quarter of a mile away. Boat No. 9 was packed. Passengers were about forty-five women and about four or five children in arms.

E. Wheelton, steward (Am. Inq.):

As I made along B Deck I met Mr. Andrews, the builder, who was opening the rooms and looking in to see if there was anyone in, and closing the doors again. Nos. 7, 5 and 9 had gone. No. 11 boat was hanging in the davits. Mr. Murdoch said: "You go too." He shouted: "Women and children first." He was then on the top deck standing by the taffrail. The boat was loaded with women and children, and I think there were eight or nine men in the boat altogether, including our crew, and one passenger.

"Have you got any sailors in?" asked Mr. Murdoch. I said: "No, sir." He told two sailors to jump into the boat. We lowered away. Everything went very smooth until we touched the water. When we pushed away from the ship's side we had a slight difficulty in hoisting the after block. We pulled away about 300 yards. We rowed around to get close to the other boats. There were about fifty-eight all told in No. 11. It took all of its passengers from A Deck except the two sailors. I think there were two boats left on the starboard side when No. 11 was lowered. The eight or nine men in the boat included a passenger. A quartermaster (Humphreys) was in charge.

C. D. MacKay, steward (Br. Inq.):

No. 11 was lowered to A Deck. Murdoch ordered me to take charge. We collected all the women (40) on the Boat Deck, and on A Deck we collected a few more. The crew were five stewards, one fireman, two sailors, one forward and one aft. There was

Wheelton, McMicken, Thessenger, Wheate and myself. The others were strangers to the ship. There were two second-class ladies, one second-class gentleman, and the rest were third-class ladies. I found out that they were all third-class passengers. We had some difficulty in getting the after-fall away. We went away from the ship about a quarter of a mile. No compass. The women complained that they were crushed up so much and had to stand. Complaints were made against the men because they smoked.

J. T. Wheate, assistant second steward (Br. Inq.):

Witness went upstairs to the Boat Deck where Mr. Murdoch ordered the boats to the A Deck where the witness and seventy of his men helped pass the women and children into boat No. 9, and none but women and children were taken in. He then filled up No. 11 with fifty-nine women and children, three male passengers and a crew of seven stewards, two sailors and one fireman. He could not say how the three male passengers got there. The order was very good. There was nobody on the Boat Deck, so the people were taken off on the A Deck.

Philip E. Mock, first-cabin passenger (letter):

No. 11 carried the largest number of passengers of any boat— about sixty-five. There were only two first-cabin passengers in the boat besides my sister, Mrs. Schabert, and myself. The remainder were second-class or stewards and stewardesses. We were probably a mile away when the *Titanic*'s lights went out. I last saw the ship with her stern high in the air going down. After the noise I saw a huge column of black smoke slightly lighter than the sky rising high into the sky and then flattening out at the top like a mushroom.

I at no time saw any panic and not much confusion. I can positively assert this as I was near every boat lowered on the starboard side up to the time No. 11 was lowered. With the exception of some stokers who pushed their way into boat No. 3 or No. 5, I saw no man or woman force entry into a lifeboat. One of these was No. 13 going down, before we touched the water.

From address of the Attorney-General,
Sir Rufus Isaacs, K. C., M. P.:

"No. 11 took seventy, and carried the largest number of any boat."

BOAT NO. 13[1]

No disorder when this boat was loaded and lowered.

Passengers: Women: Second-cabin, including Mrs. Caldwell and her child Alden. All the rest second and third-class women.

Men: Dr. Dodge only first-cabin passenger. Second-cabin, Messrs. Beasley and Caldwell. One Japanese.

Crew: Firemen: Barrett (in charge), Beauchamp, Major and two others. Stewards: Ray, Wright and another; also baker——.

Total: 64.

Incidents

Mr. Lawrence Beesley's book, already cited, gives an excellent description of No. 13's history, but for further details, see his book, *The Loss of the S.S.* Titanic, Houghton, Mifflin Co., Boston.

F. Barrett, leading stoker (Br. Inq.):

Witness then made his escape up the escape ladder and walked aft on to Deck A on the starboard side, where only two boats were left, Nos. 13 and 15. No. 13 was partly lowered when he

1. Seventh boat lowered on starboard side, 1:25 (Br. Rpt., p. 38).

got there. Five-sixths in the boat were women. No. 15 was lowered about thirty seconds later. When No. 13 got down to the water he shouted: "Let go the after-fall," but, as no one took any notice, he had to walk over women and cut the fall himself. No. 15 came down nearly on top of them, but they just got clear. He took charge of the boat until he got so cold that he had to give up to someone else. A woman put a cloak over him, as he felt so freezing, and he could not remember anything after that. No men waiting on the deck got into his boat. They all stood in one line in perfect order waiting to be told to get into the boat. There was no disorder whatever. They picked up nobody from the sea.

F. D. Ray, steward (Am. Inq., 798):

Witness assisted in the loading of boat No. 9 and saw it and No. 11 boat lowered, and went to No. 13 on A Deck. He saw it about half filled with women and children. A few men were ordered to get in; about nine to a dozen passengers and crew. Dr. Washington Dodge was there and was told that his wife and child had gone away in one of the boats. Witness said to him: "You had better get in here then," and got behind him and pushed him and followed after him. A rather large woman came along crying and saying: "Do not put me in the boat; I don't want to get in one. I have never been in an open boat in my life." He said: "You have got to go and you may as well keep quiet." After that there was a small child rolled in a blanket thrown into the boat to him. The woman that brought it got into the boat afterwards.

We left about three or four men on the deck at the rail and they went along to No. 15 boat. No. 13 was lowered away. When nearly to the water, two or three of them noticed a very large discharge of water coming from the ship's side which he thought was the pumps working. The hole was about two feet wide and about a foot deep with a solid mass of water coming out. They shouted for the boat to be stopped from being lowered and they responded promptly and stopped lowering the boat. They pushed it off from the side of the ship until they were free from this discharge. He thinks there were no sailors or quartermasters in the boat because they apparently did not know how to get free from the tackle. Knives were called for to cut loose. In the meantime they were drifting a little aft and boat No. 15 was being lowered immediately upon them about two feet from their heads and they all shouted again, and they again replied very promptly and stopped lowering boat No. 15. They elected a fireman (Barrett) to take charge. Steward Wright was in the boat; two or three children and a very young baby seven months old. Besides Nos. 9, 11, and 13, No. 15 was lowered to Deck A and filled from it. He saw no male passengers or men of the crew whatever ordered out or thrown out of these lifeboats on the starboard side. Everybody was very orderly and there was no occasion to throw anybody out. In No. 13 there were about four or five firemen, one baker, three stewards; about nine of the crew. Dr. Washington Dodge was the only first-class passenger and the rest were third-class. There was one Japanese. There was no crowd whatever on A Deck while he was loading these boats. No. 13 was full.

Extracts from Dr. Washington Dodge's address: "The Loss of the Titanic," *a copy of which he kindly sent me:*

I heard one man say that the impact was due to ice. Upon one of his listeners questioning the authority of this, he replied: "Go up forward and look down on the fo'castle deck, and you can see for yourself." I at once walked forward to the end of the promenade deck, and looking down could see, just within the starboard rail, small fragments of broken ice, amounting possibly to several cartloads. As I stood there an incident occurred which made me take a more serious view of the situation, than I otherwise would.

Two stokers, who had slipped up onto the promenade deck unobserved, said to me: "Do you think there is any danger, sir?" I replied: "If there is any danger it would be due to the vessel's having sprung a leak, and you ought to know more about it than I." They replied, in what appeared to me to be an alarmed tone: "Well, sir, the water was pouring into the stoke 'old when we came up, sir." At this time I observed quite a number of steerage passengers, who were amusing themselves by walking over the ice, and kicking it about the deck. No ice or iceberg was to be seen in the ocean.

I watched the boats on the starboard side, as they were successively filled and lowered away. At no time during this period, was there any panic, or evidence of fear, or unusual alarm. I saw no women nor children weep, nor were there any evidences of hysteria observed by me.

I watched all boats on the starboard side, comprising the odd numbers from one to thirteen, as they were launched. Not a boat was launched which would not have held from ten to twenty-five more persons. Never were there enough women or children present to fill any boat before it was launched. In all cases, as soon as those who responded to the officers' call were in the boats, the order was given to "Lower away."

What the conditions were on the port side of the vessel I had no means of observing. We were in semi-darkness on the Boat Deck, and owing to the immense length and breadth of the vessel, and the fact that between the port and the starboard side of the Boat Deck, there were officers' cabins, staterooms for passengers, a gymnasium, and innumerable immense ventilators, it would have been impossible, even in daylight, to have obtained a view of but a limited portion of this boat deck. We only knew what was going on within a radius of possibly forty feet.

Boats Nos. 13 and 15 were swung from the davits at about the same moment. I heard the officer in charge of No. 13 say: "We'll lower this boat to Deck A." Observing a group of possibly fifty or sixty about Boat 15, a small proportion of which number were women, I descended by means of a stairway close at hand to the deck below, Deck A. Here, as the boat was lowered even with the deck, the women, about eight in number, were assisted by several of us over the rail of the steamer into the boat. The officer in charge then held the boat, and called repeatedly for more women. None appearing, and there being none visible on the deck, which was then brightly illuminated, the men were told to tumble in. Along with those present I entered the boat. Ray was my table steward and called to me to get in.

The boat in which I embarked was rapidly lowered, and as it approached the water I observed, as I looked over the edge of the boat, that the bow, near which I was seated, was being lowered directly into an enormous stream of water, three or four feet in diameter, which was being thrown with great force from the side of the vessel. This was the water thrown out by the condenser pumps. Had our boat been lowered into the same it would have been swamped in an instant. The loud cries which were raised by the occupants of the boat caused those who were sixty or seventy feet above us to cease lowering our boat. Securing an oar with considerable difficulty, as the oars had been firmly lashed together by means of heavy tarred twine, and as in addition they were on the seat running parallel with the side of the lifeboat, with no less than eight or ten occupants of the boat sitting on them, none of whom showed any tendency to disturb themselves—we pushed the bow of the lifeboat, by means of the oar, a sufficient distance away from the side of the *Titanic* to clear this great stream of water which was gushing forth. We were then safely lowered to the water. During the few moments occupied by these occurrences I felt for the only time a sense of impending danger.

We were directed to pull our lifeboat from the steamer, and to follow a light which was carried in one of the other lifeboats, which had been launched prior to ours. Our lifeboat was found to contain no lantern, as the regulations require; nor was there a single sailor, or officer in the boat. Those who undertook to handle the oars were poor oarsmen, almost without exception, and our progress was extremely slow. Together with two or three other lifeboats which were in the vicinity, we endeavored to overtake the lifeboat which carried the light, in order that we might not drift away and possibly become lost. This light appeared to be a quarter of a mile distant, but, in spite of our best endeavors, we were never enabled to approach any nearer to it, although we must have rowed at least a mile.

BOAT NO. 15[1]

No disorder in loading or lowering this boat.

Passengers: All third-class women and children (53) and

Men: Mr. Haven (first-class) and three others (third-class) only. Total: 4.

Crew: Firemen: Diamond (in charge), Cavell, Taylor; Stewards: Rule, Hart. Total: 13.

Grand Total (Br. Rpt., p. 38): 70.

Incidents

G. Cavell, trimmer (Br. Inq.):

The officer ordered five of us in the boat. We took on all the women and children and the boat was then lowered. We lowered to the first-class (i. e., A) deck and took on a few more women and children, about five, and then lowered to the water. From the lower deck we took in about sixty. There were men about but we did not take them in. They were not kept back. They were third-class passengers, I think—sixty women, Irish. Fireman Diamond took charge. No other seaman in this boat. There were none left on the third-class decks after I had taken the women.

S. J. Rule, bathroom steward (Br. Inq.):

Mr. Murdoch called to the men to get into the boat. About six got in. "That will do," he said, "lower away to Deck A." At this time the vessel had a slight list to port. We sent scouts around both to the starboard and port sides. They came back and said

1. Br. Rpt., p. 38, places this next to last lowered on starboard side at 1:35.

there were no more women and children. We filled up on A Deck—sixty-eight all told—the last boat to leave the starboard side. There were some left behind. There was a bit of a rush after Mr. Murdoch said we could fill the boat up with men standing by. We very nearly came on top of No. 13 when we lowered away. A man, Jack Stewart, a steward, took charge. Nearly everybody rowed. No lamp. One deckhand in the boat, and men, women and children. Just before it was launched, no more could be found, and about half a dozen men got in. There were sixty-eight in the boat altogether. Seven members of the crew.

J. E. Hart, third-class steward (Br. Inq., 75):

Witness defines the duties and what was done by the stewards, particularly those connected with the steerage.

"Pass the women and children up to the Boat Deck," was the order soon after the collision. About three-quarters of an hour after the collision he took women and children from the C Deck to the first-class main companion. There were no barriers at that time. They were all opened. He took about thirty to boat No. 8 as it was being lowered. He left them and went back for more, meeting third-class passengers on the way to the boats. He brought back about twenty-five more steerage women and children, having some little trouble owing to the men passengers wanting to get to the Boat Deck. These were all third-class people whom we took to the only boat left on the starboard side, viz., No. 15. There were a large number already in the boat, which was then lowered to A Deck, and five women, three children and a man with a baby in his arms taken in, making about seventy people in all, including thirteen or fourteen of the crew and fireman Diamond in charge. Mr. Murdoch ordered witness into the boat. Four men passengers and fourteen crew was the complement of men; the rest were women and children.

When boat No. 15 left the boat deck there were other women and children there—some first-class women passengers and their husbands. Absolute quietness existed. There were repeated cries for women and children. If there had been any more women there would have been found places for them in the boat. He heard some of the women on the A Deck say they would not leave their husbands.

There is no truth in the statement that any of the seamen tried to keep back third-class passengers from the Boat Deck. Witness saw masthead light of a ship from the Boat Deck. He did his very best, and so did all the other stewards, to help get the steerage passengers on the Boat Deck as soon as possible.

ENGELHARDT BOAT "C"[1]

No disorder in loading or lowering this boat.

Passengers: President Ismay, Mr. Carter. Balance women and children.

Crew: Quartermaster Rowe (in charge). Steward Pearce. Barber Weikman. Firemen, three.

Stowaways: Four Chinamen, or Filipinos.

Total: 39.

Incidents

G. T. Rowe, Q. M. (Am. Inq., p. 519, and Br. Inq.):

To avoid repetition, the testimony of this witness before the two Courts of Inquiry is consolidated:

He assisted the officer (Boxhall) to fire distress signals until about five and twenty minutes past one. At this time they were getting out the starboard collapsible boats. Chief Officer Wilde wanted a sailor. Captain Smith told him to get into the boat "C" which was then partly filled. He found three women and children in there with no more about. Two gentlemen got in, Mr. Ismay and Mr. Carter. Nobody told them to get in. No one else was there. In the boat there were thirty-nine altogether. These two gentlemen,

1. Br. Rpt., p. 38, makes this last boat lowered on starboard side at 1:40.

five of the crew (including himself), three firemen, a steward, and near daybreak they found four Chinamen or Filipinos who had come up between the seats. All the rest were women and children.

Before leaving the ship he saw a bright light about five miles away about two points on the port bow. He noticed it after he got into the boat. When he left the ship there was a list to port of six degrees. The order was given to lower the boat, with witness in charge. The rub strake kept on catching on the rivets down the ship's side, and it was as much as we could do to keep off. It took a good five minutes, on account of this rubbing, to get down. When they reached the water they steered for a light in sight, roughly five miles. They seemed to get no nearer to it and altered their course to a boat that was carrying a green light. When day broke, the *Carpathia* was in sight.

In regard to Mr. Ismay's getting into the boat, the witness's testimony before the American Court of Inquiry is cited in full:

Senator Burton: Now, tell us the circumstances under which Mr. Ismay and that other gentleman got into the boat.

Mr. Rowe: When Chief Officer Wilde asked if there were any more women and children, there was no reply, so Mr. Ismay came into the boat.

Senator Burton: Mr. Wilde asked if there were any more women and children? Can you say that there were none?

Mr. Rowe: I could not see, but there were none forthcoming.

Senator Burton: You could see around there on the deck, could you not?

Mr. Rowe: I could see the fireman and steward that completed the boat's crew, but as regards any families I could not see any.

Senator Burton: Were there any men passengers besides Mr. Ismay and the other man?

Mr. Rowe: I did not see any, sir.

Senator Burton: Was it light enough so that you could see anyone near by?

Mr. Rowe: Yes, sir.

Senator Burton: Did you hear anyone ask Mr. Ismay and Mr. Carter to get in the boat?

Mr. Rowe: No, sir.

Senator Burton: If Chief Officer Wilde had spoken to them would you have known it?

Mr. Rowe: I think so, because they got in the after part of the boat where I was.

Alfred Pearce, pantryman, third-class (Br. Inq.):

Picked up two babies in his arms and went into a collapsible boat on the starboard side under Officer Murdoch's order, in which were women and children. There were altogether sixty-six passengers and five of the crew, a quartermaster in charge. The ship had a list on the port side, her lights burning to the last. It was twenty minutes to two when they started to row away. He remembers this because one of the passengers gave the time.

J. B. Ismay, President International Mercantile Marine Co. of America, New Jersey, U. S. A. (Am. Inq., pp. 8, 960):

There were four in the crew—one quartermaster, a pantryman, a butcher and another. The natural order would be women and children first. It was followed as far as practicable. About forty-five in the boat. He saw no struggling or jostling or any attempts by men to get into the boats. They simply picked the women out and put them into the boat as fast as they could—the first ones that were there. He put a great many in—also children. He saw the first lifeboat lowered on the starboard side. As to the circumstances of his departure from the ship, the boat was there. There was a certain number of men in the boat and the officer called and asked if there were any more women, but there was no response. There were no passengers left on the deck, and as the boat was in the act of being lowered away he got into it. The *Titanic* was sinking at the time. He felt the ship

going down. He entered because there was room in it. Before he
boarded the lifeboat he saw no passengers jump into the sea.
The boat rubbed along the ship's side when being lowered, the
women helping to shove the boat clear. This was when the ship
had quite a list to port. He sat with his back to the ship, rowing
all the time, pulling away. He did not wish to see her go down.
There were nine or ten men in the boat with him. Mr. Carter, a
passenger, was one. All the other people in the boat, so far as he
could see, were third-class passengers.

*Examined before the British Court of Inquiry by the Attorney-
General, Sir Rufus Isaacs, Mr. Ismay testified:*

I was awakened by the impact; stayed in bed a little time and
then got up. I saw a steward who could not say what had happened. I put a coat on and went on deck. I saw Captain Smith. I
asked him what was the matter and he said we had struck ice.
He said he thought it was serious. I then went down and saw the
chief engineer, who said that the blow was serious. He thought
the pumps would keep the water under control. I think I went
back to my room and then to the bridge and heard Captain
Smith give an order in connection with the boats. I went to the
boat deck, spoke to one of the officers, and rendered all the assistance I could in putting the women and children in. Stayed
there until I left the ship. There was no confusion; no attempts
by men to get into the boats. So far as I knew all the women and
children were put on board the boats and I was not aware that
any were left. There was a list of the ship to port. I think I remained an hour and a half on the *Titanic* after the impact. I noticed her going down by the head, sinking. Our boat was fairly
full. After all the women and children got in and there were no
others on that side of the deck, I got in while the boat was being
lowered. Before we got into the boat I do not know that any attempt was made to call up any of the passengers on the Boat
Deck, nor did I inquire.

And also examined by Mr. A. C. Edwards, M. P., counsel
for the Dock Workers' Union. Mr. Ismay's testimony
was taken as follows:

Mr. Edwards: You were responsible for determining the number of boats?

Mr. Ismay: Yes, in conjunction with the ship-builders.

Mr. Edwards: You knew when you got into the boat that the ship was sinking?

Mr. Ismay: Yes.

Mr. Edwards: Had it occurred to you apart perhaps from the captain, that you, as the representative managing director, deciding the number of lifeboats, owed your life to every other person on the ship?

The President: That is not the sort of question which should be put to this witness. You can make comment on it when you come to your speech if you like.

Mr. Edwards: You took an active part in directing women and children into the boats?

Mr. Ismay: I did all I could.

Mr. Edwards: Why did you not go further and send for other people to come on deck and fill the boats?

Mr. Ismay: I put in everyone who was there and I got in as the boat was being lowered away.

Mr. Edwards: Were you not giving directions and getting women and children in?

Mr. Ismay: I was calling to them to come in.

Mr. Edwards: Why then did you not give instructions or go yourself either to the other side of the deck or below decks to get people up?

Mr. Ismay: I understood there were people there sending them up.

Mr. Edwards: But you knew there were hundreds who had not come up?

Lord Mersey: Your point, as I understand it now, is that, having regard for his position as managing director, it was his duty to remain on the ship until she went to the bottom?

Mr. Edwards: Frankly, that is so, and I do not flinch from it; but I want to get it from the witness, inasmuch as he took it upon himself to give certain directions at a certain time, why he did not discharge his responsibility after in regard to other persons or passengers.

Mr. Ismay: There were no more passengers who would have got into the boat. The boat was being actually lowered away.

Examined by Sir Robert Finley for White Star Line:

Mr. Finley: Have you crossed very often to and from America?

Mr. Ismay: Very often.

Mr. Finley: Have you ever, on any occasion, attempted to interfere with the navigation of the vessel on any of these occasions?

Mr. Ismay: No.

Mr. Finley: When you left the deck just before getting into the collapsible boat, did you hear the officer calling out for more women?

Mr. Ismay: I do not think I did; but I heard them calling for women very often.

Mr. Edwards: When the last boat left the *Titanic* you must have known that a number of passengers and crew were still on board?

Mr. Ismay: I did.

Mr. Edwards: And yet you did not see any on the deck?

Mr. Ismay: No, I did not see any, and I could only assume that the other passengers had gone to the other end of the ship.

From an address (Br. Inq.) by Mr. A. Clement Edwards, M. P., Counsel for Dock Workers' Union:

What was Mr. Ismay's duty?

Coming to Mr. Ismay's conduct, Mr. Edwards said it was clear that that gentleman had taken upon himself to assist in getting women and children into the boats. He had also admitted that when he left the *Titanic* he knew she was doomed, that there were hundreds of people in the ship, that he didn't know whether or not there were any women or children left, and that he did not even go to the other side of the Boat Deck to see whether there were any women and children waiting to go. Counsel submitted that a gentleman occupying the position of managing director of the company owning the *Titanic*, and who had taken upon himself the duty of assisting at the boats, had certain special and further duties beyond an ordinary passenger's duties, and that he had no more right to save his life at the expense of any single person on board that ship than the captain would have had. He (Mr. Edwards) said emphatically that Mr. Ismay did not discharge his duty at that particular moment by taking a careless glance around the starboard side of the Boat Deck. He was one of the few persons who at the time had been placed in a position of positive knowledge that the vessel was doomed, and it was his clear duty, under the circumstances, to see that someone made a search for passengers in other places than in the immediate vicinity of the Boat Deck.

Lord Mersey: Moral duty do you mean?

Mr. Edwards: I agree; but I say that a managing director going on board a liner, commercially responsible for it and taking upon himself certain functions, had a special moral obligation and duty more than is possessed by one passenger to another passenger.

Lord Mersey: But how is a moral duty relative to this inquiry? It might be argued that there was a moral duty for every man on board that every woman should take precedence, and I might have to inquire whether every passenger carried out his moral duty.

Mr. Edwards agreed that so far as the greater questions involved in this case were concerned this matter was one of trivial importance.

From address of Sir Robert Finlay, K. C., M. P.,
Counsel for White Star Company (Br. Inq.):

It has been said by Mr. Edwards that Mr. Ismay had no right to save his life at the expense of any other life. He did not save his life at the expense of any other life. If Mr. Edwards had taken the trouble to look at the evidence he would have seen how unfounded this charge is. There is not the slightest ground for suggesting that any other life would have been saved if Mr. Ismay had not got into the boat. He did not get into the boat until it was being lowered away.

Mr. Edwards has said that it was Mr. Ismay's plain duty to go about the ship looking for passengers, but the fact is that the boat was being lowered. Was it the duty of Mr. Ismay to have remained, though by doing so no other life could have been saved? If he had been impelled to commit suicide of that kind, then it would have been stated that he went to the bottom because he dared not face this inquiry. There is no observation of an unfavorable nature to be made from any point of view upon Mr. Ismay's conduct. There was no duty devolving upon him of going to the bottom with his ship as the captain did. He did all he could to help the women and children. It was only when the boat was being lowered that he got into it. He violated no point of honor, and if he had thrown his life away in the manner now suggested it would be said he did it because he was conscious he could not face this inquiry and so he had lost his life.

ENGELHARDT BOAT "A"

Floated off the ship

Passengers: T. Beattie,[1] P. D. Daly,[3] G. Rheims, R. N. Williams, Jr., first-class; O. Abelseth,[3] W. J. Mellers, second-class; and Mrs. Rosa Abbott,[3] Edward Lindley,[2] third-class.

Crew: Steward: E. Brown. Firemen: J. Thompson, one unidentified body,[1] Seaman: one unidentified body.[1]

An extraordinary story pertains to this boat. At the outset of

1. Body found in boat by *Oceanic*.

2. Died in boat.

3. Pulled into boat out of sea.

my research it was called a "boat of mystery," occasioned by the statements of the *Titanic's* officers. In his conversations with me, as well as in his testimony, Officer Lightoller stated that he was unable to loosen this boat from the ship in time and that he and his men were compelled to abandon their efforts to get it away. The statement in consequence was that this boat "A" was not utilized but went down with the ship. My recent research has disabused his mind of this supposition. There were only four Engelhardt boats in all as we have already learned, and we have fully accounted for "the upset boat B," and "D," the last to leave the ship in the tackles, and boat "C," containing Mr. Ismay, which reached the *Carpathia's* side and was unloaded there. After all the mystery we have reached the conclusion that boat "A" did not go down with the ship, but was the one whose occupants were rescued by Officer Lowe in the early morning, and then abandoned with three dead bodies in it. This also was the boat picked up nearly one month later by the *Oceanic* nearly 200 miles from the scene of the wreck.

I have made an exhaustive research up to date for the purpose of discovering how Boat A left the ship. Information in regard thereto is obtained from the testimony before the British Court of Inquiry of Steward Edward Brown, from first-class passenger R. N. Williams, Jr., and from an account of William J. Mellers, a second-cabin passenger as related by him to Dr. Washington Dodge. Steward Brown, it will be observed, testified that he was washed out of the boat and yet "did not know whether he went down in the water." As he could not swim, an analysis of his testimony forces me to believe that he held on to the boat and did not have to swim and that boat "A" was the same one that he was in when he left the ship. I am forced to the same conclusion in young Williams' case after an analysis of his statement that he took off his big fur overcoat in the water and cast it adrift while he swam twenty yards to the boat, and in some unaccountable way the fur coat swam after him and also got into the boat. At any rate it was found in the boat when it was recovered later as shown in the evidence.

I also have a letter from Mr. George Rheims, of Paris, indicating his presence on this same boat with Messrs. Williams and Mellers and Mrs. Abbott and others.

Incidents

Edward Brown, steward (Br. Inq.):

Witness helped with boats 5, 3, 1 and C, and then helped with another collapsible; tried to get it up to the davits when the ship gave a list to port. The falls were slackened but the boat could not be hauled away any further. There were four or five women waiting to get into the boat. The boat referred to was the collapsible boat "A" which they got off the officers' house. They got it down by the planks, but witness does not know where the planks came from. He thinks they were with the bars which came from the other boats; yet he had no difficulty in getting the boat off the house. The ship was then up to the bridge under water, well down by the head. He jumped into the boat then and called out to cut the falls. He cut them at the aft end, but cannot say what happened to the forward fall. He was washed out of the boat *but does not know whether he went down in the water.*[1] He had his lifebelt on and came to the top. People were all around him. They tore his clothes away struggling in the water. He could not swim, but got into the collapsible boat "A." Only men were in it, but they picked up a woman and some men afterwards, consisting of passengers, stewards and crew. There were sixteen men. Fifth Officer Lowe in boat No. 14 picked them up.

O. Abelseth (Am. Inq.):

Witness describes the period just before the ship sank when an effort was made to get out the collapsible boats on the roof of the officers' house. The officer wanted help and called out: "Are there any sailors here?" It was only about five feet to the water when

1. Italics are mine. —AUTHOR.

witness jumped off. It was not much of a jump. Before that he could see the people were jumping over. He went under and swallowed some water. A rope was tangled around him. He came on top again and tried to swim. There were lots of men floating around. One of them got him on the neck and pressed him under the water and tried to get on top, but he got loose from him. Then another man hung on to him for a while and let go. Then he swam for about fifteen or twenty minutes. Saw something dark ahead of him; swam towards it and it was one of the Engelhardt boats ("A"). He had a life-preserver on when he jumped from the ship. There was no suction at all. "I will try and see." he thought, "if I can float on the lifebelt without help from swimming," and he floated easily on the lifebelt. When he got on boat "A" no one assisted him, but they said when he got on: "Don't capsize the boat," so he hung on for a little while before he got on.

Some were trying to get on their feet who were sitting or lying down; others fell into the water again. Some were frozen and there were two dead thrown overboard. On the boat he raised up and continuously moved his arms and swung them around to keep warm. There was one lady aboard this raft and she (Mrs. Abbott) was saved. There were also two Swedes and a first-class passenger. He said he had a wife and child. There was a fireman also named Thompson who had burned one of his hands; also a young boy whose name sounded like "Volunteer." He and Thompson were afterwards at St. Vincent's Hospital. In the morning he saw a boat with a sail up, and in unison they screamed together for help. Boat A was not capsized and the canvas was not raised up, and they could not get it up. *They stood all night in about twelve or fourteen inches of water*[1]—their feet in water all the time. Boat No. 14 sailed down and took them aboard and transferred them to the *Carpathia*, he helping to row. There must have been ten or twelve saved from boat A; one man was from New Jersey, with whom he came in company from London. At daybreak he seemed unconscious. He took him by the shoulder and shook him. "Who are you?" he said; "let me be; who are you?" About half an hour or so later he died.

1. Italics are mine. —AUTHOR.

• • •

In a recent letter from Dr. Washington Dodge he refers to a young man whom he met on the Carpathia, *very much exhausted, whom he took to his stateroom and gave him medicine and medical attention. This young man was a gentleman's valet and a second-cabin passenger. This answers to the description of William J. Mellers, to whom I have written, but as yet have received no response. Dr. Dodge says he believes this young man's story implicitly: He, Mellers, "was standing by this boat when one of the crew was endeavoring to cut the fastenings that bound it to the vessel just as the onrush of waters came on which tore it loose. It was by clinging to this boat that he was saved."*

R. N. Williams, Jr., in his letter writes me as follows:

"I was not under water very long, and as soon as I came to the top I threw off the big fur coat I had on. I had put my lifebelt on under the coat. I also threw off my shoes. About twenty yards away I saw something floating. I swam to it and found it to be a collapsible boat. I hung on to it and after a while got aboard and *stood up in the middle of it. The water was up to my waist.*[1] About thirty of us clung to it. When Officer Lowe's boat picked us up eleven of us were alive; all the rest were dead from cold. My fur coat was found attached to this Engelhardt boat 'A' by the *Oceanic*, and *also a cane marked 'C. Williams.'* This gave rise to the story that my father's body was in this boat, but this, as you see, is not so. How the cane got there I do not know."

Through the courtesy of Mr. Harold Wingate of the White Star Line in letters to me I have the following information pertaining to boat "A":

1. Italics are mine. —AUTHOR.

"One of the bodies found in this boat was that of Mr. Thompson Beattie. We got his watch and labels from his clothes showing his name and that of the dealer, which we sent to the executor. Two others were a fireman and a sailor, both unidentified. The overcoat belonging to Mr. Williams I sent to a furrier to be re-conditioned, but nothing could be done with it except to dry it out, so I sent it to him as it was. *There was no cane in the boat.* The message from the *Oceanic* and the words 'R. N. Williams, *care of Duane Williams,*' were twisted by the receiver of the message to 'Richard N. Williams, *cane of Duane Williams,*'[1] which got into the press, and thus perpetuated the error.

"There was also a ring found in the boat whose owner we eventually traced in Sweden and restored the property to her. We cannot account for its being in the boat, but we know that her husband was a passenger on the *Titanic*—Edward P. Lindell, a third-class passenger. The widow's address is, care of Nels Persson, Helsingborg, Sweden."

Rescue of the occupants of boat "A" at daylight Monday morning is recorded in the testimony of Officer Lowe and members of the crew of his boat No. 14 and the other boats 12, 10, 4 and "D" which were tied together. No 14 we recall was emptied of passengers and a crew taken from all the boats referred to went back to the wreck. The substance of the testimony of all of them agrees and I need only cite that of Quartermaster Bright, in charge of boat "D," as follows:

A. Bright, Q. M. (in charge) (Am. Inq., 834):

Just at daylight witness saw from his place in boat "D" one of the other collapsible boats, "A," that was awash just flush with the water. Officer Lowe came and towed witness's boat to the other collapsible one that was just awash and took from it thirteen men

---

1. Italics are mine. —AUTHOR.

and one woman who were in the water up to their ankles. They had been singing out in the dark. As soon as daylight came they could be seen. They were rescued and the boat turned adrift with two dead bodies in it, covered with a lifebelt over their faces.

Admiral Mahan on Ismay's duty:

Rear-Admiral A. T. Mahan, Retired, in a letter which the *Evening Post* publishes, has this to say of J. Bruce Ismay's duty:

In the *Evening Post* of April 24 Admiral Chadwick passes a distinct approval upon the conduct of Mr. Ismay in the wreck of the *Titanic* by characterizing the criticisms passed upon it as the "acme of emotionalism."

Both censure and approval had best wait upon the results of the investigations being made in Great Britain. Tongues will wag, but if men like Admiral Chadwick see fit to publish anticipatory opinions those opinions must receive anticipatory comment.

Certain facts are so notorious that they need no inquiry to ascertain. These are (1) that before the collision the captain of the *Titanic* was solely responsible for the management of the ship; (2) after the collision there were not boats enough to embark more than one-third of those on board, and, (3) for that circumstance the White Star Company is solely responsible, not legally, for the legal requirements were met, but morally. Of this company, Mr. Ismay is a prominent if not the most prominent member.

For all the loss of life the company is responsible, individually and collectively: Mr. Ismay personally, not only as one of the members. He believed the *Titanic* unsinkable; the belief relieves of moral guilt, but not of responsibility. Men bear the consequences of their mistakes as well as of their faults. He—and Admiral Chadwick—justify his leaving over fifteen hundred persons, the death of each one of whom lay on the company, on the ground that it was the last boat half filled; and Mr. Ismay has said, no one else to be seen.

No one to be seen; but was there none to be reached? Mr. Ismay knew there must be many, because he knew the boats could take only a third. The *Titanic* was 882 feet long; 92 broad; say, from Thirty-fourth street to a little north of Thirty-seventh. Within this space were congregated over 1,500 souls, on several decks. True, to find any one person at such a moment in the intricacies of a vessel were a vain hope; but to encounter some stragglers would not seem to be. Read in the *Sun* and *Times* of April 25 Col. Gracie's account of the "mass of humanity, men and women" that suddenly appeared before him after the boats were launched.

In an interview reported in the New York *Times* April 25 Admiral Sir Cyprian Bridge, a very distinguished officer, holds that Mr. Ismay was but a passenger, as other passengers. True, up to a certain point. He is in no sense responsible for the collision; but when the collision had occurred he confronted a wholly new condition for which he was responsible and not the captain, viz., a sinking vessel without adequate provision for saving life. Did no obligation to particularity of conduct rest upon him under such a condition?

I hold that under the conditions, so long as there was a soul that could be saved, the obligation lay upon Mr. Ismay that one person and not he should have been in the boat. More than 1,500 perished. Circumstances yet to be developed may justify Mr. Ismay's actions completely, but such justification is imperatively required. If this be "the acme of emotionalism" I must be content to bear the imputation.

Admiral Chadwick urges the "preserving a life so valuable to the great organization to which Mr. Ismay belongs." This bestows upon Mr. Ismay's escape a kind of halo of self-sacrifice. No man is indispensable. There are surely brains enough and business capacity enough in the White Star company to run without him. The reports say that of the rescued women thirty-seven were widowed by the accident and the lack of boats. Their husbands were quite as indispensable to them as Mr. Ismay to the company. His duty to the ship's company was clear and primary; that to the White Star company so secondary as to be at the moment inoperative.

We should be careful not to pervert standards. Witness the talk that the result is due to the system. What is a system, except that which individuals have made it and keep it? Whatever thus weakens the sense of individual responsibility is harmful, and so likewise is all condonation of failure of the individual to meet his responsibility.

U.S. Senate and British Inquiries
and Marconi Report

Daniel Buckley,
US Inquiry
(DAY 13)

DAB001. Mr. Buckley, where do you live?
855 Trent Avenue, Bronx.

DAB002. How old are you?
Twenty-one years old.

DAB003. Where did you get aboard the Titanic?
At Queenstown.

DAB004. Had you been living in Ireland?
Yes; I lived in King Williamstown, Town Court.

DAB005. How did you happen to come over to America?
I wanted to come over here to make some money. I came in the Titanic *because she was a new steamer. This night of the wreck I was sleeping in my room on the* Titanic, *in the steerage. There were three other boys from the same place sleeping in the same room with me.*
I heard some terrible noise and I jumped out on the floor, and the first thing I knew my feet were getting wet; the water was just coming in slightly. I told the other fellows to get up, that there was something wrong and, that the water was coming in.

They only laughed at me. One of them says: "Get back into bed. You are not in Ireland now."

I got on my clothes as quick as I could, and the three other fellows got out. The room was very small, so I got out, to give them room to dress themselves.

Two sailors came along, and they were shouting: "All up on deck! unless you want to get drowned."

When I heard this, I went for the deck as quick as I could. When I got up on the deck I saw everyone having those lifebelts on myself; so I got sorry, and said I would go back again where I was sleeping and get one of those life preservers; because there was one there for each person.

I went back again, and just as I was going down the last flight of stairs the water was up four steps, and dashing up. I did not go back into the room, because I could not. When I went back toward the room the water was coming up three steps up the stairs, or four steps; so I did not go any farther. I got back on the deck again, and just as I got back there, I was looking around to see if I could get any of those lifebelts, and I met a first class passenger, and he had two. He gave me one, and fixed it on me.

Then the lifeboats were preparing. There were five lifeboats sent out. I was in the sixth. I was holding the ropes all the time, helping to let down the five lifeboats that went down first, as well as I could.

When the sixth lifeboat was prepared, there was a big crowd of men standing on the deck. And they all jumped in. So I said I would take my chance with them.

DAB006. Who were they?

Passengers and sailors and firemen mixed. There were no ladies there at the same time.

When they jumped, I said I would go too. I went into the boat. Then two officers came along and said all of the men could come out. And they brought a lot of steerage passengers with them; and they were mixed, every way, ladies and gentlemen. And they said all the men could get out and let the ladies in. But six men were left in the boat. I think they were firemen and sailors.

I was crying. There was a woman in the boat, and she had thrown her shawl over me, and she told me to stay in there. I believe she was Mrs. Astor. Then they did not see me, and the boat was lowered down into the water, and we rowed away out from the steamer.

The men that were in the boat at first fought, and would not get out, but the officers drew their revolvers, and fired shots over our heads, and then the men got out. When the boat was ready, we were lowered down into the water and rowed away out from the steamer. We were only about 15 minutes out when she sank.

DAB014. What became of those other three boys?
I can not say. I did not see them any more after leaving the room where I parted from them.

DAB015. They were lost?
Yes; they were lost.

DAB016. Was there any effort made on the part of the officers or crew to hold the steerage passengers in the steerage?
I do not think so.

DAB017. Were you permitted to go on up to the top deck without any interference?
Yes, sir. They tried to keep us down at first on our steerage deck. They did not want us to go up to the first class place at all.

DAB018. Who tried to do that?
I can not say who they were. I think they were sailors.

DAB019. What happened then? Did the steerage passengers try to get out?
Yes; they did. There was one steerage passenger there, and he was getting up the steps, and just as he was going in a little gate

a fellow came along and chucked him down; threw him down into the steerage place. This fellow got excited, and he ran after him, and he could not find him. He got up over the little gate. He did not find him.

DAB020. *What gate do you mean?*
A little gate just at the top of the stairs going up into the first class deck.

DAB021. *There was a gate between the steerage and the first class deck?*
Yes. The first class deck was higher up than the steerage deck, and there were some steps leading up to it; 9 or 10 steps, and a gate just at the top of the steps.

DAB022. *Was the gate locked?*
It was not locked at the time we made the attempt to get up there, but the sailor, or whoever he was, locked it. So that this fellow that went up after him broke the lock on it, and he went after the fellow that threw him down. He said if he could get hold of him he would throw him into the ocean.

DAB023. *Did these passengers in the steerage have any opportunity at all of getting out?*
Yes; they had.

DAB024. *What opportunity did they have?*
I think they had as much chance as the first and second class passengers.

DAB025. *After this gate was broken?*
Yes; because they were all mixed. All the steerage passengers went up on the first class deck at this time, when the gate was broken. They all got up there. They could not keep them down.

DAB029. *Did you find any people down in the steerage when you went back the second time?*

There were a number, but I can not say how many. All the boys and girls were coming up against me. They were all going for the deck.

DAB030. *Were they excited?*
Yes; they were. The girls were very excited, and they were crying; and all the boys were trying to console them and saying that it was nothing serious.

DAB031. *Were you crying at the time?*
Not at this time. There was a girl from my place, and just when she got down into the lifeboat she thought that the boat was sinking into the water. Her name was Bridget Bradley. *She climbed one of the ropes as far as she could and tried to get back into the* Titanic *again, as she thought she would be safer in it than in the lifeboat. She was just getting up when one of the sailors went out to her and pulled her down again.*

DAB033. *Could you see many people around?*
Yes, sir; there was a great crowd of people. They were all terribly excited. They were all going for the decks as quick as they could. The people had no difficulty in stepping into the lifeboat. It was close to the ship.

DAB034. *I want to ask you whether, from what you saw that night, you feel that the steerage passengers had an equal opportunity with other passengers and the crew in getting into the lifeboats?*
Yes; I think they had as good a chance as the first and second class passengers.

DAB035. *You think they did have?*
Yes. But at the start they tried to keep them down on their own deck.

DAB036. *But they broke down this gate to which you have referred?*
Yes, sir.

DAB037. And then they went on up as others did, mingling all together?

Yes; they were all mixed up together.

DAB038. Have you told all you know, of your own knowledge, about that?

Yes.

DAB039. Were you where you could see the ship when she went down?

Yes; I saw the lights just going out as she went down. It made a terrible noise, like thunder.

DAB040. I wish you would tell the committee in what part of the ship this steerage was located.

Down, I think, in the lower part of the steamer, in the after part of the ship; at the back.

Senator Smith: That is all. Thank you.

John Collins,
US Inquiry
(DAY 7)

(Testimony taken separately before Senator Bourne on behalf of
the subcommittee.)
   (The witness was sworn by Senator Bourne.)

JOC001. State your residence?
No. 65 Bally Carry Street, Belfast.

JOC002. How old are you?
I will be 18 next November.

JOC003. What is your occupation?
Assistant cook, first class galley.

JOC004. How long have you followed the sea?
This was my first voyage, on the Titanic.

JOC006. Your first voyage, then, was on the Titanic?
Yes.

JOC007. You were on it at the time of the accident?
I was, sir.

JOC008. I wish you would tell the committee just what you
were doing immediately prior to, and what you did after, the

time that the catastrophe on the Titanic *took place, in your own language?*

I stopped work at 9 o'clock on Sunday night, and I came up again and walked up and down the alleyway. I went into my bunk and fell asleep. That was about 10 o'clock—about a quarter to 10. I fell asleep, and was sound asleep, and exactly at a quarter past 11 I was wakened up. I had a clock by me, by my bed, and my clock was five minutes fast, and it was exactly a quarter past 11 when the ship struck the iceberg, and it wakened me. I put on my trousers, got out of bed, and they were letting off steam in the stoke hole. I asked what was the matter, and it seemed she struck an iceberg. The word came down the alleyway that there was no harm, and everyone returned to their bunks.

JOC015. *Now, go on with your description.*

I went back into the bedroom and was told to lie down, and I got up again. I did not take off any of my clothes, and I came out again and saw the stewards in their white jackets in the passageway; the passengers were running forward, the stewards were steering them, and they made a joke of it, and we all turned in then and the word came in that we were to get out of our beds and get the lifebelts on and get up to the upper deck.

JOC016. *At what time was it that this word came? How long after the ship struck?*

Well, it was exactly—I am sure—half an hour, sir. Quite half an hour, it was.

JOC017. Go on.

We went up to the deck when the word came. Then I met a companion of mine, a steward, and I asked him what number my boat was, and he said No. 16; so I went up to No. 16 boat, and I seen both firemen and sailors with their bags ready for No. 16 boat. I said to myself, "There is no chance there," and I ran back to the deck, ran to the port side on the saloon deck with another steward and a woman and two children, and the steward had one of the children in his arms and the woman was crying. I took the child off of the woman and made for one of the boats. Then the word came around from the starboard side there was a collapsible boat getting launched on the starboard side and that all women and children were to make for it. So me and another steward and the two children and the woman came around on that side, the starboard side, and when we got around there we saw then that it was forward. We saw the collapsible boat taken off of the saloon deck, and then the sailors and the firemen that were forward seen the ship's bow in the water and seen that she was intending to sink her bow, and they shouted out for all they were worth we were to go aft, and word came there was a boat getting launched, so we were told to go aft, and we were just turning around and making for the stern end when the wave washed us off the deck—washed us clear of it— and the child was washed out of my arms; and the wreckage and the people that was around me, they kept me down for at least two or three minutes under the water.

JOCo18. Two or three minutes?
Yes; I am sure.

JOCo19. Were you unconscious?
No; not at all. It did not affect me much, the salt water.

JOCo20. But you were under the water. You can not stay under the water two or three minutes, can you?
Well, it seemed that to me. I could not exactly state how long, but it seemed that to me. When I came to the surface I saw this boat that had been taken off. I saw a man on it. They had been working on it taking it off of the saloon deck, and when the waves washed it off the deck they clung to that; then I made for it when I came to the surface and saw it, and I swam over to it.

JOCo21. Did you have a lifebelt on?
I had, sir. I was only about 4 or 5 yards off of it, and I swam over to it and I got on to it.

JOC022. How many were on the collapsible boat?

Well, sir, I could not exactly say; but I am sure there was more than 15 or 16.

JOC023. Did those who were on help you get on?

No, sir; they were all watching the ship. I had not much to do. All I had to do was to give a spring and I got onto it; and we were drifting about for two hours on the water.

JOC024. When you had the child in your arms and went to this collapsible boat that you understood was being launched, why did you not get into it?

Sir, we had not time, sir; they had not got it off the deck until we were washed off the deck.

JOC040. How far were you from the stern end of the ship when you came up and got into the collapsible boat, would you judge?

We were about—I could not exactly state how far I was from the Titanic when I come up to the surface. I was not far, because her lights went out then. Her lights went out until the water almost got to amidships on her.

JOC052. If it was dark, how could you see?

We were not too far off. I saw the white of the funnel. Then she turned over again, and down she went.

JOC053. There was not much of a sea on at the time of the accident?

It was as calm as that board.

JOC054. How do you account for this wave that washed you off amidships?

By the suction which took place when the bow went down in the water.

JOC055. And the waves broke over the deck and washed you off?

Washed the decks clear.

JOCo56. How many were around you at that time that were washed off?

There were hundreds on the starboard side.

JOCo57. And you think every one of the hundreds were washed in the water?

Yes, sir; they were washed off into the water.

JOCo58. The order had been given that every passenger and member of the crew should put on a lifebelt?

Yes, sir.

JOCo59. What became of those hundreds that were washed off at the same time you were?

I got on to the raft. I could see when I got on to the raft. I saw the stern of the boat, and I saw a mass of people and wreckage, and heard cries.

JOCo60. In the water?

In the water.

JOCo65. How many of the hundreds that were washed off of the ship at the same time with you got into the collapsible boat with you?

Well, sir, the boat was taken off the saloon deck, and the wave came up and washed the boat right off, and she was upside down, sir, and the water washed over her. She was turned over, and we were standing on her.

JOCo66. You were standing on the bottom of the boat?

Yes, sir.

JOCo75. Did the men on the bottom of the collapsible boat refuse to let others get on from the water?

Only one, sir. If a gentleman had got on we would all have been turned over. We were all on the boat. One was running from one side to the other to keep her steady. If this man had caught hold of her he would have tumbled the whole lot of us off.

JOC076. Who prevented him?

We were all telling him not to get on. He said, "That is all right, boys, keep cool," he said; "God bless you," and he bid us good-by and he swam along for about two minutes and we seen him, but did not see him moving off; we saw his head, but we did not see him moving his hands.

Charles Joughin,
British Inquiry
(DAY 6)

6040.—*I went to the deck pantry, and while I was in there I thought I would take a drink of water, and while I was getting the drink of water I heard a kind of a crash as if something had buckled, as if part of the ship had buckled, and then I heard a rush overhead.*

6045. *People running—yes?*
When I got up on top I could then see them clambering down from those decks. Of course, I was in the tail end of the rush.

6048. *Did you see them clambering down to get on to the A deck so as to get further aft?*
Their idea was to get on to the poop.

6049. *You say that you heard this sound of buckling or crackling. Was it loud; could anybody in the ship hear it?*
You could have heard it, but you did not really know what it was. It was not an explosion or anything like that. It was like as if the iron was parting.

6050. *Like the breaking of metal?*
Yes.

6051. Was it immediately after that sound that you heard this rushing of people and saw them climbing up?
Yes.

6052. What did you do?
I kept out of the crush as much as I possibly could, and I followed down—followed down getting towards the well of the deck, and just as I got down towards the well she gave a great list over to port and threw everybody in a bunch except myself. I did not see anybody else besides myself out of the bunch.

6053. That was when you were in the well, was it?
I was not exactly in the well, I was on the side, practically on the side then. She threw them over. At last I clambered on the side when she chucked them.

6054. You mean the starboard side?
The starboard side.

6055. The starboard was going up and she took a lurch to port?
It was not going up, but the other side was going down.

6056. It is very difficult to say how many, I daresay, but could you give me some idea, of how many people there were in this crush?
I have no idea, Sir; I know they were piled up.

6057. What do you mean when you say, "No idea." Were there hundreds?
Yes, there were more than that—many hundreds, I should say.

6059. She took a lurch and she did not return?
She did not return.

6060. Can you tell us what happened to you?
Yes, I eventually got on to the starboard side of the poop.

6064. *On the side of the ship?*
Yes.

6070. *Did you find anybody else holding that rail there, on the poop?*
No.

6071. *You were the only one?*
I did not see anybody else.

6072. *Were you holding the rail so that you were inside the ship, or were you holding the rail so that you were on the outside of the ship?*
On the outside.

6073. *So that the rail was between you and the deck?*
Yes.

6074. *Then what happened?*
Well, I was just wondering what next to do. I had tightened my belt and I had transferred some things out of this pocket into my stern pocket. I was just wondering what next to do when she went.

6075. *And did you find yourself in the water?*
Yes.

6076. *Did you feel that you were dragged under or did you keep on the top of the water?*
I do not believe my head went under the water at all. It may have been wetted, but no more.

Harold S. Bride,
Report to his Employer, Marconi Co.,
APRIL 27, 1912

Here is a paper, sir, that may be of interest to you. It is a report which I have made to Mr. Cross, the traffic manager of the Marconi Co.
Senator Smith: Yes; this is interesting. (Reading):

NO. 294 WEST NINETY-SECOND STREET,
NEW YORK CITY, N. Y., APRIL 27, 1912.
W. R. CROSS, ESQ.,

DEAR SIR: Hearing of the conflicting reports concerning the loss of the *Titanic*, which are being spread around, I think it is advisable for me to give you, to the best of my ability, a true account of the disaster, so that the Marconi Co. may be in full possession of all the facts.

I regret to say my memory fails me with regard to the time of the occurrence or any of the preceding incidents; but otherwise I am sure of all my statements.

The night before the disaster Mr. Phillips and myself had had a deal of trouble, owing to the leads from the secondary of the transformer having burnt through inside the casing and make contact with certain iron bolts holding the woodwork and frame together, thereby earthing the power to a great extent. After binding these leads with rubber tape, we once more had the apparatus in perfect working order, but not before we had put in nearly six hours' work, Mr. Phillips being of the opinion that, in the first place, it was the condensers which had broken, and these we had had out and examined before locating the damage in the transformer.

Owing to this trouble, I had promised to relieve Mr. Phillips on the following night at midnight instead of the usual time, 2 o'clock, as he seemed very tired.

During Sunday afternoon, toward 5 o'clock, I was called by the *Californian* (call letters MWL) with an ice report, but I did not immediately answer, as I was writing up the abstracts; and also it used to take us some considerable time to start up the motor and alternator, it not being advisable to leave them working, as the alternator was liable to run hot.

I, however, acknowledged the receipt of the report when "MWL" transmitted it to the *Baltic*, and took it myself to the officer on watch on the bridge.

Neither Mr. Phillips nor I, to my knowledge, received any further ice reports.

About 9 p.m. I turned in and woke on my own accord just about midnight, relieving Mr. Phillips, who had just finished sending a large batch of telegrams to Cape Race.

Mr. Phillips told me that apparently we had struck something, as previous to my turning out he had felt the ship tremble and stop, and expressed an opinion that we should have to return to Belfast.

I took over the telephone from him, and he was preparing to retire when Capt. Smith entered the cabin and told us to get assistance immediately.

Mr. Phillips resumed the phones, after asking the captain if he should use the regulation distress call "C Q D." The captain said "Yes," and Mr. Phillips started in with "C Q D," having obtained the latitude and longitude of the *Titanic.*

The *Frankfurt* was the first to answer. We gave him the ship's position, which he acknowledged by "OK, stdbi."

The second answer was from the *Carpathia,* who immediately responded with his position and informed us he was coming to our assistance as fast as possible.

These communications I reported myself to the captain, who was, when I found him, engaging in superintending the filling and lowering of the lifeboats.

The noise of escaping steam directly over our cabin caused a deal of trouble to Mr. Phillips in reading the replies to our distress call, and this I also reported to Capt. Smith, who by some means managed to get it abated.

The *Olympic* next answered our call, but as far as I know, Mr. Phillips did not go to much trouble with her, as we now realized the awful state of affairs, the ship listing heavily to port and forward.

The captain also came in and told us she was sinking fast and could not last longer than half an hour.

Mr. Phillips then went outside to see how things were progressing, and meanwhile I established communication with the *Baltic*, telling him we were in urgent need of assistance.

This I reported to Mr. Phillips on his return, but suggested "M B C" was too far away to be of any use.

Mr. Phillips told me the forward well deck was under water, and we got our lifebelts out and tied on each other, after putting on additional clothing.

Again Mr. Phillips called "C Q D" and "S O S" and for nearly five minutes got no reply, and then both the *Carpathia* and the *Frankfurt* called.

Just at this moment the captain came into the cabin and said, "You can do nothing more; look out for yourselves." Mr. Phillips resumed the phones and after listening a few seconds jumped up and fairly screamed, "The ----- fool. He says, 'What's up old man?'" I asked "Who?" Mr. Phillips replied the *Frankfurt* and at that time it seemed perfectly clear to us that the *Frankfurt's* operator had taken no notice or misunderstood our first call for help.

Mr. Phillips' reply to this was "You fool, stdbi and keep out."

Undoubtedly both Mr. Phillips and I were under a great strain at this time, but though the committee inquiring into the facts on this side are inclined to censure that reply, I am still of the opinion that Mr. Phillips was justified in sending it.

Leaving Mr. Phillips operating, I went to our sleeping cabin, and got all our money together, returning to find a fireman or coal trimmer gently relieving Mr. Phillips of his lifebelt. There immediately followed a general scrimmage with the three of us.

I regret to say that we left too hurriedly to take the man in question with us, and without a doubt he sank with the ship in the Marconi cabin as we left him.

I had up to this time kept the PV entered up, intending when we left the ship to tear out the lot and each to take a copy, but now we could hear the water washing over the boat deck, and Mr. Phillips said, "Come, let's clear out."

We had nearly the whole time been in possession of full power from the ship's dynamo, though toward the end the lights sank and we were ready to stand by, with emergency apparatus and candles, but there was no necessity to use them.

Leaving the cabin, we climbed on top of the house comprising the officers' quarters and our own, and here I saw the last of Mr. Phillips, for he disappeared walking aft.

I now assisted in pushing off a collapsible lifeboat, which was on the port side of the forward funnel, onto the boat deck. Just as the boat fell I noticed Capt. Smith dive from the bridge into the sea.

Then followed a general scramble down on the boat deck, but no sooner had we got there than the sea washed over. I managed to catch hold of the boat we had previously fixed up and was swept overboard with her.

I then experienced the most exciting three or four hours anyone could reasonably wish for, and was in due course, with the rest of the survivors picked up by the *Carpathia*.

As you have probably heard, I got on the collapsible boat a second time, which was, as I felt it, upturned.

I called Phillips several times, but got no response, but learned later from several sources that he was on this boat and expired even before we were picked off by the *Titanic*'s boat.

I am told fright and exposure was the cause of his death.

As far as I can find out, he was taken on board the *Carpathia* and buried at sea from her, though for some reason the bodies of those who had died were not identified before burial from the *Carpathia*, and so I can not vouch for the truth of this.

After a short stay in the hospital of the *Carpathia* I was asked to assist Mr. Cottam, the operator, who seemed fairly worn out with work.

Hundreds of telegrams from survivors were waiting to go as soon as we could get communication with shore stations.

Regarding the working of the *Carpathia*.

The list of survivors, Mr. Cottam told me, had been sent to the *Minnewaska* and the *Olympic*.

When we established communication with the various coast stations, all of which had heavy traffic for us, in some cases running into hundreds of messages, we told them we would only accept service and urgent messages, as we knew the remainder would be press and messages inquiring after some one on the *Titanic*.

It is easy to see we might have spent hours receiving messages inquiring after some survivor, while we had messages waiting from that survivor for transmission.

News was not withheld by Mr. Cottam or myself with the idea of making money, but because, as far as I know, the captain of the *Carpathia* was advising Mr. Cottam to get off the survivors' traffic first.

Quite 75 percent of this we got off.

On arrival in New York Mr. Marconi came on board with a reporter of the *New York Times*. Also Mr. Sammis was present, and I received $500 for my story, which both Mr. Marconi and Mr. Sammis authorized me to tell.

I have forgotten to mention that the United States Government sent out a ship, as they said, to assist us named the *Chester*.

Several messages passed between the commander of that vessel and the *Carpathia*, and resulted in the captain telling us to transmit the names of the third class passengers to the *Chester*.

Though it has since been reported that the most expert operator in the United States Navy was on board the *Chester*, I had to repeat these names, nearly in all, several times to him taking up nearly a couple of hours of valuable time, though I sent them in the first place slowly and carefully.

I am now staying with relatives and waiting orders from the Marconi Co. here, who have been most considerate and kind, buying me much needed clothes and looking after me generally.

I am glad to say I can now walk around, the sprain in my left foot being much better, though my right foot remains numbed from the exposure and cold, but causes me no pain or inconvenience whatever.

I greatly appreciate the cable the company so kindly sent me and thank them for the same.

Trusting this report will be satisfactory until my return to England, I beg to remain.

Yours, obediently,

HAROLD S. BRIDE

Newspaper First Accounts

Harold S. Bride,
New York Times,
APRIL 19, 1912

The following thrilling statement was dictated today by Mr. Bride, the assistant Marconi operator on board the *Titanic,* to the *New York Times* representative, in the presence of Mr. Marconi, who is now staying in New York:

"I joined the *Titanic* at Belfast. I was born in Nunhead, London, S. E., twenty-two years ago, and joined the Marconi staff last July. I first worked on the *Haverford,* and then on the *Lusitania,* and was transferred to the *Titanic* at Belfast. I didn't have much to do aboard the *Titanic,* except to relieve Phillips, the senior operator, from midnight until some time in the morning, when he finished sleeping." "There were three rooms in the wireless cabin. One was a sleeping room, one a dynamo room, and one an operating room. I took off my clothes and went to sleep in the bed. Then I was conscious of waking up and hearing Phillips sending to Cape Race. I read what he was sending. It was only routine matter. I remembered how tired he was, and got out of bed without my clothes on to relieve him. I didn't even feel the shock. I hardly knew it had happened until after the captain had come to us. There was no jolt whatever."

THE HELP SIGNAL, "C.Q.D."

"I was standing by Phillips, telling him to go to bed, when the captain put his head in the cabin, 'We've struck an iceberg,' the captain said, 'and I'm having an inspection made to tell what it has done for us. You had better get ready to send out a call for assistance, but don't send it until I tell you. 'The captain went away, and in ten minutes, I should estimate, he came back. We could hear terrible confusion outside, but not the least thing to indicate any trouble. The wireless was working perfectly. 'Send a call for assistance,' ordered the captain, barely putting his head in the door. 'What call should I send?' Phillips asked. 'The regulation international call for help, just that.' Then the captain was gone." "Phillips began to send 'C.Q.D.' He flashed away at it, and we joked while he did so. All of us made light of the disaster. We joked that way while we flashed the signals for about five minutes. Then the captain came back. 'What are you sending?' he asked. 'C.Q.D.,' Phillips replied."

JOKING ABOUT THE COLLISION

"The humour of the situation appealed to me, and I cut in with a little remark that made us all laugh, including the captain. Send 'S.O.S.,' I said, 'it's the new call, and it may be your last chance to send it.' Phillips, with a laugh, changed the signal to 'S.O.S.' The captain told us we had been struck amidships, or just aft of amidships. It was ten minutes, Phillips told me, after he noticed the iceberg, but the slight jolt was the only signal to us that a collision had occurred. We thought we were a good distance away. We said lots of funny things to each other in the next few minutes. We picked up the first steamship *Frankfurt*; gave her our position, and said we had struck an iceberg, and needed assistance. The *Frankfurt* operator went away to tell his captain. He came back, and we told him we were sinking by the head, and that we could observe a distinct list forward." "The *Carpathia* answered our signal, and we told her our position, and said we were sinking by the head. The operator went to tell the captain, and in five minutes returned, and told us the *Carpathia* was putting about and heading for us."

SCENE ON THE DECK

"Our captain had left us at this time, and Phillips told me to run and tell him what the *Carpathia* had answered. I did so, and I went through an awful mass of people to his cabin. The decks were full of scrambling men and women." "I came back and heard Phillips giving the *Carpathia* further directions. Phillips told me to put on my clothes. Until that moment I forgot I wasn't dressed. I went to my cabin and dressed. I brought an overcoat to Phillips, and as it was very cold I slipped the overcoat upon him while he worked." "Every few minutes Phillips would send me to the captain with little messages. They were merely telling how the *Carpathia* was coming our way, and giving her speed.

HEROIC TELEGRAPHIST

"I noticed as I came back from one trip that they were putting off the women and children in lifeboats, and that the list forward was increasing. Phillips told me the wireless was growing weaker. The captain came and told us our engine rooms were taking water, and that the dynamos might not last much longer. We sent that word to the *Carpathia*." "I went out on deck and looked around. The water was pretty close up to the boat deck. There was a great scramble aft, and how poor Phillips worked through it I don't know. He was a brave man. I learned to love him that night, and I suddenly felt for him a great reverence to see him standing there sticking to his work while everybody else was raging about. I will never live to forget the work Phillips did for the last awful fifteen minutes." "Phillips clung on, sending and sending. He clung on for about ten minutes, or maybe fifteen minutes, after the captain released him. The water was then coming into our cabin." "From aft came the tunes of the ship's band, playing the ragtime tune, 'Autumn.' Phillips ran aft, and that was the last I ever saw of him alive." "I went to the place where I had seen the collapsible boat on the boat deck, and to my surprise I saw the boat, and the men still trying to push it off. I guess there wasn't a sailor in the crowd. They couldn't do it. I went up to them, and was just lending a hand when a large wave came awash of the deck. The big wave carried the boat off. I had hold of an oar-lock and I went off with it. The next I knew I was in the boat. But that wasn't all; I was in the boat, and the boat was upside down, and I was under it. I remember realising I was wet through, and that whatever happened I must breathe, for I was under water. I knew I had to fight for it, and I did. How I got out from under the boat I don't know, but I felt a breath of air at last. There were men all around me—hundreds of them. The sea was dotted with them, all depending on their lifebelts."

LAST GLIMPSE OF THE *TITANIC*

"I felt I simply had to get away from the ship. She was a beautiful sight then. Smoke and sparks were rushing out of her funnels. There must have been an explosion, but we heard none. We only saw a big stream of sparks. The ship was gradually turning on her nose—just like a duck does that goes down for a dive. I had only one thing on my mind—to get away from the suction." "The band was still playing. I guess all the band went down. They were heroes. They were still playing 'Autumn.' Then I swam with all my might. I suppose I was 150 ft. away when the *Titanic*, on her nose, with her after quarter sticking straight up in the air, began to settle slowly. When at last the waves washed over her rudder there wasn't the least bit of suction I could feel. She must have kept going down just as flowing as she had been." "I felt after a little while like sinking. I was very cold. I saw a boat of some kind near me, and put all my strength into an effort to swim to it. It was hard work, and I was all alone when a hand reached out from the boat and pulled me aboard. It was our same collapsible boat and the same crowd was on it. There was just room for me to roll on the edge. I lay there not caring what happened. Somebody sat on my legs. They were wedged in between the slats, and were being wrenched. I hadn't the heart left to ask the man to move. There was a terrible sight all around; men swimming and sinking everywhere." "I saw some lights off in the distance, and knew a steamship was coming to our aid. I didn't care what happened. I just lay and gasped when I could, and felt the pain in my feet. I feel it still. At last the *Carpathia* was alongside, and the people were being taken up a rope ladder. Our boat drew near, and one by one the men were taken off of it. One man was dead. I passed him, and went to a ladder, although my feet pained me terribly." "The dead man was Phillips. He died on the raft from exposure and cold. I guess he had been all in from work before the wreck came. He stood his ground until the crisis passed and then collapsed. But I hardly thought of that then; I didn't think much about anything. I tried the rope ladder. My feet pained me terribly, but I got to the top, and felt hands reaching out to me. The next I know a woman was leaning over me in a cabin, and I felt her hand waving in my hair and rubbing my face. I felt somebody at my feet, and felt the warmth of liquor. Somebody got me under the arms, and then I was carried down below to the hospital. That was early in the day. I guess I lay in hospital until near night, when they told me the *Carpathia*'s wireless man was acting 'queer,' and would I help?" "After that I never was out of the wireless room, so I don't know what happened to the passengers."

Laura Cribb,
New York Evening Journal,
APRIL 19, 1912

My father and I were travelling third class in order to save as much money as possible so that he would have sufficient means to go into business when we reached this country. However, we were very comfortable. The first few days of the voyage were glorious, and we made many friends among the passengers who were coming to this country to start their lives new in what my father had always termed the Land of Promise. He was a highly educated man, and for years he had been desirous of coming to America, but it was only a month ago that we decided to leave our home in Dorset.

I was in my berth early Sunday night and was thrown violently to the floor by the impact of the boat when it struck the iceberg. It was then about 11:30 o'clock, and for a moment I was so stunned that I was unable to imagine what had occurred until I heard one of the officers of the ship shouting that the boat had struck an iceberg. He gave hurried instructions that we should dress and go up on the second deck.

Ah, the courage and bravery of those officers was glorious to see. They seemed to be everywhere at once, shouting instructions, giving advice, quieting those who were terrified and lending aid and assistance to those who were too frightened to help themselves.

Why, I saw one officer who stood on the second deck with his revolver in his hand and threatened to shoot any man who attempted to enter a boat before every woman was cared for.

And he shot three.

It would have been a horrible sight at any other time, but in that hour of chaos and excitement I don't think there was a single person who didn't, inwardly at least, glory in his deed.

Shortly after we left the third deck we were lowered in a lifeboat, all women and children except six members of the crew, and we pushed away far enough to be out of the suction zone. We were so fascinated by the sights on the *Titanic*, however, that we could not keep our eyes off her until the last lights went out and the final notes of the band were drowned in the hiss and roar that came with the final plunge of the great ship as she sank bow first.

Each of us knew that with the sinking we had lost some dear one—my father went down with those other brave men who stuck to their posts and gave their lives that we women and children might be saved—but each of us was glad and proud, I think, to know that they were real men, the kind of men who are heroes.

We were in the boat for nearly four hours before we were picked up by the four sailing vessels from the *Titanic*, which had been lashed together for greater safety. It was then some time before we reached the *Carpathia*—I don't know how long, for I had become so benumbed by then that I was unable to correctly keep track. We saw the *Carpathia* for a great distance, but it seemed hours and hours before we reached her and were finally hauled over her side to safety.

Hugh Woolner,
New York Sun,
APRIL 19, 1912

We were sitting, a party of about six, drinking hot whiskey and water. On Sunday night I noticed that everyone was drinking hot drinks. The previous nights we had iced drinks, but on Sunday everybody seemed to be drinking grog. It had suddenly become deadly cold in the lounge and restaurant and the lady of our party had gone off to her room.

Then we men strolled up just above to the smoking room and had been seated only a few minutes when there came a heavy grinding sort of shock beginning far ahead of us in the bows and rapidly passing along the ship and away under our feet. Everyone sprang up and ran out through the swing doors astern.

A man in front of me called out that he had seen an iceberg towering fifty feet above the deck, which was 100 ft above the sea, and passing away astern. This was the explanation.

I went with a Swedish friend whose acquaintance I made on board, Björnström Steffanson of the Swedish Embassy in Washington. We sought out the lady who had been recommended to my care, Mrs. Churchill Candee, who was returning from Paris to see her son after an aeroplane accident.

We found her and I took her up on to the A deck to see how things were going. We found the engines stopped and the officers and crew making preparations to lower the boats. The officers were assuring everyone that there was no danger to life, but that the ladies were to be put into the boats as a precautionary measure.

We continued our walk awhile, and then I saw passengers coming up with life belts on. I got Mrs. Candee's tied on to her and then went off to my room and got on mine and brought away an extra one which I soon gave to some scared person who had none. Bjornstrom and I took Mrs. Candee up to the upper A deck where the boats were hung and we put her safely with a rug into the first boat, which gradually was filled with women and children and a few of the crew were put in, three I think, and a youth with a broken arm.

Not enough men were put into the first boats really. We then bade her a cheery good-bye and told her we should help her onboard again when the ship had steadied herself. She wanted us to come too but we laughed this off.

We then went and helped with several more life boats, bundling in the women and children. Meanwhile several gentlemen were standing calmly by and looking on. Several men crept into these few boats, as it came out, and they give fatuous explanations how they came to do so. They were forced in by zealous friends against their own wish, and so on.

The calm courage of the passengers was most inspiring. Many women refused to leave without their husbands. Björnström and I took many of them at their husbands' desire and bodily chucked them into the boats. Eventually all the lifeboats on the port side were launched, and while the crew were putting a big Berthon collapsible boat on the davits he and I went down to the lower deck and around to look for stray women.

We found three ladies close together and then we rushed them into a boat on the starboard side by sheer bluff. We shouted our way through the press; "Make way for ladies!" and then we hoisted them up, one of us on each side, and giving them a final heave in they had to go, head over heels. We then turned our attention to a boat ready on the starboard side, where there was shouting going on.

We saw the first officer twice fire a pistol in the air ordering a crowd of the crew out of the boat. We ran in and helped bundle the men out onto the deck and then we got a lot, about ten, Italian and other foreign women into that boat and when we saw it was being safely lowered we went away and made a final search on the deck below.

The electric lights were beginning to turn red and not a soul was to be seen on the whole deck of 160 yards. The thick glass windows were all closed and Björnström said to me: "I think we may now make a try for ourselves." I replied: "All right."

We walked along through an open door beyond the glass windows, where there was an open gunwale. Looking out we saw the sea pouring over the bows and through the captain's bridge. Just opposite us was the collapsible boat which we had seen being hooked onto the last davits on the port side. She was being lowered into the sea and hung about nine feet away from us. I said: "Let's make a jump for it! There is plenty of room in her bows!" Björnström replied "Right you are!"

We skipped on the gunwale, balanced ourselves for a moment and leaped into the air. He landed fair and square into the boat. I landed on my chest and caught hold with my hands on the gunwale and slipped off backward. I hauled myself up with my arms and got my right foot over the gunwale.

Björnström said, "All right, I've got you," and levered me up by my right foot. But that time my left leg was in the sea, so it was a near thing.

The water was pouring in through the door we had just walked through. It rose so rapidly that if we had waited another minute we should have been pinned between the deck and its roof. We first hauled in another man passenger who was in the sea, and then I climbed over a number of women and children and got out two oars. Björnström took one, I took another, a steward got another and another man took the fourth.

I handed him a rowlock so that he could steer and we began to pull like the deuce to get clear of the ship, which I knew was doomed; but I was anxious to get away from the suction when the big ship when under. I never pulled harder in my life. About thirty women and children were in the boat, with only three oars to pull. However we got away from her and got clear, but only about 150 yards, when I saw the monster take a huge tilt forward and her stern came clean out of the water at least eighty feet.

Lights were still burning and she settled forward still further, then stopped for about thirty seconds. Suddenly, with a terrific roar, like thousands of tons of rocks rumbling down a metal chute, she plunged bodily down, head first. Every light went out and the roaring went on for about a minute.

Then arose the most fearful and bloodcurdling wail. It was awful. One thousand seven hundred men in the dark, going down amid that ghastly turmoil! I can never forget it.

We continued our course, for it would have been sheer madness to have returned and tried to pick up any more. It would have meant all of us perishing.

The sea was as smooth as a pond or none of us would be alive. The *Titanic* struck at 11:45 p.m. on a starry, clear night. She sank finally at 2:22 a.m. I believe seventeen boats got away. I was in the seventeenth.

It got colder and colder. Fortunately I had on my fur coat and under that my dress clothes. The only thing I saved was my money. I worked all through the excitement with Björnström at my side. We spoke with strong authority and people simply stood aside and made way for us when we came up with women in tow. It was remarkable!

There were scenes of magnificent unselfishness and devotion; women who absolutely refused to go without their husbands; dozens of husbands who simply obeyed orders and remained silent and quiet on deck while their wives were put into safety. In particular a very handsome old gentleman, Mr. Isidor Straus, and his wife were there and declined to be separated and when we suggested that so old a man was justified in going into the boat that was waiting, Mr. Straus said: "Not before the other men."

His wife tightened her grasp on his arm and patted it and smiled up at him and then smiled at us.

In our boat we floated around for a long time in the dark, the cries getting fainter and fewer in the distance. Then a boat with an officer came along and he gave us orders for us to form a string by making fast our painter's head and tail, so as to make a more conspicuous mark on the ocean for a passing ship to see. This we did and it gave us something to do.

After a while orders were given to lighten the officer's boat, so that he could go and help some poor wretches on an upturned boat, which by now was faintly visible in the distance. We got seven more into our already pretty full boat, but we could stand them upright. Other boats got others, and the officer went away with his sail up and got in about twenty shivering men who had been balancing themselves for over three hours up to their ankles on an upturned collapsible boat. Think of it!

Faint streaks of light began in the east by this time and I saw a breeze coming towards us, which was a serious matter in our heavily loaded condition. I advised throwing off the painter and keeping her head into the sea. This was done. The wind continued to freshen.

Looking around, I saw about twenty icebergs that looked like photographs of the Antarctic expedition. The whole horizon was snow—the edge of a floe, which turned out to be at least forty miles long and yet our lookout on the *Titanic* had seen nothing and we had been going full speed ahead all through the night.

Then I saw a rocket and a little later the lights of a steamer coming our way. This cheered us mightily, as you may imagine. Very slowly she seemed to come on, picking her way through the ice. Eventually she slowed down and then stopped and we saw boats about her sides and I understood that our first boatloads were being taken aboard.

The officer in the sailboat bore down on us and seeing we were being rather roughly knocked about by the sea, gave us a tow, but started away from the steamer and we then saw he was making for another set of unfortunates, who were standing up, apparently in the water. They were a party of fourteen or so, among them a black haired woman and two corpses.

The living having been taken aboard, we wore around and made for the ship, the breeze freshening all the while. It seemed a very long time, but eventually we came alongside the *Carpathia* on her way with a crowd of tourists on their way to Gibraltar. Getting under the lee side, we made fast and soon had the women hoisted in a sling, and then we men clambered stiffly up the rope ladders.

Stewards steered us to the dining saloon, where hot brandy and water and biscuits awaited us. Seven hundred, about, were saved out of, I believe, 2,500.

Everything possible has been done on board to make us comfortable, and nothing could exceed the kindness the passengers on the *Carpathia* showed to the shivering people who came up out of the sea. I was given a sofa in the first officer's cabin. We had fogs nearly all the time since we were rescued and our speed was therefore moderate.

This general description will serve to show that the behavior of the American and English passengers and of the whole crew was admirable with very few exceptions.

HUGH WOOLNER

Margaret Brown,
Newport Herald,
MAY 28 & 29, 1912

A special boat train (train deluxe) from Paris reached Cherbourg at 5 p.m. April 10th. When we arrived, no steamer in sight. She was late, having met with some difficulty in leaving the docks at Liverpool. We all boarded the tender that was waiting to convey the hundreds of passengers to the master palace of the sea, that proved later to be the tomb of many of them.

After an hour or more of waiting in the cold, gray atmosphere, the funnels of the *Titanic*, the world's greatest masterpiece of modern ocean liners appeared over the other side of the break-water.

In a few minutes more this wonderful floating palace hove in sight around the curve of the dike and dropped anchor. The tender put on steam, and after half an hour in a running sea we were alongside the keel of the *Titanic*. The tossing of the small craft in the choppy sea caused most of the passengers to be uncomfortable and actively ill. All were chilled through.

On boarding the vessel, the greater number of passengers immediately sought their staterooms. The bugle for dinner sounded a half-hour later, but it was unsuccessful in calling forth many to its magnificent dining room. The electric heater and warm covering were found too comfortable to be deserted even for the many course dinner, even at the craving of the inner man.

The second day out broke clearer and less crisp, and half-after twelve found most of the passengers promenading the deck or basking in the warm sun outside the Palm Garden. There were long benches on the long bow of the boat for those who found the sway-back steamer chairs uncomfortable.

The last half-hour lapsing between the first and second gongs, when all take their exercise before descending to the dining hall, most of the passengers are to be found walking enveloped in heavy wraps. The women were in luxurious furs, and the men in heavy overcoats buttoned closely around their necks and partly disguised in steamer caps. In passing to and fro they discovered old friends on board, and some made new ones. Small groups were standing here and there, discussing the ship and its marvels, its possibility for speed and all its wonderful advantages over anything of its kind heretofore put afloat. Each and all seemed to have consulted the log as to the distance covered that day and each successive day. The number of knots covered was registered there each day at noon, and was the topic of conversation on deck and at the table at the luncheon hour.

After luncheon, or about two-thirty, the favorite and popular place was the reading room, where the passengers settled themselves comfortably with some chosen book from the well-equipped library on the ship. Others were taking a quiet siesta on the deck, wrapped in heavy steamer rugs. Few remained in their staterooms, for the sea was perfectly calm and no vibration was felt. Consequently, there was little or no mal-de-mer.

Thus Thursday, Friday and Saturday were passed.

Sunday services were held at ten-thirty, quite one-half of the passengers attending. Later the passengers went outside to promenade on deck, but much more briskly as the temperature had dropped perceptibly lower. After luncheon a few remained on deck, but all were restlessly searching for a warm place. The comfortable chairs in the lounge held but few, as a shaft of cold air seemed to penetrate every nook and corner, and chill the marrow. Heavy furs and warm clothing were donned.

Dinner time found few inclined to shed their warm clothing for dinner dress. Even the innumerable brides, who on various occasions appeared in a different Paris creation each night, could not be induced to change. Though the board groaned with viands, the passengers found it uncomfortable to sit through the many-course dinner. Many sought their staterooms immediately afterwards.

The writer sought some exceedingly intellectual and much traveled acquaintances, a Mrs. Bucknell, whose husband has founded the Bucknell University of Philadelphia, and Dr. Brew of Philadelphia, who had done much in scientific research. During our conversation that I had with her on the tender while waiting for the *Titanic*, she said she feared boarding the ship, she had evil forebodings that something might happen. We laughed at her premonitions, and shortly afterwards sought our quarters.

Anxious to finish a book, I stretched on the brass bed at the side of which was a lamp. So completely absorbed in my reading, I gave little thought to the crash that struck at my window overhead and threw me to the floor. Picking myself up I proceeded to see what the steamer had struck. On emerging from the stateroom, I found many men in the gangway in their pajamas, whom I had overheard a few moments before entering their staterooms saying that they were nearly frozen and had to leave the smoking-rooms. They, while standing, were chaffing each other, one of them remarked, "Are you prepared to swim in those things?" referring to the pajamas. Women were standing along the corridors in their kimonos. All seemed to be quietly listening, thinking nothing serious had occurred, though realizing at the time that the engines had stopped immediately after the crash and the boat was at a standstill, and as there was no confusion of any kind, the book was again picked up.

On overhearing the occupants of the adjoining stateroom say, "We will go on deck and see what has happened," I again arose and saw six or more stewards and one officer in the corridor forcing an auger through a hole in the floor, while treating the whole thing with levity. Again returning to my book, presently I saw the curtains moving, but no-one was visible.

I again looked out and saw a man whose face was blanched, his eyes protruding, wearing the look of a haunted creature. He was gasping for breath, and in an undertone he gasped, "Get your life-saver." I immediately reached above and dragged all out, as I thought some others might need them. Snatching up furs and placing a silk capote on my head, I hurriedly mounted the stairs to A deck, and there I found possibly fifty passengers, all putting on their life-belts. Strapping myself into mine, I afterwards was told to go up on the storm deck.

My party that I was traveling with had already gone up. On reaching A deck, Mrs. Bucknell approached and whispered to me, "Didn't I tell you something was going to happen?" On reaching the storm deck we found a number of men trying to unravel the tackle of the boats to let them down, which seemed at the time very difficult. We were approached by an officer and told to descend to the deck below. We found the lifeboats there were being lowered from the falls and were at that time flush with the deck. Madame DeVallier [de Villiers; *i.e.* Berthe Mayne], of Paris, appeared from below in a night dress and evening slippers with no stockings, over which she wore a woolen motor coat. She clutched at my arm and in a terrified voice said she was going below for her money and jewels. After much persuasion I prevailed upon her not to go down but to get into the boat. As she hesitated and became very excited, I told her it was all only a precaution and she would be able to return to the then-sinking steamer later. After she got on, I turned and found the lady of my party in a lowering boat. I was walking away eager to see what was being done with the boats on the other side, not fearing any immediate danger, thinking if the worst should happen I could swim out. Suddenly I saw a shadow, and a few seconds later I was taken hold of, and with the words, "You are going, too," I was dropped fully four feet into the lowering life-boat. When I got in, on looking around I saw but one man, who was in charge of the boat.

While being lowered by jerks by an officer from above, I discovered that a great gush of water was spouting through the porthole from D deck, and our lifeboat was in grave danger of being submerged. I immediately grasped an oar and held the lifeboat away from the ship. While being lowered we were conscious of strains of music being wafted on the night air. As we reached a sea as smooth as glass, we looked up and saw the benign, resigned countenance, the venerable white hair, and the Chesterfieldian bearing of our beloved Captain (with whom I had crossed twice before—only three months previous, on the *Olympic*, our party sat at his table), as he peered down upon us like a solicitous father, directing us to row to the light in the distance, and all boats keep together. With but one man in the boat, and possibly fourteen women, I saw that it was necessary for someone to bend to the oars. I placed mine in the rowlocks and asked a young woman near me to hold one while I placed the other one on the further side. To my surprise she immediately began to row like a galley-slave, every stroke counting. Myself on the other side we managed to pull out from the steamer. All the time while rowing we were facing the starboard side of the sinking vessel. By that time E & C decks were completely submerged, and the strains of music became fainter, as though the instruments were filling up with water. Suddenly all ceased when the heroic musicians could play no more.

The only seaman in our boat was the quartermaster. He was at the rudder, and standing much higher than we were. He was shivering like an aspen. As we pulled away from the boat, we heard sounds of firing, and were told later that it was officers shooting as they were letting down the boats from the steamer, trying to prevent those from the lower decks jumping into the lifeboats. Others said it was the boilers.

The quartermaster in command of our boat burst out in a frightened voice and warned us of the fate that awaited us, telling us our task in rowing away from the sinking ship was futile, as she was so large that in sinking she would draw everything for miles around down with her suction, and if we escaped that the boilers would burst and rip up the bottom of the sea, tearing the icebergs asunder and completely submerge us. We were truly doomed either way. He dwelt on the dire fate awaiting us, narrating at great length the incidents that happened at Liverpool— how two large steamers, the *New York* and one other, were drawn under and almost capsized, we all the while bending to the oars with a vengeance, tugging on. All occupants of the lifeboats remained as mute as the dead, all standing erect clustered in the middle of the boat.

Presently we heard shouts and cries of terror from the fast sinking ship. We were told the shouts were from the trunk men on the collapsible boats. Our quartermaster haggled long and loud. The splash of the oars partly drowned the voices of the perishing men on the doomed steamer. The ladies all seemed terrified. Those having husbands, sons or fathers buried their heads on the shoulders of those near them, and moaned and groaned only.

While my eyes were glued on the fast disappearing ship, I particularly watched the broad promenade deck. It was fully lighted but not one moving object was visible. Suddenly a rift in the water, the sea opened up and the surface foamed like giant arms spread around the ship, and the vessel disappeared from sight, and not a sound was heard.

When none of the calamities that were predicted by our terrified boatman was experienced, we asked him to return and pick up those in the water. Again we were admonished and told how the frantic drowning victims would grapple the sides of our boat and capsize us. He not yielding to our entreaties, we pulled away vigorously toward the faintly glimmering light on the horizon. After three hours of pulling at the oars, the light grew fainter and then completely disappeared. Then our quartermaster, who stood on his pinnacle trembling, with an attitude like someone preaching to the multitude, fanning the air with his hands, recommenced the tirade of evil foreboding, telling us we were likely to drift for days, all the while reminding us that we were surrounded by icebergs, pointing to a pyramid of ice looming up in the distance, possibly seventy feet high reflected by the myriad stars in the sky, that looked like a black shaft. He most forcibly impressed upon us that there was no water in the casks in the lifeboats and no bread, no compass and no chart. No one answered him. They all seemed to be stricken dumb.

One of the ladies in the boat had had the presence of mind to procure her silver brandy flask. As she held it in her hand, the silver glittered and he being attracted to it implored her to give it to him, saying he was frozen. She refused the brandy, but removed the steamer blanket and put it around his shoulders, while another lady wrapped a second blanket around his head and limbs, he looking "as snug as a bug in a rug."

We asked him to relieve one or the other at the oars, saying to him that we would manage the rudder. He flatly refused and continued to rampoon us at the oars, bursting out, "Here, you fellow on the starboard side, your oar is not being put in the water at the right angle!" No one made any protest to his outbursts, as he broke the monotony, but we continued to pull at the oars, with no goal in sight. Presently he raised his voice, shouting to another lifeboat to pull near and lash to, commanding some of the other ladies to take the light and signal to the other lifeboats. His command was immediately obeyed. That and one other command—that we drop the oars and lie fallow until we were rescued. Some time later, after hearing shouts, a lifeboat hove to and obeyed his orders to throw a rope and be tied to ours. Alongside she dropped oars, and on the cross-seat of that boat stood a man in white pajamas. He looked like a snowman in that icy region. His teeth were chattering, and he appeared quite numb. Seeing his predicament, I told him he had better get to rowing to keep his blood in circulation, which was met with forcible protest from our quartermaster.

We, after the exercise, felt the bluest from the icy fields and demanded that we be allowed to keep warm. Immediately over into our boat jumped a half-frozen stoker, black and covered with coal dust, dressed as he was in thin jumpers. I picked up a large sable stole that I had dropped in the boat, and from his waist down wrapped it around his limbs, tying the tails around his ankles. I handed him an oar and then told the pajama man to cut loose, and a howl arose from our seaman. He moved to prevent it, and I said if he did he would be thrown overboard. Then I felt a hand laid on my shoulder to stay my threats, knowing it would not be necessary to push him over, had I only moved in his direction he would have tumbled into the sea, so paralyzed was he with fright. He had by this time worked himself up to such a pitch of sheer despair, fearing that a scramble of any kind would remove the plug from the bottom of the boat (that it had taken three of us some length of time to feel around, find it and place it in the hole), and if it were displaced the water would sweep in and there was grave danger of filling the boat. The quartermaster became very impertinent and our fur-enveloped stoker, in as broad a cockney as one hears in the Haymarket, shouted, "Soy, don't you know you are talking to a loidy?"

For the time being the seaman was silenced, and we again set at our task.

Two other ladies came to the rescue of those rowing and caught hold of the oars and backed the water. Thus we aimlessly tugged on over the vast waste of water. Lights were flashed from other lifeboats miles away.

While glancing around, watching the edge of the horizon, the beautiful modulated voice of the young English woman at the oar exclaimed, "There is a flash of light!" All looked in the direction pointed out, and our pessimistic seaman said, "That is a falling star." It became brighter and later was multiplied by those on the lighted deck. He was convinced then that it was a ship (or said it was the *Olympic*, as she had to have passed after midnight; the *Olympic* passed two days later.) Then he gave a sigh of relief and again ordered us to drop the oars.

We saw this steamer approaching the small lifeboats near her, while we were then possibly six or eight miles off. However, the distance seemed interminable. We saw she was anchored.

Again a declaration was made that we, regardless of what our quartermaster said, would row toward her. Again the young Englishwoman from the Thames got to work, accompanying her strokes with cheerful words to the wilted occupants of the boat.

A little while later dawn disclosed our awful situation. There were fields of ice on which, like points on the landscape, rested innumerable pyramids of icy peaks. Seemingly half an hour later the sun, like a ball of molten lead, appeared at its background. The hand of Nature portrayed a scenic effect beyond the ken of the human mind. The heretofore smooth sea became choppy, which seemed to retard our progress. All the while we saw the small lifeboats being hauled aboard.

By the time we reached the *Carpathia* a heavy sea was running. Our boat being the last to approach, we found it difficult to get close. Three or four unsuccessful attempts were made. Each time we were dashed against the keel and bounded off like a rubber ball. A rope was then thrown to us, which was spliced in four at the bottom, where a wide board was held in four large knots. Feet first, we got on and sat on the seat that formed a swing. Catching hold of the one thick rope, we were hoisted up to where a dozen of the crew and officers and doctors were waiting. Stimulants were given those who needed them and hot coffee was provided for all the survivors.

Everything was done for our comfort, the *Carpathia* passengers sharing their staterooms, clothes and toilet articles, they, then retiring to the far corner of the ship where their deck chairs were placed, giving the lounge up completely to the survivors, and the two succeeding foggy murky days, when the deck was too damp to sit out, they remained in their stuffy staterooms rather than use up the space there.

After picking up the lifeboats, only half filled, the ship reconnoitered for hours around the place where the *Titanic* had sunk. In doing so they passed fifty miles of icefields, so I was told, endangering their own safety in their endeavor to rescue more.

On entering the dining salon, I saw in one corner our brave and heroic quartermaster with a cluster of people around him. He was wildly gesticulating, trying to impress upon them what difficulty he had had in disciplining the occupants of his boat. On seeing a few of us near, he did not tarry long but made a hasty retreat.

On the swivel chairs in the dining salon were seated the *Titanic* survivors. They were speechless, half-clad, their eyes protruding, hair streaming down those who, only twelve hours before, were immaculately groomed and richly gowned and furred — evidence of "Vanity, vanity, all is vanity." Here they sat, shaven and shorn and in utter hopelessness and despair, almost all bereft of husbands and sons, fathers and brothers. Unable to grasp the situation, they sat moist, not being able to realize in the one short hour between a quarter of twelve, when the boat struck, and somewhat after one, when she sank, that their dear ones were swallowed up in the jaws of death.

Sprinkled among the affluent were our sisters of the second class, and for a time there was that social leveling caused only by the close proximity of death.

While getting the addresses from many of the survivors of their relatives that they might be apprised by Marconi of their safety, I was grappled by a poor woman of the second class, who held in her closed hand long strands of hair she had pulled from her head. Holding them on high, as though measuring them with her eyes, she frantically shouted to me to find her baby. I promised her I would. Seeing she was mentally unbalanced, a doctor was called and she was put under opiates. When she had gotten into the boat her baby was being handed to her and somehow was dropped into the sea and drowned.

Fortunately the *Carpathia* was carrying something more than half she usually accommodates so the second morning found a greater number of the *Titanic* survivors provided for. The overflow beds were made on the couches in the lounge, and pallets of blankets were made on the floor. The first night many of the men slept on the deck in steamer chairs, others slept in the smoking room and dining salon. The Captain gave up his stateroom, it accommodating four of the socially representative ladies.

The barber, fortunately, had in stock a few dozen toothbrushes, combs and other toilet articles. The *Carpathia's* objective points being ports on the Mediterranean, she was carrying on an extra large supply of food. In that line there was nothing left to be desired.

On reaching the *Carpathia* the first thing found necessary to be done was to relieve the anxiety of relatives of the survivors. Immediately on obtaining the addresses, I visited the Marconi quarters and left the written messages that had to be paid before sending, though there were many who had little or no funds.

The system was so glutted in sending messages of the wreck and names of surviving passengers, it was the third day before the private ones could be sent, their Marconi system being limited, so I was told, to 250 miles.

The kindly spirit and tender solicitation of officers, crew and passengers elicited the thought that we, the survivors, should in some substantial way express our gratitude to the Captain to the form of a loving-cup and to compensate the crew for their efficiency and double hours of labor on our behalf.

At breakfast the second morning, when I suggested to the gentlemen at the table that immediate action should be taken, I found they were eager to express gratitude but made a protest at funds being collected. A committee was later formed, and a typed notice was tacked up that a meeting of the survivors would be held in the dining salon at three in the afternoon. Almost the full list of survivors were present. Resolutions of gratitude, first to God, and then to the captain and officers, were framed and read.

A subscription list was immediately started, and about $4,000 was subscribed in money and checks. The names and amounts subscribed were typed and tacked on the wall at the foot of the stairs and an open list for those not having yet given in their names and amounts. The day before reaching New York the fund was augmented to the extent of $10,000 so I was informed by the Secretary.

The gravity of the situation was there and then relieved, if the expression on faces was any criterion. The tense mental anxiety was perceptibly mitigated. A large number of the passengers living out of New York were momentarily embarrassed for funds and only needed enough to tide them over. The Committee waited upon the owner; the survivors' demands being made known, he conceded all. The demand was that the White Star Line furnish transportation and other necessities to their destination.

The second officer, who acted as spokesman for the crew of the *Titanic*, stated that their services were at an end when the *Titanic* sank, and upon reaching New York they would be set adrift. It was immediately seen to that their transportation to England would be given, and also employment on reaching there.

The three succeeding days were spent among the passengers, listing their needs and making provision in the way of clothes, as many escaped in their night-clothing, over which was drawn a cloak. A number who were in our boat had only sandals on and no stockings.

The day before landing three Irish girls were found in the steerage, they having kept their berths since the rescue, having no clothes and refusing to rise with blankets only to wrap around them, they were among the passengers going to New York.

As the *Carpathia* was nearing the harbor, it was surrounded by smaller boats that went out to meet it, in which were newspaper men and photographers to take flashlights. They impeded the progress of the *Carpathia*. The excitement of this and the Captain calling through a megaphone to the pilot to disperse the drafts or he would be unable to reach the dock, and the seeing and hearing of the multitude of humanity on the wharf so frightened these women that they refused to quit the ship and go with the ladies of the Travelers Aid Society, who came on to take them to a place of safety until friends were found and arrangements were made for them to either return to their homes in Europe, or other destinations in America. Feeling it a duty to remain with those, and after the army of Red Cross doctors and nurses, White Star Line officials and general Aid Corps, had taken leave of the ship, we found it was necessary to improvise beds in the lounge, so I remained with them on board all night. There were many who had friends on the dock but did not know them, so with each one was sent an escort and the names called out, and there, finding their friends, would return to the ship and report, and we kept a list of their whereabouts. For some of those remaining, telegrams were sent that night and the next morning. Friends of many came aboard, and the others, less fortunate, consented to go with the ladies of the Travelers Aid conditionally that they would be allowed to see me at the Ritz-Carleton, where I would be, and I promised to have their various consuls there and we would try to find their friends, whose addresses their husbands had when the ship sank. This took some days afterwards.

The next morning, on the ship, I was joined with five members of the committee, who brought on $5,000 so they said, in funds to be distributed among the much overworked crew of the *Carpathia*. This being done, an order was given for the loving-cup to be presented to the captain on the return of his ship from Naples. Having taken a list of those of the survivors who were to be assisted, a copy was made and given to the White Star agents who came on the boat.

The further work of the committee of the survivors of the *Titanic* was to see, by keeping check, that the company were keeping their promise and that all were cared for.

The only comment that could be made was that the *Carpathia* did not follow the customary procedure on boats. Where there is death on board, they usually bury them at night in place of adding to the horror of passengers by burying the men who died on board after being rescued from the collapsible boat at the hour of four in the afternoon when the passengers were around. They possibly may have had a good and sufficient reason for such a departure from the usual procedure. The men who died were rescued by the lifeboat in which were the four prominent lady personages.

In rescuing these, the plug in their lifeboat was dislodged and a foot of water covered the bottom of their boat, which, to prevent the filling of the boat, it was needful that they bail it out with a large dipper hanging from the seat. In the boat two of the men rescued, I was told, died and lay for hours in the bottom of the boat during the six hours on the open sea before the passengers were rescued by the *Carpathia*.

It was very apparent that the consideration and solicitation shown toward the unfortunate survivors had been taken exception to from some sources. On one occasion, when ladies of the committee stopped to inquire the way to reach the second and third class, they were intercepted by the doctor as he emerged from the quarters of the secluded plutocrat. He approached one of the ladies and said, "Madam, we have the situation under perfect control. Blankets have been cut up and we are having clothes made. Cutting up blankets would not soothe their tortured minds." Then and there we were more determined, and a notice was posted that the hours of eleven to one and three to six the committee would be in the dining salon. During those hours the survivors came in twos and fours and poured out their grief and story of distress. Between flows of tears they unburdened their sorrows that lay like a weight upon their breasts. The gratitude shown by these people and the evidence that the great mental strain they were under was partly relieved when they knew that someone was interested in their welfare, was proof conclusive to the committee that they were working along the right lines regardless of how the doctor felt in the matter, feeling that he was voicing only the sentiment of the secluded autocrat, as a number of these foreign women of the first and second class were told that now they had no funds, their arrival in America would be under the Allen Law. They were terrified at their being subject to such humiliation. They were fully convinced that such was not the case that they would be provided with means and transportation. They arose and said their lodestone was then and there lifted and their minds were very much relieved.

Another instance when the ladies were made to feel that they were overstepping their bounds in their endeavor to relieve the situation for those people was when the resolutions were read. They were told emphatically it was an absolute affront to the owners and manager who was on board. We replied we were only compelled to do what he had neglected as his duty. If this interest had been shown by him, it would have placed him in a very different light than that of doing as he did, concealing himself behind closed doors to the exclusion of everyone. The contrast was extremely noticeable, as he was the most conspicuous figure on the *Titanic* before she went down. He was six feet tall and of the oriental type, with manner of pacing the deck with an expression of intensity of purpose and determination, he had always been in extreme evidence. Assuming this attitude at this time was extremely ridiculous.

In passing up the stairs at noon on the day we were rescued, two tall men stood aside for me to pass. Looking up, I saw the face of the man and his friend who had told me to get my life-

preserver and who later put me into the boat when I was walking away on the *Titanic*. Putting out my hand, it is needless to
say how profuse I was in expressing my gratitude. I asked to
whom I was indebted for my life and safety. He handed me their
cards, reading "Calderhead and Bough, buyers for Kimball
Brothers, New York." They stated that, in seeing the distress of
many women who were bereft of their husbands and some who
had perished, it made them feel extremely embarrassed, and
their attitude in keeping out of sight other than when they came
to the dining salon for meals, was that of men feeling that their
lives being saved was somewhat of a stigma, and the worn expression of their faces, as though they continually asked themselves the question, what woman's place in the lifeboat did they
fill, and in an apologetic manner they told how inadvertently they
caught the last boat being lowered half-empty. They told me of
the navigation laws restricting men from the boats when women
and children were on board. I replied that such must have been
the ancient law, and now that equal rights existed, truly all should
be relieved, as I chance; that their conscience on that score
should be relieved, as I was a living evidence of their thoughtful-
ness to womankind, as at the time they placed me in the boat I
had no intention of getting off, but was most concerned in
knowing what was taking place on the other side of the steamer,
and marveling all the while at the clumsiness of the crew in letting down the lifeboats, comparing the discipline of what I had
seen in my travels on German liners, where a daily drill of military tactics in handling lifeboats took place. It was truly shown
at the time that the crew of the *Titanic* were amateurs in comparison to what I had seen on a German ship on the China seas,
when we encountered the outer forces of a typhoon that set us
aground until the tide took us out to the rescue of those floating
around in the wreckage of a submerged tramp steamer. The
comparison seemed crude indeed, as there was no organization
or discipline shown at the time, though it was known, as soon as
she struck the high iceberg and when riding over the submerged
one, the bottom of the boat was ripped off, as immediately
trunks began to float about in the hold and an officer was seen

dragging the mailbags a few minutes after she struck, giving them time to realize the worst had happened and for the crew to be at their posts.

On the contrary, it was plain to be seen that of the seventy stewards who were saved, none attempted to warn those in the staterooms of their danger.

One of the heroes on board was the eighteen-year-old son of the Thayers of Philadelphia. He and his father, after having taken an affectionate farewell of his mother after placing her in the lifeboat, while walking on the deck of the *Titanic* plunged off. While swimming, he was drawn twice under the keel by the suction. In his struggles he grasped hold of the collapsible boat and was among those who were rescued. He was on board the *Carpathia* when his mother was hoisted from the lifeboat. She was under the impression that both her husband and son had perished on the *Titanic*, but, to her supreme joy, she was clasped in her son's arms. In her great thankfulness in having one spared her, for the rest of the voyage not more than a few minutes at a time would she permit him to be separate from her.

The attitude of the men who were rescued was indeed pathetic. Each and all seemed as though they were trying to efface themselves when they were encountered passing to and fro. It was noticed how they all tried to explain how it came about like a miracle that their lives were saved, with an expression of apology as though it were a blight on their manhood. One man displaying an order he had demanded from the officer when asked to get into the lifeboat half-filled with women that he might row, all stating that they took the boats when there was no one around to get in.

The third day on the *Carpathia* I talked at great length with one of the officers of the *Titanic* [Fifth Officer Lowe] who had had in his command five lifeboats, he having the one that went back and rescued those on the collapsible. In talking it over, he stated that they saw to it that, among those who were saved would not be any of the rich nabobs, again reiterating the same, adding, "We saw to it that they would take their chances with good men." While preening his feathers over this fact, he stated

that there was one who got through without the officers knowing it. He later displayed his weapon and told how with that, he
made one who persistently attempted to get in the boat with his
wife, was told in the strong expletive of the masculine lexicon to
"chase himself around the deck." He stated the only thing he regretted was the oaths he had used towards the ladies in the
boats.

William T. Sloper,
Hartford Times,
APRIL 19, 1912

While it is still on my mind I shall try to set down here for the benefit of my friends and those interested, as clearly as I can, what I saw and experienced as a passenger on the ill-fated ship *Titanic.*

I did not book passage on this ship until the day before she sailed, and I should not have done so had I not met friends who came over with me in January and with whom I had been more or less in Egypt during the winter. There were fourteen of us who were on the *Titanic,* who had been in Egypt together, and as I write this there are only seven survivors.

On Sunday evening a gentleman who I had not met previously, asked me if I would make a fourth at bridge. A mother and her daughter from New York and himself. I accepted his invitation, and to this fact I feel that I owe my life, as I had been going to bed early every night previously and I should probably have been in bed when the accident happened.

We played in the "Lounge," and at 11:30 the steward asked us to finish our game, as everyone else had gone to bed and the lights were going to be put out in the room. We finished the game, and at 11:40 I said good-night to the ladies and was on the stairway going down to my cabin. Suddenly there was a lurch and a creaking crash; the boat seemed to shiver and keel over to port.

A half-dozen room stewards and I rushed out onto the promenade deck and peered into the starlit darkness. We could see
what appeared to be a sail or something white standing out off
our starboard side, astern. It was very cold, and we soon went
back into the companionway, where it was warmer.

Meanwhile the engines had stopped and frightened faced people commenced to appear, many scantily attired, inquiring anxiously as to what had happened. They told them that the ship
had struck an iceberg, but as it was apparently a glancing blow
that it could not have done much damage and that there was no
danger.

I was not so sure, however, about there being no danger, and
when the ladies, with whom I had been playing cards, appeared
I told them to go to their cabins and change their evening
clothes for heavier ones. It being Sunday night I had not dressed
for dinner, so that I had on a very heavy sack suit. I went for my
sweater and heavy overcoat and took my pocket-book from another coat pocket—this was all that I saved, but I'm not com-
plaining.

When I left my cabin, which was in the bow of the ship, I noticed that the floor seemed uneven and that the ship was listing
toward the starboard bow. Meeting the ladies again on the stairs
and the gentleman who had been playing cards with us, we went
out on deck together and took a turn about the deck. As we
started forward from the stern my heart sank to see that there
was really quite a pitch downward of the deck under our feet.
Many more people had appeared on deck, some clad only in
night clothes and dressing gowns.

There was no confusion, however, or anything resembling a
panic. The stewards assured everyone who asked them that the
water tight bulkheads were closed and that while there was a
hole in her, she could not possibly sink, and many who had got
out of bed to ascertain the trouble returned satisfied. All this
time the steam from the boilers was blowing off furiously overhead, and the noise on the deck was deafening. We went back
into the companionway, and Miss ——, who had only just re-

covered from an attack of nervous prostration, and was greatly alarmed and excited, stopped everyone as they came out from the lower deck and asked them if there was any danger. The designer of the *Titanic*, who was aboard, came rushing up from below at this minute, and although he said nothing about the seriousness of the trouble, one look at his face convinced me he was worried.

Someone else appeared at this moment and said that the water was rushing in through the squash court wall, and that she was filling rapidly. We were now ordered by the stewards to put on life preservers in case anything should happen that should make it necessary for us to leave the ship. We returned to our staterooms for our life preservers and assembled on the upper stairway leading out on the top deck. The feeling which came over me as I stood in the companionway with these people while we tied on our life preservers cannot be put down adequately on paper. As long as I live I shall never forget that feeling. I had read many stories and accounts of just this thing, and here I was going through the terrible experience myself.

I could only think that I must be asleep and in an awful dream. As a man, I was bound to cheer up the ladies and act as calm as I could, but to say that I felt that way underneath would be untrue. All this time there was no sign of panic or distress among passengers or crew. Everyone behaved wonderfully calm and cheerful. I felt as certain as anyone could feel that we had come to the end, and that many, if not all, would soon be gone. All of the people who were there in this companionway at this time, passed out quietly onto the deck where the lifeboats were. I remember distinctly that there was no crowding through the doorway—everyone was over polite.

The covers had been taken off the lifeboats and they were quickly swung off on the davits and lowered to the level of the deck. From this deck, we were, if I remember correctly, somewhere about eighty feet above the water, and to leave a well-lighted ship that at the time seemed to have listed slightly, and step into a small boat that might plunge down into the darkness below, or, if it reached the sea safely, be capsized by the water, was a question which made some people hold back.

Miss G—, who was now in a state of high nervous excitement, made toward the first boat, and for fear that she might misstep or jump, I kept hold of her arm, and I remember tried to quiet her by saying "Keep a stiff upper lip." When the officers in charge of the first boat motioned for us to step in she stepped forward with her mother and the gentleman who had been playing cards with us, and I helped them into the boat and followed after them. People sort of hung back at this time. Many men wouldn't leave the ship or let their friends, as they couldn't believe that the ship could really go down.

Colonel Astor was directly behind me, with Mrs. Astor, and he suddenly drew back and pulled his wife back with him. Someone spoke to him, but I did not overhear what was said. At any rate they did not follow us into the boat. When twenty-nine people, including three of the crew, were in the boat, and as nobody else seemed ready to follow, the officer on the deck gave word to "lower away."

We might have taken a few more people and managed somehow, although the boat was pretty well filled. While we were being lowered I expected one end of the boat would drop faster than the other and that we should be thrown out into the sea, but we were finally in the water without any mishap. Cutting loose from the ship we pulled away as quickly as we could, as other boats were being lowered overhead and we wished to get out of the way of them. When the people above on the *Titanic* saw the first two or three lifeboats get away safely they eventually decided to come, too, for the rest of the boats on our side quickly filled and were lowered.

Fortunately, the sea was as smooth as a mill pond, and for the time being I felt that we were safe. It was very cold and I was glad to take an oar and help row. As we left the deck somebody had thrown in a number of steamer rugs which were wrapped around the women. The people in our boat were evenly divided, as half were men and half women. Most of the boats that followed afterward had only two or three men in them and had a hard time making headway with so few to manage the boat. One of the three sailors took our tiller and the command of the boat. After we had rowed 300 yards or so we rested on our oars and waited to see what should happen.

The *Titanic* was settling rapidly in the bow and it was evident that it was only a question of a few minutes when the largest and finest ship in the world would go down. Every one began to question the three sailors in our boat as to whether there were boats for everyone to get off in, whether the wireless operator had been at his post and whether he had been in communication with other ships when we struck the iceberg. When we realized that there were at least 2,200 souls and that the lifeboats filled with the same number as ours would only accommodate 800, we began to realize the awfulness of the situation. The sailors told us that there were rafts and collapsible boats enough to take nearly every one, but that in the confusion and at the rate that the *Titanic* was filling they were afraid that these rafts and boats would not be gotten ready in time.

We were rapidly drifting away from the ship and we could dimly see other lifeboats around us full of people. I looked at my watch at this time and it was a quarter of two in the morning. As we sat there on the calm sea with the stars overhead and watched the big ship's bow sinking lower and lower, suddenly the lights dimmed and we knew that the end was near. In a minute the lights went out entirely and then the stern seemed to rise up perpendicularly in the air.

There were two loud explosions, a grinding crash, and the big ship plunged down out of sight. Then followed the most awful thing that I have ever listened to—the screams and cries of all of the hundreds of poor people who were not instantly killed by the explosion, and who were struggling in the water. The ship's barber (whom I didn't know had been saved for two days afterwards, as he was quite badly injured) told me that he was on the upper deck trying to unfasten one of the collapsible boats when the plunge came, which preceded the two explosions. He was thrown off the ship and fell onto several deck chairs which were floating in the sea. He lay there on his stomach and when the explosions came he was badly injured by something heavy falling on his back and across his legs.

Just before he was pitched off the ship he saw hundreds of the third class passengers and some of the officers, with the ship's two doctors, standing on the top deck near the stern of the vessel. When the stern stood up perpendicularly these people were flung helter skelter against a barrier which divided first class from the second class portion of the deck. Then when the explosions came many of these people were blown up into the air along with a lot of debris. The barber was picked up in one of the last boats which left the ship just before the end and brought to the *Carpathia*.

I might tell here of many other thrilling escapes from death, such as the barber had, but I will not take the space to do so, as this account is supposed to be just my own experience. We made fast to another lifeboat full of people which drew alongside of our boat and waited for what should follow. Except for a ground swell the sea was motionless and we sat there anxiously scanning the horizon for the lights of a ship which should come to rescue us from our perilous position. As the other lifeboat had thirty-five people we took three people and a baby over into our boat. We had no lights and we sat there in darkness and silence, wondering if the wireless operator had succeeded in reaching anybody before the *Titanic* went down.

One of the lifeboats kept burning green fire, which I afterward learned one of the stewards had brought in his pocket, he having been shipwrecked once before. We kept close behind this boat and just before dawn we saw the mast lights of a ship on the horizon, and we felt sure that they must have seen the green fire or the rockets that were sent up from the *Titanic*'s bridge just before she sank. At any rate we felt pretty sure that we should be rescued.

Casting off from the other boat we each rowed with renewed strength for the ship which we could see more and more clearly with every passing moment. As the dawn approached we could see that the sea around us was dotted here and there with icebergs and in one direction there seemed to be an ice field of some miles in length. Here and there was a lifeboat, all headed toward the ship; a breeze sprang up with the rising sun, making the sea rougher, and it was very difficult for landlubbers like myself to manage the long heavy oars with which we were trying to row the boat. As lifeboats were approaching the ship from all directions she lay to and waited for us to row alongside. We finally pulled up under the lee of the vessel, which proved to be the *Carpathia,* and after waiting for half an hour for our turn we were at last safely on board.

All of the harrowing details will have been told by others, so that I need go into them only briefly. Just to say that the two gentlemen who sat with me at the small table in the dining-room, a Mr. W. C. Dulles from Goshen, N. Y., and a Mr. Hoyt of New York City were not saved. The horror of it all is forced upon one by the sight of these poor people who such a short time ago were so happy on board that splendid ship, but who are now mourning the loss of people dear to them. Most of the life-boats were filled with women, as when it became apparent that the ship was really sinking, and people were anxious to leave, the officers stood by the lifeboats with revolvers, I am told, and would let only enough men get in each boat to row it.

I feel that I owe my life to the fact that the young lady lost control of herself and went into the first boat, pulling me after her. There is also the fact that at first when we left the ship people hung back and they had difficulty in filling the first two or three lifeboats. My inclination was to stay aboard and wait a while until we saw whether there really was danger of the ship sinking. Later on when they wouldn't let the men go I could not have left. Many husbands and sons were separated from their women folks by this rule. One young lad whom I knew was with his father on the ship to the last. They were both thrown into the sea by the plunge which preceded the explosion. They clung to a collapsible boat to which fifty or sixty others were trying to cling until his father's strength gave out and he was forced to let go, leaving his son to be rescued some time later. One family of

Canadians from Winnipeg, whom I knew—three girls and a mother—are here, but the father and son are gone, held back at pistol point.

A poor little lady in the next room to me on the *Carpathia* last night was hysterical all night and between her sobs I could hear her say: "He said he would shoot him if he followed me." She lost her husband and I think they had not been long married. The heartbroken people, as they leaned over the rail of the *Carpathia* looking down into each lifeboat as it came alongside to see if their missing dear ones were aboard, were pitiful objects to behold. It was terrible to look down into these boats as they came alongside, into the upturned faces of these women, in some cases standing in water up to their ankles with dead men lying in the bottom of the boat anxiously scanning our faces at the rail to see if their dear ones were safe on board.

Some of the rescued people who were the last to leave the ship told me that when they left the orchestra was playing in the "Lounge," and that it was brave but ghastly to hear them. The stewards and crew were wonderful, and I didn't hear of anyone who lost his head or nerve. Only those who have been as near to death in a shipwreck as we were can realize the awfulness of some of the scenes which the rescued witnessed, or how thankful they feel to have been saved.

I can hardly realize now that the great ship and all those brave ladies and gentlemen have really gone down while I am here alive. It was a beautiful night and the sunrise the next morning from our small boat was the most glorious sunrise I have ever seen. Truly the ways of the Almighty are beyond our feeble understanding.

In finishing this account I wish to give testimony to the kindness and sympathy of the passengers and crew of the Cunard steamship *Carpathia*, which rescued us. In ten minutes the wireless operator on this ship would have gone to bed and our message would not have reached this vessel. We might still have been on the sea in small boats or swamped and drowned. The stewards and crew have worked ceaselessly to make us comfortable and feed us while the passengers have given up their berths and submitted without a murmur to having their trip terminate in New York when they expected to be in Naples at that time.

WILLIAM T. SLOPER

Vera Dick,
Washington Post,
APRIL 19, 1912

The night on which the big steamship *Titanic* crushed out its life against the iceberg juggernaut was very clear, and there was a tang in the air. I was on deck and was almost thrown from my feet by the shock of the collision. I have heard it said that the sinking of the *Titanic* was caused by an explosion in the engine room. This is untrue.

I saw the iceberg that brought down the *Titanic*. The ship officers saw it, too, and the bells were rung to reverse the course. The boat actually escaped the exposed part of the berg, but grounded on the unexposed part.

There were terrified screams from all parts of the boat. Women came rushing upon deck with hardly any clothes upon them. Half a score were in their night gowns, and many were in their bare feet. Capt. Smith and a man who was said to be the personal aide to the President of the United States were among the coolest men on board.

They ordered the men into line, and then the women were called to one side. I saw a number of immigrants rushing up the stairs, yelling and screaming and fighting to get to the boats. Officers drew guns and told them that if they moved toward the boats they would be shot dead.

There were some terrible scenes. I saw fathers parting from their children and giving them an encouraging pat on the shoulders.

VERA DICK, *WASHINGTON POST*, APRIL 19, 1912287

I saw men kissing their wives and telling them that they would be with them shortly.

One man said there was absolutely no danger, that the boat was the finest ever built, with water-tight compartments, and that it could not sink. That seemed to be the general impression.

One of the most interesting sidelights on the whole tragedy is the way some of the women in evening dress faced the tragedy. It was evident that they did not appreciate the danger.

One man handed a life-saver to a woman with the remark, "We are wearing these this season. They are most becoming."

One woman had a fox terrier in her arms, and the man told her to try a life-saver on the dog.

"Everybody is wearing them now," he laughed.

It was evident that many people thought that there was too much agitation, and that for a boat of that kind to sink was absolutely impossible.

Some of the people on the boat have said I was brave because I wanted to remain on board until the last, and refused to take a seat in the first boat when the captain wanted to put me in. As a matter of fact, there were women older and more nervous than I, and I thought they should have the first chance. I realized the danger, but I am young and felt equal to the situation.

Capt. Smith, or maybe it was Mr. Moore—I don't know which—finally insisted that I leave. "This is no place for a woman, and you will have to go in the next boat," they told me. I then allowed myself to be put off the *Titanic*, although I would like to have stayed until the last. I could have jumped overboard as some of the men did.

A band was playing on the *Titanic* when it went down. The captain had ordered the band to play, and to play continuously, so that the women would not feel that they were in danger. The bandsmen were loyal. They kept on playing jolly, happy tunes. They were playing some American air when the guards shot the jaw off an immigrant who tried to crowd into one of the boats, brushing the women aside.

They played, and their airs were mingled with the shrieks of terrified women. And as I went over the side, they were still playing—discordantly it seemed—and I guess they kept on until the *Titanic* was swallowed up by the ocean.

The boat in which I was placed was rowed quickly away from the *Titanic*. We kept looking back, like Lot's wife. It might have cost us our lives, or it might have delayed us, but still we looked back at the great *Titanic*, with its lines of light indicating the floors like a skyscraper when the occupants are at work.

It was about 11:45 when we struck the iceberg, and it was 2:20 when the boat went down.

As we looked back, we saw the lowest floor of lights wiped out by the waterline. Then another floor went out, then another, and another, one floor of lights after another, as the *Titanic* settled. There was no suddenness about it. It was rhythmic— tragically, heart-rendingly rhythmic.

In the boat in which I was there were women in their night gowns and bare feet. The night was very clear, starlight, but very, very cold. Many of them shivered horribly. Some of them talked of suicide—those who had lost loved ones. We drifted about all that night, subsisting on bread and water—that was all we had— and then were picked up by the *Carpathia*. When we took an account of the people who were saved, we found 44 deck hands, 73 engineers, 210 first-class passengers, 125 second-class, 144 third class, 16 stewardesses, and 38 stewards.

Some of the rescued passengers died afterward on the *Carpathia*, and were buried at sea. There were none of the usual formalities. It was desired that no attention be directed to the occurrences. The rescued passengers were frantic enough already.

Walter Nichols,
Brooklyn Daily Eagle,
APRIL 19, 1912

I've been a sailor for twenty years, and I've crossed about 300 times, but this!

We left Southampton on Wednesday, April 10, with fine weather. Everything aboard was ship shape. We got to Cherbourg at about six that night and took on a lot of people there, though not quite so many as we took on at Southampton, counting steerage and all. We only stopped for a little at Queenstown, leaving there between 2 and 2:30 on Thursday afternoon. Our first day's run was 488 knots. This was counting from the time we left Queenstown until 12 o'clock on Friday. From Friday noon to Saturday noon she ran 544 knots, and the next day 546. She wasn't trying for a record because she was a new ship, and this was her first trip.

All day Sunday it was very cold, although the weather was fine. There was ice all around us. There were services on board that day, in the first and second cabins. I was busy with my work and didn't go. Sunday night was my night off, and I went to bed at about 10 o'clock. I got off at 9, but I fooled around for a couple of hours before I turned in. I didn't go on deck. On a big boat like that a man working inside doesn't go on deck often. Sometimes you don't get a peep at the water for days at a time. It's just like working in a big hotel. But I knew that it was mighty cold outside and I knew what the reason was, too. I've crossed enough to know that when it gets cold like that at this season it's because there's icebergs around. And if we fellows down below knew it I guess the navigating officers knew it, too.

My bunk was amidships on deck E, the main thoroughfare of the boat. There are still two decks below that, F and G. At 11:40 I was awakened by feeling a bit of a vibration. The ship went on for a bit and then the engines stopped. Nobody was frightened and some of the men in the room with me didn't want to trouble to get up to look out and see what had happened. I put on my coat and took a run out to look. It was all black outside and I couldn't see anything except that there was some ice on the deck forward.

Half of the men went back to bed. Nobody believed anything could be wrong. They had such faith in the ship. Everybody believed in her.

It was bitter cold outside, and I was glad enough to get back into the cabin where I bunked. It's located not far from the engine room—the engine rooms are just behind and below us—and within a few minutes of the time we struck I could hear the engineers passing along the order to close the watertight doors. One man would tell it to the next and he would pass it on to someone else.

Well, as I say, some of the men went back to bed. I stayed up and sat around talking with some of the fellows for I should say three-quarters of an hour after the collision, when the second steward in charge of our cabin came in and gave us orders to report up on deck. That meant that we were to report to the positions assigned to us in the lifeboat drill. My place was with lifeboat No. 15. So I went up on deck A, where the lifeboats are. On my way up I noticed some of the passengers about, but no one seemed to be worried or excited. I passed by the gymnasium on my way. Inside were a number of passengers amusing themselves. One man was riding the bicycle, one of those exercise machines, and another was punching the bag.

No. 15, my boat, was the after boat on the starboard side. All the odd numbered boats are on one side of the ship and the even numbered boats on the other. There were ten of us to man the boat, which is a big one, holding about seventy to eighty persons. When I got on deck it was still dark, but I could hear the wireless machine sputter. I didn't see any icebergs or anything. Up on deck A, which is the boat deck, there were only the boat crews. At least that is all I could see. I saw them working away at Boat No. 11 and Boat No. 13. When I looked down I saw that several of the boats were already in the water. The ship was brightly lit and I could see the boats, with people in them, floating about in the reflection of the light from the ship.

The officer in charge of the boats on that part of the deck had a revolver in his hand. He gave his orders quietly and we didn't realize even then that anything serious was the matter. The ship was down in the water a little forward but you couldn't notice it much from where I was.

We stood in line waiting for orders while boats 11 and 13 were swung out on the davits and lowered. The crews would make them ready and get into them. Then they would lower them to deck B, where the passengers were. The boats are held by three ropes, one on either end and one in the middle. They are cut loose by knocking out a block in the center after she is in the water.

I guess we waited for some minutes while they were getting the two other boats away. They were mighty careful not to let one boat go before the other had got clear. It's a drop of some ninety or a hundred feet from the boat deck to the water, and they had to look sharp to keep one boat from fouling the other.

After we got in our boat and were waiting to be lowered to deck B I heard the band playing. I was looking sharp after what I was doing and I don't remember what they played. I could just hear a sort of confused sound of the instruments, enough to know that they were playing. Someone told me afterward that the last piece they played was "Nearer, My God, to Thee." They didn't have a chance, poor devils. They were cooped up in one of the reception rooms, and they were drowned like rats, every one of them.

Altogether it took us about twenty minutes to fill our lifeboat and get away. There was no confusion and no rush. On deck B, where we loaded the passengers, First Officer Murdoch was in charge. He saw to the giving of the orders to the men that handled the boats. The order was to take women only, and the officers kept saying, "We can only take women. No man is allowed to get in."

But no one seemed particularly anxious to get in. The officer kept on talking to the women, sort of urging them. "Come, now," he'd say. "Get in or we'll have to leave you behind. The boat's going to leave and we can't wait for you." Several women stepped back as they saw the boat and refused to leave their men folks when they saw that they would have to go alone. One woman stepped up to the rail against which we holding the boat, looked into it and then stepped back as though she didn't like it. I saw Colonel Astor kiss his wife good-bye. I knew him because he had been pointed out to me in the saloon. I didn't know any of the rest.

All the time we were there the officer kept talking quiet like, urging women to get in. He didn't say anything about danger. I guess he didn't want to have any rush and he just talked, quiet like, and kept sort of joking them along, telling them to hurry or they'd be left, and things like that. But they all seemed to think that the ship was a better place to be than in a lifeboat. Many of the boats weren't full. We only had about fifty people in ours. Some of the men passengers had to urge the women to go, and some of the women whose men folks didn't happen to be close to them refused to go.

Our boat was one of the last to get away. We held on until we were sure No. 13 was clear. Then we dropped to the water. None of us was excited and some of the men seemed to take it as a sort of little excursion in the boat. None of us had any idea that the *Titanic* would sink. We knew that the *Olympic* was on the way to us and we expected that she would come in the morning to pick up the boats and to take off the people that were left on the *Titanic*.

As soon as we struck the water we started to pull away from the ship, so as not to foul against her side. As soon as we got a little distance off I could see that she was down a good deal by the head because the propeller was sticking half way out of the water. When we were a couple of hundred yards away from the ship I saw two flashes and heard two revolver shots coming from near the bridge. All the boats had been lowered and I didn't know what the shots meant. By this time it must have been about 1 o'clock in the morning and the lights were still going on the main part of the ship. The other boats were all about us and we kept shouting to one another to keep close together. After we left the ship about four other boats got away. I kept pulling away at my oar and we rowed around just to keep warm. The women we had on board were huddled down in the center of the boat. Some of them were standing, but most of them were squatting down.

We saw the ship gradually settling down at the bow, until the forepart of the ship wasn't visible. Part of the time the band was still playing and we could hear the wireless. About an hour after we left her the fore part of the boat was going under and that was the first time we realized that she was going to sink. Because up to this time the men in the boat had taken the whole thing as a sort of holiday.

The ship sank slowly and steadily and then we heard a little explosion that must have been the first boiler. After that the lights began to go out in different parts of the ship. Then came a big explosion. We could see a mass of black smoke. The boat seemed to lift right up out of the water and tilt up on end, and then seemed to break and drop back. For one moment she was right up in the air standing on her nose.

That's when the people left on board went into the water. There were 1,500 to 1,700 left on the ship and most of them were thrown into the water by this explosion. Then a horrible shriek went up, cries for help and weird shouts. You can imagine what it was like, 1,500 of them. If you're ever been around when they were feeding a kennel of dogs, that's the only thing I can think of that it sounded like—and that kept up for half an hour, growing fainter and fainter as the minutes passed. There was no other sound—just the crying of the people.

The ship quietly sank out of sight without a sound. We could

see black spots of wreckage and hundreds of people struggling
in the water. Some of the boats were near enough to help and
pull some of the people in. One of the women in our boat wanted
us to go back, but we wouldn't do it. Had we gotten in among
that crowd struggling in the water it might have meant the end
of us. With twenty of them grabbing the boat on one side it
would have swamped us in a minute. It was awful, but there was
nothing to do but wait. I won't forget those shrieks. The women
in our boat crouched down and murmured. No one spoke. For
half an hour we could hear those cries for help. Some of those
left on the boat had managed to get on bits of wreckage. Some
were on rafts so loaded down that they were partly under water.
Some of the women in our boat started to move around. We had
to keep them quiet, for with their shifting about we might have
gone over.

Gradually those voices died away, and in something like half
an hour everything was quiet and dark. We could see the other
boats drifting about and kept close to them. Every now and then
we passed a body floating on the water.

Just as it was getting light, a few hours later, I don't know just
how many, we saw the lights of the *Carpathia*. We hadn't suffered any, because we kept warm by rowing. Every man that
was saved was in one of the boats. The cold water killed the others. No one could stand the water for six or seven hours. Every
one of the bodies had on a lifebelt. We didn't try to pick them
up; what was the use? We had all we could tend to with the living without bothering about the dead ones. The women in our
boat didn't see the bodies. They were too far down in the bottom of the boat. They kept talking quietly, just as though they
were still on the ship.

In some of the boats, I heard later, there was a lot of weeping,
but not in ours. I guess those must have been Continentals. The
women in our boat were mostly English stock, and they're a
braver sort. The kind makes a big difference.

By the time we started to row toward the *Carpathia*—we
didn't know it was she until later; we thought it was the
Olympic—it was getting light enough so we could look about

us. Then, for the first time, we saw that there were big icebergs all about us. We counted fifteen or sixteen big bergs. They loomed up through the light, which wasn't strong yet, like sailing craft, and they were shaped like schooner sails, too. In all my sailing I've never seen so many icebergs in one place. A little farther off was a big ice floe; I guess it must have been ten to fifteen miles long. There was a cold, freezing wind blowing toward us from this shoal.

When we got up to the *Carpathia* they were all ready for us. The men climbed on board up a rope ladder. The women were hoisted up in a bo'sun's chair and the children were put in sacks.

After we got on board and the strain was over I felt weak for the first time. [illegible] . . . a lot of the women became hysterical. The people on the *Carpathia* were surprised that there were so few of us left. They had expected to pick up everybody. If they had I guess there wouldn't have been room enough on board to stand up. The passengers were distributed all about and we were told to bunk wherever we could. After the *Carpathia* had got us all on board from the lifeboats she started to cruise about. Bodies were floating all around and bits of wreckage. I saw chairs, cushions and pillows floating on the water. The *Californian* came along a short time after we were on board the *Carpathia*. The *Carpathia* cruised among the wreckage until 9 or 10 o'clock. We didn't pick up anyone. All those that were alive were in the boats. And several of the men in the boats that had been fished up out of the water were dead. They dropped them over the side a little later. Nobody could have lived long in that cold water.

On board the *Carpathia* things were pretty crowded. The passengers were put wherever there was room in the steerage and anywhere. The *Titanic* crew waited on the *Titanic* passengers. Many of the women stayed in their rooms during the whole trip. I heard that Mr. Ismay stayed in his cabin all the time. I didn't see him. Orders came to us that no news of any kind was to be given out. The captain handled all the news that was received or sent out. The first thing some of the passengers tried to do after getting on the *Carpathia* was to send wireless messages telling their people they were safe, but they weren't allowed to do it.

They kept asking questions, but they weren't told anything. These were the orders: Don't give any information. I suppose a lot of the *Titanic*'s passengers on the *Carpathia* knew less about the accident than anyone else. They took all our names soon after we got aboard. But a lot of them were never sent ashore. My name wasn't sent in and my sister Ruth didn't know I was safe until I went to see her at 16 East Eleventh street, where she is working. My brother Frank came down to the boat to see if I was there, but he missed me.

Whatever news may have come to the ship we didn't know anything about it. All the news went to the captain through the Marconi man. We were a sorry looking lot on the *Carpathia*. You wouldn't have known them to be the same people that were on the *Titanic*. All the clothes anyone had were those they wore in the boats. Some of the women only had on their nightdresses and their outer coats which they put on when they came up on deck. A lot of the men, like myself, threw on their clothes over their pajamas. I'm still wearing mine.

After we got on board the *Carpathia* we heard all sorts of experiences that others had had. I was told of one woman who took off her coat and insisted on giving it to a man who had been pulled out of the water into one of the boats. One man who was saved had jumped down 150 feet into the water from the stern of the ship just after the explosion. The baker, who was also picked up by a boat, jumped from one of the top decks into the water just before the big explosion.

As to the cause of the accident, I think someone must have been careless. There was no excuse for their not seeing the berg. We who were below knew there were icebergs about and the officers of the ship must have known of it. The collision must have torn out the bottom of the ship beyond the first line of watertight bulkhead doors. She must have had hundreds of tons of water in her forward part to make her propellers stick up out of the water the way they did.

There were a lot of life rafts aboard the *Titanic* that were not used. If the people on board had only realized that. Some of the men did throw the life rafts into the water and jumped in after them. Then they climbed up on them and some of them were afterwards picked up by the small boats.

All the engineers were drowned—thirty-two or thirty-six of them. Not one was saved. The Marconi man who was saved was hurt about the legs. They had to carry him to the wireless room on the *Carpathia*, but he worked most of the time. Some of the men picked up by the boats died after they got on board the *Carpathia*. I think there were three or four. They were buried on Monday. The *Carpathia* didn't meet any ships until we were off Sandy Hook this afternoon. Then we were met by a couple of newspaper tugs. But orders were given to allow no communication and a couple of bo'suns manned the rail to see that the order was carried out. I was surprised the way they let us through. No quarantine stop and no bother with the customs. I didn't expect that they would let us members of the crew off the ship. But I just walked off and no one interfered with me. Now I guess I'll have to start in and look for another job.

The Tragic Home-Coming

Logan Marshall,
The Sinking of the Titanic
and
Great Sea Disasters

CHAPTER XV

Jack Thayer's Own Story of the Wreck

SEVENTEEN-YEAR-OLD SON OF PENNSYLVANIA RAILROAD
OFFICIAL TELLS MOVING STORY OF HIS RESCUE—TOLD MOTHER TO BE
BRAVE—SEPARATED FROM PARENTS—JUMPED WHEN VESSEL SANK—
DRIFTED ON OVERTURNED BOAT—PICKED UP BY *CARPATHIA*

One of the calmest of the passengers was young Jack Thayer, the seventeen-year-old son of Mr. and Mrs. John B. Thayer. When his mother was put into the life-boat he kissed her and told her to be brave, saying that he and his father would be all right. He and Mr. Thayer stood on the deck as the small boat in which Mrs. Thayer was a passenger made off from the side of the *Titanic* over the smooth sea.

The boy's own account of his experience as told to one of his rescuers is one of the most remarkable of all the wonderful ones that have come from the tremendous catastrophe:

"Father was in bed, and mother and myself were about to get into bed. There was no great shock. I was on my feet at the time and I do not think it was enough to throw anyone down. I put on an overcoat and rushed up on A deck on the port side. I saw nothing there. I then went forward to the bow to see if I could see any signs of ice. The only ice I saw was on the well deck. I could not see very far ahead, having just come out of a brightly lighted room.

"I then went down to our room and my father and mother came on deck with me, to the starboard side of A deck. We could not see anything there. Father thought he saw small pieces of ice floating around, but I could not see any myself. There was no big berg. We walked around to the port side, and the ship had then a fair list to port. We stayed there looking over the side for about five minutes. The list seemed very slowly to be increasing.

"We then went down to our rooms on C deck, all of us dressing quickly, putting on all our clothes. We all put on life-preservers, and over these we put our overcoats. Then we hurried up on deck and walked around, looking out at different places until the women were all ordered to collect on the port side.

SEPARATED FROM PARENTS

"Father and I said good-bye to mother at the top of the stairs on A deck. She and the maid went right out on A deck on the port side and we went to the starboard side. As at this time we had no idea the boat would sink we walked around A deck and then went to B deck. Then we thought we would go back to see if mother had gotten off safely, and went to the port side of A deck. We met the chief steward of the main dining saloon and he told us that mother had not yet taken a boat, and he took us to her.

"Father and mother went ahead and I followed. They went down to B deck and a crowd got in front of me and I was not able to catch them, and lost sight of them. As soon as I could get through the crowd I tried to find them on B deck, but without success. That is the last time I saw my father. This was about one half an hour before she sank. I then went to the starboard side, thinking that father and mother must have gotten off in a boat. All of this time I was with a fellow named Milton C. Long, of New York, whom I had just met that evening.

"On the starboard side the boats were getting away quickly. Some boats were already off in a distance. We thought of getting into one of the boats, the last boat to go on the forward part of the starboard side, but there seemed to be such a crowd around I thought it unwise to make any attempt to get into it. He and I stood by the davits of one of the boats that had left. I did not no-tice anybody that I knew except Mr. Lindley, whom I had also just met that evening. I lost sight of him in a few minutes. Long and I then stood by the rail just a little aft of the captain's bridge.

THOUGHT SHIP WOULD FLOAT

"The list to the port had been growing greater all the time. About this time the people began jumping from the stern. I thought of jumping myself, but was afraid of being stunned on hitting the water. Three times I made up my mind to jump out and slide down the davit ropes and try to make the boats that were lying off from the ship, but each time Long got hold of me and told me to wait a while. He then sat down and I stood up waiting to see what would happen. Even then we thought she might possibly stay afloat.

"I got a sight on a rope between the davits and a star and noticed that she was gradually sinking. About this time she straightened up on an even keel and started to go down fairly fast at an angle of about 30 degrees. As she started to sink we left the davits and went back and stood by the rail about even with the second funnel.

"Long and myself said good-bye to each other and jumped up on the rail. He put his legs over and held on a minute and asked me if I was coming. I told him I would be with him in a minute. He did not jump clear, but slid down the side of the ship. I never saw him again.

"About five seconds after he jumped I jumped out, feet first. I was clear of the ship; went down, and as I came up I was pushed away from the ship by some force. I came up facing the ship, and one of the funnels seemed to be lifted off and fell towards me about 15 yards away, with a mass of sparks and steam coming out of it. I saw the ship in a sort of a red glare, and it seemed to me that she broke in two just in front of the third funnel.

"This time I was sucked down, and as I came up I was pushed out again and twisted around by a large wave, coming up in the midst of a great deal of small wreckage. As I pushed my hand from my head it touched the cork fender of an overturned life-boat.

I looked up and saw some men on the top and asked them to give me a hand. One of them, who was a stoker, helped me up. In a short time the bottom was covered with about twenty-five or thirty men. When I got on this I was facing the ship.

"The stern then seemed to rise in the air and stopped at about an angle of 60 degrees. It seemed to hold there for a time and then with a hissing sound it shot right down out of sight with people jumping from the stern. The stern either pivoted around towards our boat, or we were sucked towards it, and as we only had one oar we could not keep away. There did not seem to be very much suction and most of us managed to stay on the bottom of our boat.

"We were then right in the midst of fairly large wreckage, with people swimming all around us. The sea was very calm and we kept the boat pretty steady, but every now and then a wave would wash over it.

SAID THE LORD'S PRAYER

"The assistant wireless operator was right next to me, holding on to me and kneeling in the water. We all sang a hymn and said the Lord's Prayer, and then waited for dawn to come. As often as we saw the other boats in a distance we would yell, 'Ship ahoy!' But they could not distinguish our cries from any of the others, so we all gave it up, thinking it useless. It was very cold and none of us were able to move around to keep warm, the water washing over her almost all the time.

"Toward dawn the wind sprang up, roughening up the water and making it difficult to keep the boat balanced. The wireless man raised our hopes a great deal by telling us that the Carpathia would be up in about three hours. About 3:30 or 4 o'clock some men on our boat on the bow sighted her mast lights. I could not see them, as I was sitting down with a man kneeling on my leg. He finally got up and I stood up. We had the second officer, Mr. Lightoller, on board. We had an officer's whistle and whistled for the boats in the distance to come up and take us off.

"It took about an hour and a half for the boats to draw near. Two boats came up. The first took half and the other took the balance, including myself. We had great difficulty about this time in balancing the boat, as the men would lean too far, but we were all taken aboard the already crowded boat, and in about a half or three-quarters of an hour later we were picked up by the *Carpathia*.

"I have noticed Second Officer Lightoller's statement that 'J. B. Thayer was on our overturned boat,' which would give the impression that it was father, when he really meant it was I, as he only learned my name in a subsequent conversation on the *Carpathia*, and did not know I was 'junior.'"

CHAPTER XVI

Incidents Related by James McGough

WOMEN FORCED INTO THE LIFE-BOATS—WHY SOME MEN WERE
SAVED BEFORE WOMEN—ASKED TO MAN LIFE-BOATS

Surrounded by his wife and members of his family, James Mc-Gough, of Philadelphia, a buyer for the Gimbel Brothers, whose fate had been in doubt, recited a most thrilling and graphic picture of the disaster.

As the *Carpathia* docked, Mrs. McGough, a brother and several friends of the buyer, met him, and after the touching reunion had taken place the party proceeded to Philadelphia.

Vivid in detail, Mr. McGough's story differs essentially from one the imagination would paint. He declared that the boat was driving at a high rate of speed at the time of the accident, and seemed impressed by the calmness and apathy displayed by the survivors as they tossed on the frozen seas in the little life-boats until the *Carpathia* picked them up.

The *Titanic* did not plunge into the water suddenly, he declared, but settled slowly into the deep with its hundreds of passengers.

"The collision occurred at 20 minutes of 12," said Mr. Mc-Gough. "I was sleeping in my cabin when I felt a wrench, not severe or terrifying.

"It seemed to me to be nothing more serious than the racing of the screw, which often occurs when a ship plunges her bow deep into a heavy swell, raising the stern out of water. We dressed hurriedly and ran to the upper deck. There was little noise or tumult at the time.

"The promenade decks being higher from the base of the ship and thus more insecure, strained and creaked; so we went to the lower decks. By this time the engines had been reversed, and I could feel the ship backing off. Officers and stewards ran through the corridors, shouting for all to be calm, that there was no danger. We were warned, however, to dress and put life-preservers on us. I had on what clothing I could find and had stuffed some money in my pocket.

PARTING OF ASTOR AND BRIDE

"As I passed the gymnasium I saw Colonel Astor and his young wife together. She was clinging to him, piteously pleading that he go into the life-boat with her. He refused almost gruffly and was attempting to calm her by saying that all her fears were groundless, that the accident she feared would prove a farce. It proved different, however.

"None, I believe, knew that the ship was about to sink. I did not realize it just then. When I reached the upper deck and saw tons of ice piled upon our crushed bow the full realization came to me.

"Officers stood with drawn guns, ordering the women into the boats. All feared to leave the comparative safety of a broad and firm deck for the precarious smaller boats. Women clung to their husbands, crying that they would never leave without them, and had to be torn away.

"On one point all the women were firm. They would not enter a life-boat until men were in it first. They feared to trust themselves to the seas in them. It required courage to step into the frail crafts as they swung from the creaking davits. Few men were willing to take the chance. An officer rushed behind me and shouted:

"'You're big enough to pull an oar. Jump into this boat or we'll never be able to get the women off.' I was forced to do so, though I admit that the ship looked a great deal safer to me than any small boat.

"Our boat was the second off. Forty or more persons were crowded into it, and with myself and members of the crew at the oars, were pulled slowly away. Huge icebergs, larger than the Pennsylvania depot at New York, surrounded us. As we pulled away we could see boat after boat filled and lowered to the waves. Despite the fact that they were new and supposedly in excellent working order, the blocks jammed in many instances, tilting the boats, loaded with people, at varying angles before they reached the water.

BAND CONTINUED PLAYING

"As the life-boats pulled away the officers ordered the bands to play, and their music did much to quell panic. It was a heartbreaking sight to us, tossing in an eggshell three-fourths of a mile away, to see the great ship go down. First she listed to the starboard, on which side the collision had occurred, then she settled slowly but steadily, without hope of remaining afloat.

"The *Titanic* was all aglow with lights as if for a function. First we saw the lights of the lower deck snuffed out. A while later and the second deck illumination was extinguished in a similar manner. Then the third and upper decks were darkened, and without plunging or rocking the great ship disappeared slowly from the surface of the sea.

"People were crowded on each deck as it lowered into the water, hoping in vain that aid would come in time. Some of the life-boats caught in the merciless suction were swallowed with her.

"The sea was calm—calm as the water in a tumbler. But it was freezing cold. None had dressed heavily, and all, therefore, suffered intensely. The women did not shriek or grow hysterical while we waited through the awful night for help. We men stood at the oars; stood because there was no room for us to sit, and kept the boat headed into the swell to prevent her capsizing. Another boat was at our side, but all the others were scattered around the water.

"Finally, shortly before 6 o'clock, we saw the lights of the *Carpathia* approaching. Gradually she picked up the survivors in the other boats and then approached us. When we were lifted to the deck the women fell helpless. They were carried to whatever quarters offered themselves, while the men were assigned to the smoking room.

"Of the misery and suffering which was witnessed on the rescue ship I know nothing. With the other men survivors I was glad to remain in the smoking room until New York was reached, trying to forget the awful experience.

"To us aboard the *Carpathia* came rumors of misstatements which were being made to the public. The details of the wreck were wofully misunderstood.

"Let me emphasize that the night was not foggy or cloudy. There was just the beginning of the new moon, but every star in the sky was shining brightly, unmarred by clouds. The boats were lowered from both sides of the *Titanic* in time to escape, but there was not enough for all."

CHAPTER XI

Preparations on Land to Receive the Sufferers

POLICE ARRANGEMENTS—DONATIONS OF MONEY AND SUPPLIES—
HOSPITALS AND AMBULANCES MADE READY—PRIVATE HOUSES THROWN
OPEN—WAITING FOR THE *CARPATHIA* TO ARRIVE—THE SHIP SIGHTED!

New York City, touched to the heart by the great ocean calamity and desiring to do what it could to lighten the woes and relieve the sufferings of the pitiful little band of men and women rescued from the *Titanic*, opened both its heart and its purse.

The most careful and systematic plans were made for the reception and transfer to homes, hotels or institutions of the *Titanic*'s survivors. Mayor Gaynor, with Police Commissioner Waldo, arranged to go down the bay on the police boat *Patrol*, to come up with the *Carpathia* and take charge of the police arrangements at the pier.

In anticipation of the enormous number that would, for a variety of reasons, creditable or otherwise, surge about the Cunard pier at the coming of the *Carpathia*, Mayor Gaynor and the police commissioner had seen to it that the streets should be rigidly sentineled by continuous lines of policemen. Under Inspector George McClusky, the man of most experience, perhaps, in handling large crowds, there were 200 men, including twelve mounted men and a number in citizens' clothes. For two blocks to the north, south and east of the docks lines were established through which none save those bearing passes from the Government and the Cunard Line could penetrate.

With all arrangements made that experience or information could suggest, the authorities settled down to await the docking of the *Carpathia*. No word had come to either the White Star Line or the Cunard Line, they said, that any of the *Titanic*'s people had died on that ship or that bodies had been recovered from the sea, but in the afternoon Mayor Gaynor sent word to the Board of Coroners that it might be well for some of that body to meet the incoming ship. Coroners Feinberg and Holtzhauser with Coroner's Physician Weston arranged to go down the bay on the Patrol, while Coroner Hellenstein waited at the pier. An undertaker was notified to be ready if needed. Fortunately there was no such need.

EVERY POSSIBLE MEASURE THOUGHT OF

Every possible measure of relief for the survivors that could be thought of by officials of the city, of the Federal Government, by the heads of hospitals and the Red Cross and relief societies was arranged for. The Municipal Lodging House, which has accommodations for 700 persons, agreed to throw open its doors and furnish lodging and food to any of the survivors as long as they should need it. Commissioner of Charities Drummond did not know, of course, just how great the call would be for the services of his department. He went to the Cunard pier to direct his part of the work in person. Meanwhile he had twenty ambulances ready for instant movement on the city's pier at the foot of East Twenty-sixth Street. They were ready to take patients to the reception hospital connected with Bellevue or the Metropolitan Hospital on Blackwell's Island. Ambulances from the Kings County Hospital in Brooklyn were also there to do their share. All the other hospitals in the city stood ready to take the *Titanic*'s people and those that had ambulances promised to send them. The Charities ferryboat, *Thomas S. Brennan*, equipped as a hospital craft, lay off the department pier with nurses and physicians ready to be called to the Cunard pier on the other side of the city. St. Vincent's Hospital had 120 beds ready, New York

Hospital twelve, Bellevue and the reception hospital 120 and Flower Hospital twelve.

The House of Shelter maintained by the Hebrew Sheltering and Immigrant Aid Society announced that it was able to care for at least fifty persons as long as might be necessary. The German Society of New York, the Irish Immigrant Society, the Italian Society, the Swedish Immigrant Society and the Young Men's Christian Association were among the organizations that also offered to see that no needy survivor would go without shelter.

Mrs. W. A. Bastede, whose husband is a member of the staff of St. Luke's Hospital, offered to the White Star Line the use of the newly opened ward at St. Luke's, which will accommodate from thirty to sixty persons. She said the hospital would send four ambulances with nurses and doctors and that she had collected clothing enough for fifty persons. The line accepted her offer and said that the hospital would be kept informed as to what was needed. A trustee of Bellevue also called at the White Star offices to offer ambulances. He said that five or six, with two or three doctors and nurses on each, would be sent to the pier if required.

Many other hospitals as well as individuals called at the mayor's office, expressing willingness to take in anybody that should be sent to them. A woman living in Fiftieth Street just off Fifth Avenue wished to put her home at the disposal of the survivors. D. H. Knott, of 102 Waverley Place, told the mayor that he could take care of 100 and give them both food and lodging at the Arlington, Holly and Earl Hotels. Commissioner Drummond visited the City Hall and arranged with the mayor the plans for the relief to be extended directly by the city. Mr. Drummond said that omnibuses would be provided to transfer passengers from the ship to the Municipal Lodging House.

MRS. VANDERBILT'S EFFORTS

Mrs. W. K. Vanderbilt, Jr., spent the day telephoning to her friends, asking them to let their automobiles be used to meet the *Carpathia* and take away those who needed surgical care. It was announced that as a result of Mrs. Vanderbilt's efforts 100 limousine automobiles and all the Fifth Avenue and Riverside Drive automobile buses would be at the Cunard pier.

Immigration Commissioner Williams said that he would be at the pier when the *Carpathia* came in. There was to be no inspection of immigrants at Ellis Island. Instead, the commissioner sent seven or eight inspectors to the pier to do their work there and he asked them to do it with the greatest possible speed and the least possible bother to the shipwrecked aliens. The immigrants who had no friends to meet them were to be provided for until their cases could be disposed of. Mr. Williams thought that some of them who had lost everything might have to be sent back to their homes. Those who were to be admitted to the United States were to be cared for by the Women's Relief Committee.

RED CROSS RELIEF

Robert W. de Forest, chairman of the Red Cross Relief Committee of the Charity Organization Society, after conferring with Mayor Gaynor, said that in addition to an arrangement that all funds received by the mayor should be paid to Jacob H. Schiff, the New York treasurer of the American Red Cross, the committee had decided that it could turn over all the immediate relief work to the Women's Relief Committee.

The Red Cross Committee announced that careful plans had been made to provide for every possible emergency.

The emergency committee received a telegram that Ernest P. Bicknell, director of the American Red Cross, was coming from Washington. The Red Cross Emergency Relief Committee was to have several representatives at the pier to look out for the passengers on the *Carpathia*. Mr. Persons and Dr. Devine were to be there and it was planned to have others.

The Salvation Army offered, through the mayor's office, accommodation for thirty single men at the Industrial Home, 533 West Forty-eighth Street, and for twenty others at its hotel, 18 Chatham Square. The army's training school at 124 West Fourteenth

Street was ready to take twenty or thirty survivors. R. H. Farley, head of the White Star Line's third class department, said that the line would give all the steerage passengers railroad tickets to their destination.

Mayor Gaynor estimated that more than 5,000 persons could be accommodated in quarters offered through his orders. Most of these offers of course would have to be rejected. The mayor also said that Colonel Conley of the Sixty-ninth Regiment offered to turn out his regiment to police the pier, but it was thought that such service would be unnecessary.

CROWDS AT THE DOCKS

Long before dark on Thursday night a few people passed the police lines and with a yellow card were allowed to go on the dock; but reports had been published that the *Carpathia* would not be in till midnight, and by 8 o'clock there were not more than two hundred people on the pier. In the next hour the crowd with passes trebled in number. By 9 o'clock the pier held half as many as it could comfortably contain. The early crowd did not contain many women relatives of the survivors. Few nervous people could be seen, but here and there was a woman, usually supported by two male escorts, weeping softly to herself.

On the whole it was a frantic, grief-crazed crowd. Laborers rubbed shoulders with millionaires.

The relatives of the rich had taxicabs waiting outside the docks. The relatives of the poor went there on foot in the rain, ready to take their loved ones.

A special train was awaiting Mrs. Charles M. Hays, widow of the president of the Grand Trunk Railroad. A private car also waited Mrs. George D. Widener.

EARLY ARRIVALS AT PIER

Among the first to arrive at the pier was a committee from the Stock Exchange, headed by R. H. Thomas, and composed of

Charles Knoblauch, B. M. W. Baruch, Charles Holzderber and J. Carlisle. Mr. Thomas carried a long black box which contained $5,000 in small bills, which was to be handed out to the needy steerage survivors of the Titanic as they disembarked.

With the early arrivals at the pier were the relatives of Frederick White, who was not reported among the survivors, though Mrs. White was; Harry Mock, who came to look for a brother and sister; and Vincent Astor, who arrived in a limousine with William A. Dobbyn, Colonel Astor's secretary, and two doctors. The limousine was kept waiting outside to take Mrs. Astor to the Astor home on Fifth Avenue.

EIGHT LIMOUSINE CARS

The Waldorf-Astoria had sent over eight limousine car to convey to the hotel these survivors:

Mrs. Mark Fortune and three daughters, Mrs. Lucien P. Smith, Mrs. J. Stewart White, Mrs. Thornton Davidson, Mrs. George C. Douglass, Mrs. George D. Widener and maid, Mrs. George Wick, Miss Bonnell, Miss E. Ryerson, Mrs. Susan P. Ryerson, Mrs. Arthur Ryerson, Miss Mary Wick, the Misses Howell, Mrs. John P. Snyder and Mr. and Mrs. D. H. Bishop.

THIRTY-FIVE AMBULANCES AT THE PIER

At one time there were thirty-five ambulances drawn up outside the Cunard pier. Every hospital in Manhattan, Brooklyn and the Bronx was represented. Several of the ambulances came from as far north as the Lebanon Hospital, in the Bronx, and the Brooklyn Hospital, in Brooklyn.

Accompanying them were seventy internes and surgeons from the staffs of the hospitals, and more than 125 male and female nurses.

St. Vincent's sent the greatest number of ambulances, at one time, eight of them from this hospital being in line at the pier.

Miss Eva Booth, direct head of the Salvation Army, was at the pier, accompanied by Miss Elizabeth Nye and a corps of her officers, ready to aid as much as possible. The Sheltering Society and various other similar organizations also were represented, all ready to take care of those who needed them.

An officer of the Sixty-ninth Regiment, N. G. N. Y., offered the White Star Line officials the use of the regiment's armory for any of the survivors.

Mrs. Thomas Hughes, Mrs. August Belmont and Mgrs. Lavelle and McMahon, of St. Patrick's Cathedral, together with a score of black-robed Sisters of Charity, representing the Association of Catholic Churches, were on the pier long before the *Carpathia* was made fast, and worked industriously in aiding the injured and ill.

The Rev. Dr. William Carter, pastor of the Madison Avenue Reformed Church, was one of those at the pier with a private ambulance awaiting Miss Sylvia Caldwell, one of the survivors, who is known in church circles as a mission worker in foreign fields.

FREE RAILROAD TRANSPORTATION

The Pennsylvania Railroad sent representatives to the pier, who said that the railroad had a special train of nine cars in which it would carry free any passenger who wanted to go immediately to Philadelphia or points west. The Pennsylvania also had eight taxicabs at the pier for conveyance of the rescued to the Pennsylvania Station, in Thirty-third Street.

Among those who later arrived at the pier before the *Carpathia* docked were P. A. B. Widener, of Philadelphia, two women relatives of J. B. Thayer, William Harris, Jr., the theatrical man, who was accompanied by Dr. Dinkelspiel, and Henry Arthur Jones, the playwright.

RELATIVES OF SAVED AND LOST

Commander Booth, of the Salvation Army, was there especially to meet Mrs. Elizabeth Nye and Mrs. Rogers Abbott, both *Titanic* survivors. Mrs. Abbott's two sons were supposed to be among the lost. Miss Booth had received a cablegram from London saying that other Salvation Army people were on the *Titanic*. She was eager to get news of them.

Also on the pier was Major Blanton, U. S. A., stationed at Washington, who was waiting for tidings of Major Butt, supposedly at the instance of President Taft.

Senator William A. Clark and Mrs. Clark were also in the company. Dr. John R. MacKenty was waiting for Mr. and Mrs. Henry S. Harper. Ferdinand W. Roebling and Carl G. Roebling, cousins of Washington A. Roebling, Jr., whose name is among the list of dead, went to the pier to see what they could learn of his fate.

J. P. Morgan, Jr., arrived at the pier about half an hour before the *Carpathia* docked. He said he had many friends on the *Titanic* and was eagerly awaiting news of all of them.

Fire Commissioner Johnson was there with John Peel, of Atlanta, Ga., a brother of Mrs. Jacques Futrelle. Mrs. Futrelle has a son twelve years old in Atlanta, and a daughter Virginia, who has been in school in the North and is at present with friends in this city, ignorant of her father's death.

A MAN IN HYSTERICS

There was one man in that sad waiting company who startled those near him about 9 o'clock by dancing across the pier and back. He seemed to be laughing, but when he was stopped it was found that he was sobbing. He said that he had a relative on the *Titanic* and had lost control of his nerves.

H. H. Brunt, of Chicago, was at the gangplank waiting for A. Saalfeld, head of the wholesale drug firm of Sparks, White &

Co., of London, who was coming to this country on the *Titanic* on a business trip and whose life was saved.

WAITING FOR *CARPATHIA*

During the afternoon and evening tugboats, motor boats and even sailing craft, had been waiting off the Ambrose Light for the appearance of the *Carpathia*.

Some of the waiting craft contained friends and anxious relatives of the survivors and those reported as missing.

The sea was rough and choppy, and a strong east wind was blowing. There was a light fog, so that it was possible to see at a distance of only a few hundred yards. This lifted later in the evening.

First to discover the incoming liner with her pitiful cargo was one of the tugboats. From out of the mist there loomed far out at sea the incoming steamer.

RESCUE BOAT SIGHTED

"Liner ahead!" cried the lookout on the tug to the captain.

"She must be the *Carpathia*," said the captain, and then he turned the nose of his boat toward the spot on the horizon.

Then the huge black-hull and one smokestack could be distinguished.

"It's the *Carpathia*," said the captain. "I can tell her by the stack."

The announcement sent a thrill through those who heard it. Here, at the gate of New York, was a ship whose record for bravery and heroic work would be a familiar name in history.

CHAPTER XII

The Tragic Home-Coming

THE *CARPATHIA* REACHES NEW YORK—AN INTENSE AND
DRAMATIC MOMENT—HYSTERICAL REUNIONS AND CRUSHING
DISAPPOINTMENTS AT THE DOCK—CARING FOR THE SUFFERERS—FINAL
REALIZATION THAT ALL HOPE FOR OTHERS IS FUTILE—
LIST OF SURVIVORS—ROLL OF THE DEAD

It was a solemn moment when the *Carpathia* heaved in sight.
There she rested on the water, a blur of black—huge, mysteri-
ous, awe-inspiring—and yet withal a thing to send thrills of pity
and then of admiration through the beholder.

It was a few minutes after seven o'clock when she arrived at
the entrance to Ambrose Channel. She was coming fast, steam-
ing at better than fifteen knots an hour, and she was sighted long
before she was expected. Except for the usual side and masthead
lights she was almost dark, only the upper cabins showing a glimmer here and there.

Then began a period of waiting, the suspense of which proved
almost too much for the hundreds gathered there to greet friends
and relatives or to learn with certainty at last that those for
whom they watched would never come ashore.

There was almost complete silence on the pier. Doctors and
nurses, members of the Women's Relief Committee, city and
government officials, as well as officials of the line, moved ner-
vously about.

Seated where they had been assigned beneath the big customs
letters corresponding to the initials of the names of the survivors
they came to meet, sat the mass of 2,000 on the pier.

Women wept, but they wept quietly, not hysterically, and the sound of the sobs made many times less noise than the hum and bustle which is usual on the pier among those awaiting an incoming liner.

Slowly and majestically the ship slid through the water, still bearing the details of that secret of what happened and who perished when the *Titanic* met her fate.

Convoying the *Carpathia* was a fleet of tugs bearing men and women anxious to learn the latest news. The *Cunarder* had been as silent for days as though it, too, were a ship of the dead. A list of survivors had been given out from its wireless station and that was all. Even the approximate time of its arrival had been kept a secret.

NEARING PORT

There was no response to the hail from one tug, and as others closed in, the steamship quickened her speed a little and left them behind as she swung up the channel.

There was an exploding of flashlights from some of the tugs, answered seemingly by sharp stabs of lightning in the northwest that served to accentuate the silence and absence of light aboard the rescue ship. Five or six persons, apparently members of the crew or the ship's officers, were seen along the rail; but otherwise the boat appeared to be deserted.

Off quarantine the *Carpathia* slowed down and, hailing the immigration inspection boat, asked if the health officer wished to board. She was told that he did, and came to a stop while Dr. O'Connell and two assistants climbed on board. Again the newspaper men asked for some word of the catastrophe to the *Titanic*, but there was no answer, and the *Carpathia* continued toward her pier.

As she passed the revenue cutter *Mohawk* and the derelict destroyer *Seneca* anchored off Tompkinsville the wireless on the Government vessels was seen to flash, but there was no answering spark from the *Carpathia*. Entering the North River she laid her course close to the New Jersey side in order to have room to swing into her pier.

By this time the rails were lined with men and women. They were very silent. There were a few requests for news from those on board and a few answers to questions shouted from the tugs.

The liner began to slacken her speed, and the tugboat soon was alongside. Up above the inky blackness of the hull figures could be made out, leaning over the port railing, as though peering eagerly at the little craft which was bearing down on the *Carpathia*.

Some of them, perhaps, had passed through that inferno of the deep sea which sprang up to destroy the mightiest steamship afloat.

"*Carpathia*, ahoy!" was shouted through a megaphone.

There was an interval of a few seconds, and then, "Aye, aye," came the reply.

"Is there any assistance that can be rendered?" was the next question.

"Thank you, no," was the answer in a tone that carried emotion with it. Meantime the tugboat was getting nearer and nearer to the *Carpathia*, and soon the faces of those leaning over the railing could be distinguished.

TALK WITH SURVIVORS

More faces appeared, and still more.

A woman who called to a man on the tugboat was asked, "Are you one the *Titanic* survivors?"

"Yes," said the voice, hesitatingly.

"Do you need help?"

"No," after a pause.

"If there is anything you want done it will be attended to."

"Thank you. I have been informed that my relatives will meet me at the pier."

"Is it true that some of the life-boats sank with the *Titanic?*"

"Yes. There was some trouble in manning them. They were not far enough away from her."

All of this questioning and receiving replies was carried on with the greatest difficulty. The pounding of the liner's engines, the washing of the sea, the tugboat's engines, made it hard to understand the woman's replies.

ALL CARED FOR ON BOARD

"Were the women properly cared for after the crash?" she was asked.

"Oh, yes," came the shrill reply. "The men were brave—very brave." Here her voice broke and she turned and left the railing, to reappear a few moments later and cry:

"Please report me as saved."

"What name?" was asked. She shouted a name that could not be understood, and, apparently believing that it had been, turned away again and disappeared.

"Nearly all of us are very ill," cried another woman. Here several other tugboats appeared, and those standing at the railing were besieged with questions.

"Did the crash come without warning?" a voice on one of the smaller boats megaphoned.

"Yes," a woman answered. "Most of us had retired. We saved a few of our belongings."

"How long did it take the boat to sink?" asked the voice.

TITANIC CREW HEROES

"Not long," came the reply. "The crew and the men were very brave. Oh, it is dreadful—dreadful to think of!"

"Is Mr. John Jacob Astor on board?"

"No."

"Did he remain on the *Titanic* after the collision?"

"I do not know."

Questions of this kind were showered at the few survivors who stood at the railing, but they seemed too confused to answer them intelligibly, and after replying evasively to some they would disappear.

RUSHES ON TO DOCK

"Are you going to anchor for the night?" Captain Rostron was asked by megaphone as his boat approached Ambrose Light. It was then raining heavily.

"No," came the reply. "I am going into port. There are sick people on board."

"We tried to learn when she would dock," said Dr. Walter Kennedy, head of the big ambulance corps on the mist-shrouded pier, "and we were told it would not be before midnight and that most probably it would not be before dawn to-morrow. The childish deception that has been practiced for days by the people who are responsible for the *Titanic* has been carried up to the very moment of the landing of the survivors."

She proceeded past the Cunard pier, where 2,000 persons were waiting her, and steamed to a spot opposite the White Star piers at Twenty-first Street.

The ports in the big inclosed pier of the Cunard Line were opened, and through them the waiting hundreds, almost frantic with anxiety over what the *Carpathia* might reveal, watched her as with nerve-destroying leisure she swung about in the river, dropping over the life-boats of the *Titanic* that they might be taken to the piers of the White Star Line.

THE *TITANIC* LIFE-BOATS

It was dark in the river, but the lowering away of the life-boats could be seen from the *Carpathia*'s pier, and a deep sigh arose from the multitude there as they caught this first glance of anything associated with the *Titanic*.

Then the *Carpathia* started for her own pier. As she approached it the ports on the north side of pier 54 were closed that the *Carpathia* might land there, but through the two left open to accommodate the forward and after gangplanks of the big liner the watchers could see her looming larger and larger in the darkness till finally she was directly alongside the pier.

As the boats were towed away the picture taking and shouting of questions began again. John Badenoch, a buyer for Macy & Co., called down to a representative of the firm that neither Mr. nor Mrs. Isidor Straus were among the rescued on board the *Carpathia*. An officer of the *Carpathia* called down that 710 of the *Titanic*'s passengers were on board, but refused to reply to other questions.

The heavy hawsers were made fast without the customary shouting of ship's officers and pier hands. From the crowd on the pier came a long, shuddering murmur. In it were blended sighs and hundreds of whispers. The burden of it all was: "Here they come."

ANXIOUS MEN AND WOMEN

About each gangplank a portable fence had been put in place, marking off some fifty feet of the pier, within which stood one hundred or more customs officials. Next to the fence, crowded close against it, were anxious men and women, their gaze strained for a glance of the first from the ship, their mouths opened to draw their breaths in spasmodic, quivering gasps, their very bodies shaking with suppressed excitement, excitement which only the suspense itself was keeping in subjection.

These were the husbands and wives, children, parents, sweethearts and friends of those who had sailed upon the *Titanic* on its maiden voyage.

They pressed to the head of the pier, marking the boats of the wrecked ship as they dangled at the side of the *Carpathia* and were revealed in the sudden flashes of the photographers upon the tugs. They spoke in whispers, each group intent upon its own sad business. Newspaper writers, with pier passes showing in their hat bands, were everywhere.

A sailor hurried outside the fence and disappeared, apparently on a mission for his company. There was a deep-drawn sigh as he walked away, shaking his head toward those who peered eagerly at him. Then came a man and woman of the *Carpathia*'s own passengers, as their orderly dress showed them to be.

Again a sigh like a sob swept over the crowd, and again they turned back to the canopied gangplank.

THE FIRST SURVIVORS

Several minutes passed and then out of the first cabin gangway, tunneled by a somber awning, streamed the first survivors. A young woman, hatless, her light brown hair disordered and the leaden weight of crushing sorrow heavy upon eyes and sensitive mouth, was in the van. She stopped, perplexed, almost ready to drop with terror and exhaustion, and was caught by a customs official.

"A survivor?" he questioned rapidly, and a nod of the head answering him, he demanded:

"Your name."

The answer given, he started to lead her toward that section of the pier where her friends would be waiting.

When she stepped from the gangplank there was quiet on the pier. The answers of the woman could almost be heard by those fifty feet away, but as she staggered, rather than walked, toward the waiting throng outside the fence, a low wailing sound arose from the crowd.

"Dorothy, Dorothy!" cried a man from the number. He broke through the double line of customs inspectors as though it was composed of wooden toys and caught the woman to his breast. She opened her lips inarticulately, weakly raised her arms and would have pitched forward upon her face had she not been supported. Her fair head fell weakly to one side as the man picked her up in his arms, and, with tears streaming down his face, stalked down the long avenue of the pier and down the long stairway to a waiting taxicab.

The wailing of the crowd—its cadences, wild and weird—grew steadily louder and louder till they culminated in a mighty shriek, which swept the whole big pier as though at the direction of some master hand.

RUMORS AFLOAT

The arrival of the *Carpathia* was the signal for the most sensational rumors to circulate through the crowd on the pier.

First, Mrs. John Jacob Astor was reported to have died at 8:06 o'clock, when the *Carpathia* was on her way up the harbor.

Captain Smith and the first engineer were reported to have shot themselves when they found that the *Titanic* was doomed to sink. Afterward it was learned that Captain Smith and the engineer went down with their ship in perfect courage and coolness.

Major Archibald Butt, President Taft's military aide, was said to have entered into an agreement with George D. Widener, Colonel John Jacob Astor and Isidor Straus to kill them first and then shoot himself before the boat sank. It was said that this agreement had been carried out. Later it was shown that, like many other men on the ship, they had gone down without the exhibition of a sign of fear.

MRS. CORNELL SAFE

Magistrate Cornell's wife and her two sisters were among the first to leave the ship. They were met at the first cabin pier entrance by Magistrate Cornell and a party of friends. None of the three women had hats. One of those who met them was Magistrate Cornell's son. One of Mrs. Cornell's sisters was overheard to remark that "it would be a dreadful thing when the ship began really to unload."

The three women appeared to be in a very nervous state. Their hair was more or less dishevelled. They were apparently fully dressed save for their hats. Clothing had been supplied them in their need and everything had been done to make them comfortable. One of the party said that the collision occurred at 9:45.

Following closely the Cornell party was H. J. Allison, of Montreal, who came to meet his family. One of the party, who was weeping bitterly as he left the pier, explained that the only one of the family that was rescued was the young brother.

MRS. ASTOR APPEARED

In a few minutes young Mrs. Astor with her maid appeared. She came down the gangplank unassisted. She was wearing a white sweater. Vincent Astor and William Dobbyn, Colonel Astor's secretary, greeted her and hurried her to a waiting limousine which contained clothing and other necessaries of which it was thought she might be in need. The young woman was white-faced and silent. Nobody cared to intrude upon her thoughts. Her stepson said little to her. He did not feel like questioning her at such a time, he said.

LAST SEEN OF COLONEL ASTOR

Walter M. Clark, a nephew of the senator, said that he had seen Colonel Astor put his wife in a boat, after assuring her that he would soon follow her in another. Mr. Clark and others said that Colonel and Mrs. Astor were in their suite when the crash came, and that they appeared quietly on deck a few minutes afterward.

Here and there among the passengers of the *Carpathia* and from the survivors of the *Titanic* the story was gleaned of the rescue. Nothing in life will ever approach the joy felt by the hundreds who were waiting in little boats on the spot where the *Titanic* foundered when the lights of the *Carpathia* were first distinguished. That was at 4 o'clock on Monday morning.

DR. FRAUENTHAL WELCOMED

Efforts were made to learn from Dr. Henry Frauenthal something about the details of how he was rescued. Just then, or as he was leaving the pier, beaming with evident delight, he was surrounded by a big crowd of his friends.

"There's Harry! There he is!" they yelled and made a rush for him.

All the doctor's face that wasn't covered with red beard was aglow with smiles as his friends hugged him and slapped him on the back. They rushed him off bodily through the crowd and he too was whirled home.

A SAD STORY

How others followed—how heartrending stories of partings and of thrilling rescues were poured out in an amazing stream—this has all been told over and over again in the news that for days amazed, saddened and angered the entire world. It is the story of a disaster that nations, it is hoped, will make impossible in the years to come.

In the stream of survivors were a peer of the realm, Sir Cosmo Duff Gordon, and his secretary, side by side with plain Jack Jones, of Birmingham, able seaman, millionaires and paupers, women with bags of jewels and others with nightgowns their only property.

MORE THAN SEVENTY WIDOWS

More than seventy widows were in the weeping company. The only large family that was saved in its entirety was that of the Carters, of Philadelphia. Contrasting with this remarkable salvage of wealthy Pennsylvanians was the sleeping eleven-months-old baby of the Allisons, whose father, mother and sister went down to death after it and its nurse had been placed in a life-boat.

Millionaire and pauper, titled grandee and weeping immi-grant, Ismay, the head of the White Star Company, and Jack Jones from the stoke hole were surrounded instantly. Some would gladly have escaped observation. Every man among the survivors acted as though it were first necessary to explain how he came to be in a life-boat. Some of the stories smacked of Munchausen. Others were as plain and unvarnished as a pike staff. Those that were most sincere and trustworthy had to be fairly pulled from those who gave their sad testimony.

Far into the night the recitals were made. They were told in the rooms of hotels, in the wards of hospitals and upon trains that sped toward saddened homes. It was a symposium of horror and heroism, the like of which has not been known in the civi-lized world since man established his dominion over the sea.

STEERAGE PASSENGERS

The two hundred and more steerage passengers did not leave the ship until 11 o'clock. They were in a sad condition. The women were without wraps and the few men there were wore very little clothing. A poor Syrian woman who said she was Mrs. Habush, bound for Youngstown, Ohio, carried in her arms a six-year-old baby girl. This woman had lost her husband and three brothers. "I lost four of my men folks," she cried.

TWO LITTLE BOYS

Among the survivors who elicited a large measure of sympathy were two little French boys who were dropped, almost naked, from the deck of the sinking *Titanic* into a life-boat. From what place in France did they come and to what place in the New World were they bound? There was not one iota of information to be had as to the identity of the waifs of the deep, the orphans of the *Titanic.*

The two baby boys, two and four years old, respectively, were in the charge of Miss Margaret Hays, who is a fluent speaker of French, and she had tried vainly to get from the lisping lips of the two little ones some information that would lead to the finding of their relatives.

Miss Hays, also a survivor of the *Titanic,* took charge of the almost naked waifs on the *Carpathia.* She became warmly attached to the two boys, who unconcernedly played about, not understanding the great tragedy that had come into their lives.

The two little curly-heads did not understand it all. Had not their pretty nineteen-year-old foster mother provided them with pretty suits and little white shoes and playthings a-plenty? Then, too, Miss Hays had a Pom dog that she brought with her from Paris and which she carried in her arms when she left the *Titanic* and held to her bosom through the long night in the life-boat, and to which the children became warmly attached. All three became aliens on an alien shore.

Miss Hays, unable to learn the names of the little fellows, had dubbed the older Louis and the younger "Lump." "Lump" was all that his name implies, for he weighed almost as much as his brother. They were dark-eyed and brown curly-haired children, who knew how to smile as only French children can.

On the fateful night of the *Titanic* disaster and just as the last boats were pulling away with their human freight, a man rushed to the rail holding the babes under his arms. He cried to the passengers in one of the boats and held the children aloft. Three or four sailors and passengers held up their arms. The father dropped the older boy. He was safely caught. Then he dropped the little fellow and saw him folded in the arms of a sailor. Then the boat pulled away.

The last seen of the father, whose last living act was to save his babes, he was waving his hand in a final parting. Then the *Titanic* plunged to the ocean's bed.

BABY TRAVERS

Still more pitiable in one way was the lot of the baby survivor, eleven-months-old Travers Allison, the only member of a family of four to survive the wreck. His father, H. J. Allison, and mother and Lorraine, a child of three, were victims of the catastrophe. Baby Travers, in the excitement following the crash, was separated from the rest of the family just before the *Titanic* went down. With the party were two nurses and a maid.

Major Arthur Peuchen, of Montreal, one of the survivors, standing near the little fellow, who, swathed in blankets, lay blinking at his nurse, described the death of Mrs. Allison. She had gone to the deck without her husband, and, frantically seeking him, was directed by an officer to the other side of the ship.

She failed to find Mr. Allison and was quickly hustled into one of the collapsible life-boats, and when last seen by Major Peuchen she was toppling out of the half-swamped boat. J. W. Allison, a cousin of H. J. Allison, was at the pier to care for Baby Travers and his nurse. They were taken to the Manhattan Hotel.

Describing the details of the perishing of the Allison family, the rescued nurse said they were all in bed when the *Titanic* hit the berg.

"We did not get up immediately," said she, "for we had not thought of danger. Later we were told to get up, and I hurriedly dressed the baby. We hastened up on deck, and confusion was all about. With other women and children we clambered to the life-boats, just as a matter of precaution, believing that there was no immediate danger. In about an hour there was an explosion and the ship appeared to fall apart. We were in the life-boat about six hours before we were picked up."

THE RYERSON FAMILY

Probably few deaths have caused more tears than Arthur Ryerson's, in view of the sad circumstances which called him home

from a lengthy tour in Europe. Mr. Ryerson's eldest son, Arthur
Larned Ryerson, a Yale student, was killed in an automobile accident Easter Monday, 1912.

A cablegram announcing the death plunged the Ryerson family into mourning and they boarded the first steamship for this
country. It happened to be the *Titanic*, and the death note came
near being the cause of the blotting out of the entire family.

The children who accompanied them were Miss Susan P. Ryerson, Miss Emily B. Ryerson and John Ryerson. The latter is 12
years old.

They did not know their son intended to spend the Easter hol-
idays at their home at Haverford, Pa. until they were informed
of his death. John Lewis Hoffman, also of Haverford and a student of Yale, was killed with young Ryerson.

The two were hurrying to Philadelphia to escort a fellow-
student to his train. In turning out of the road to pass a cart the
motor car crashed into a pole in front of the entrance to the estate of Mrs. B. Frank Clyde. The college men were picked up unconscious and died in the Bryn Mawr Hospital.

G. Heide Norris of Philadelphia, who went to New York to
meet the surviving members of the Ryerson family, told of a
happy incident at the last moment as the *Carpathia* swung close
to the pier. There had been no positive information that young
"Jack" Ryerson was among those saved—indeed, it was feared
that he had gone down with the *Titanic*, like his father, Arthur
Ryerson.

Mr. Norris spoke of the feeling of relief that came over him
as, watching from the pier, he saw "Jack" Ryerson come from a
cabin and stand at the railing. The name of the boy was missing
from some of the lists and for two days it was reported that he
had perished.

CAPTAIN ROSTRON'S REPORT

Less than 24 hours after the Cunard Line steamship *Carpathia*
came in as a rescue ship with survivors of the *Titanic* disaster,

she sailed again for the Mediterranean cruise which she originally started upon last week. Just before the liner sailed, H. S. Bride, the second Marconi wireless operator of the *Titanic*, who had both of his legs crushed on a life-boat, was carried off on the shoulders of the ship's officers to St. Vincent's Hospital.

Captain A. H. Rostron, of the *Carpathia*, addressed an official report, giving his account of the *Carpathia*'s rescue work, to the general manager of the Cunard Line, Liverpool. The report read: "I beg to report that at 12:35 a.m. Monday 18th inst. I was informed of urgent message from *Titanic* with her position. I immediately ordered ship turned around and put her in course for that position, we being then 58 miles S. 52—E. 'T' from her; had heads of all departments called and issued what I considered the necessary orders, to be in preparation for any emergency.

"At 2:40 a.m. saw flare half a point on port bow. Taking this for granted to be ship, shortly after we sighted our first iceberg. I had previously had lookouts doubled, knowing that Titanic had struck ice, and so took every care and precaution. We soon found ourselves in a field of bergs, and had to alter course several times to clear bergs; weather fine, and clear, light air on sea, beautifully clear night, though dark.

"We stopped at 4 a.m., thus doing distance in three hours and a half, picking up the first boat at 4:10 a.m.; boat in charge of officer, and he reported that *Titanic* had foundered. At 8:30 a.m. last boat picked up. All survivors aboard and all boats accounted for, viz., fifteen life-boats, one boat abandoned, two Berthon boats alongside (saw one floating upwards among wreckage), and according to second officer (senior officer saved) one Berthon boat had not been launched, it having got jammed, making sixteen life-boats and four Berthon boats accounted for. By the time we had cleared first boat it was breaking day, and I could see all within area of four miles. We also saw that we were surrounded by icebergs, large and small, huge field of drift ice with large and small bergs in it, the ice field trending from N. W. round W. and S. to S. E., as far as we could see either way.

"At 8 a.m. the Leyland S. S. *California* came up. I gave him the principal news and asked him to search and I would proceed to New York; at 8:50 proceeded full speed while researching over vicinity of disaster, and while we were getting people aboard I gave orders to get spare hands along and swing in all our boats, disconnect the fall and hoist up as many *Titanic* boats as possible in our davits; also get some on forecastle heads by derricks. We got thirteen life-boats, six on forward deck and seven in davits. After getting all survivors aboard and while searching I got a clergyman to offer a short prayer of thankfulness for those saved, and also a short burial service for their loss, in saloon.

"Before deciding definitely where to make for, I conferred with Mr. Ismay, and as he told me to do what I thought best, I informed him, I considered New York best. I knew we should require clean blankets, provisions and clean linen, even if we went to the Azores, as most of the passengers saved were women and children, and they hysterical, not knowing what medical attention they might require. I thought it best to go to New York. I also thought it would be better for Mr. Ismay to go to New York or England as soon as possible, and knowing I should be out of wireless communication very soon if I proceeded to Azores, it left Halifax, Boston and New York, so I chose the latter.

"Again, the passengers were all hysterical about ice, and I pointed out to Mr. Ismay the possibilities of seeing ice if I went to Halifax. Then I knew it would be best to keep in touch with land stations as best I could. We have experienced great difficulty in transmitting news, also names of survivors. Our wireless is very poor, and again we have had so many interruptions from other ships and also messages from shore (principally press, which we ignored). I gave instructions to send first all official messages, then names of passengers, then survivors' private messages. We had haze early Tuesday morning for several hours; again more or less all Wednesday from 5:30 a.m. to 5 p.m.; strong south-southwesterly winds and clear weather Thursday, with moderate rough sea.

"I am pleased to say that all survivors have been very plucky.

The majority of women, first, second and third class, lost their husbands, and, considering all, have been wonderfully well. Tuesday our doctor reported all survivors physically well. Our first class passengers have behaved splendidly, given up their cabins voluntarily and supplied the ladies with clothes, etc. We all turned out of our cabins and gave them to survivors— saloon, smoking room, library, etc., also being used for sleeping accommodation. Our crew, also turned out to let the crew of the *Titanic* take their quarters. I am pleased to state that owing to preparations made for the comfort of survivors, none were the worse for exposure, etc. I bet to specially mention how willing and cheerful the whole of the ship's company behaved, receiving the highest praise from everybody. And I can assure you I am very proud to have such a company under my command.

"A. H. ROSTRON"

The following list of the survivors and dead contains the latest revisions and corrections of the White Star Line officials, and was furnished by them exclusively for this book.

LIST OF SURVIVORS

FIRST CABIN

Anderson, Harry.
Antoinette, Miss.
Appieranelt, Miss.
Appleton. Mrs. E. D.
Abbott, Mrs. Rose.
Allison, Master, and nurse.
Andrews, Miss Cornelia I.
Allen, Miss. E. W.
Astor, Mrs. John Jacob, and maid.
Aubeart, Mme. N., and maid.
Barratt, Karl B.
Besette, Miss.
Barkworth, A. H.
Bucknell, Mrs. W.
Bowerman, Miss E.
Brown, Mrs. J. J.
Burns, Miss C. M.
Bishop, Mr. and Mrs. D. H.
Blank, H.

Bessina, Miss A.
Baxter, Mrs. James.
Brayton, George.
Bonnell, Miss Lily.
Brown, Mrs. J. M.
Bowen, Miss G. C.
Beckwith, Mr. and Mrs. R. L.
Bisley, Mr. and Mrs.
Bonnell, Miss C.
Cassebeer, Mrs. H. A.
Cardeza, Mrs. J. W.
Candell, Mrs. Churchill.
Case, Howard B.
Camarion, Kenard.
Casseboro, Miss D. D.
Clark, Mrs. W. M.
Chibinace, Mrs. B. C.
Charlton, W. M.
Crosby, Mrs. E. G.

Carter, Miss Lucille.
Calderhead, E. P.
Chandanson, Miss Victorine.
Cavendish, Mrs. Turrell, and maid.
Chafee, Mrs. H. I.
Cardeza, Mr. Thomas.
Cummings, Mrs. J.
Chevre, Paul.
Cherry, Miss Gladys.
Chambers, Mr. and Mrs. N. C.
Carter, Mr. and Mrs. W. E.
Carter, Master William.
Compton, Mrs. A. T.
Compton, Miss S. R.
Crosby, Mrs. E. G.
Crosby, Miss Harriet.
Cornell, Mrs. R. C.
Chibnall, Mrs. E.
Douglas, Mrs. Fred.
De Villiers, Mme.
Daniel, Miss Sarah.
Daniel, Robert W.
Davidson, Mr. and Mrs. Thornton, and family.
Douglas, Mrs. Walter, and maid.
Dodge, Miss Sarah.
Dodge, Mrs. Washington, and son.
Dick, Mr. and Mrs. A. A.
Daniell, H. Haren.
Drachensted, A.
Daly, Peter D.
Endres, Miss Caroline.
Ellis, Miss.
Earnshaw, Mrs. Boulton.
Eustis, Miss E.
Emmock, Philip E.
Flagenheim, Mrs. Antoinette.
Franicatelli, Miss.
Flynn, J. I.
Fortune, Miss Alice.
Fortune, Miss Ethel.
Fortune, Mrs. Mark.
Fortune, Miss Mabel.
Frauenthal, Dr. and Mrs. H. W.
Frauenthal, Mr. and Mrs. T. G.
Frolicher, Miss Margaret.
Frolicher, Max and Mrs.
Frolicher, Miss N.
Futrelle, Mrs. Jacques.
Gracie, Colonel Archibald.
Graham, Mr. and Mrs. William.

Graham, Miss M.
Gordon, Sir Cosmo Duff.
Gordon, Lady.
Gibson, Miss Dorothy.
Goldenberg, Mr. and Mrs. Samuel.
Goldenberg, Miss Ella.
Greenfield, Mrs. L. P.
Greenfield, G. B.
Greenfield, William.
Gibson, Mrs. Leonard.
Googht, James.
Haven, Mr. Henry B.
Harris, Mrs. H. B.
Holverson, Mrs. Alex.
Hogeboom, Mrs. J. C.
Hawksford, W. J.
Harper, Henery, and man servant.
Harper, Mrs. H. S.
Hold, Miss J. A.
Hope, Nina.
Hoyt, Mr. and Mrs. Fred.
Horner, Henry R.
Harder, Mr. and Mrs. George.
Hays, Mrs. Charles M., and daughter.
Hippach, Miss Jean.
Hippach, Mrs. Ida S.
Ismay, J. Bruce.
Jenasco, Mrs. J.
Kimball, Mr. and Mrs. Ed. N.
Kennyman, F. A.
Kenchen, Miss Emile.
Longley, Miss G. F.
Leader, Mrs. A. F.
Leahy, Miss Nora.
Lavory, Miss Bertha.
Lines, Mrs. Ernest.
Lines, Miss Mary.
Lindstrom, Mrs. Singird.
Lesneur, Gustave, Jr.
Madill, Miss Georgette A.
Mahan, Mrs.
Melicard, Mme.
Menderson, Miss Letta.
Maimy, Miss Roberta.
Marvin, Mrs. D. W.
Marechell, Pierre.
Maroney, Mrs. R.
Meyer, Mrs. E. I.
Mock, Mr. P. E.
Middle, Mme. M. Olive.

Minahan, Miss Daisy.
Minahan, Mrs. W. E.
McGough, James.
Newell, Miss Alice.
Newell, Miss Madeline.
Newell, Washington.
Newson, Miss Helen.
O'Connell, Miss R.
Ostby, E. C.
Ostby, Miss Helen.
Omund, Fieunam.
Panhart, Miss Ninette.
Pears, Mrs. E.
Pomroy, Miss Ellen.
Potter, Mrs. Thomas, Jr.
Peuchen, Major Arthur.
Peercault, Miss A.
Ryerson, John.
Renago, Mrs. Mamam.
Ranelt, Miss Appie.
Rothschild, Mrs. Lord Martin.
Rosenbaum, Miss Edith.
Rheims, Mr. and Mrs George.
Rosible, Miss H.
Rothes, Countess.
Robert, Mrs. Edna.
Rolmane, C.
Ryerson, Miss Susan P.
Ryerson, Miss Emily.
Ryerson, Mrs. Arthur, and maid.
Stone, Mrs. George M.
Skeller, Mrs. William.
Segesser, Miss Emma.
Seward, Fred. K.
Shutter, Miss.
Sloper, William T.
Swift, Mrs. F. Joel.
Schabert, Mrs. Paul.
Sheddel, Robert Douglass.
Snyder, Mr. and Mrs. John.
Serepeca, Miss Augusta.
Silverthorn, R. Spencer.

Saalfeld, Adolf.
Stahelin, Max.
Simoinus, Alfonsius.
Smith, Mrs. Lucien P.
Stephenson, Mrs. Walter.
Solomon, Abraham.
Silvey, Mrs. William B.
Stenmel, Mr. and Mrs. Heleery.
Spencer, Mrs. W. A., and maid.
Slayter, Miss Hilda.
Spedden, Mr. and Mrs. F. O., and
    child.
Steffanson, H. B.
Straus, Mrs., maid of.
Schabert, Mrs. Emma.
Slinter, Mrs. E.
Simmons, A.
Taylor, Miss.
Tucker, Mrs., and maid.
Thayer, Mrs. J. B.
Thayer, J. B., Jr.
Taussig, Miss Ruth.
Taussig, Mrs. E.
Thor, Miss Ella.
Thorne, Mrs. G.
Taylor, Mr. and Mrs. E. Z.
Trout, Miss Jessie.
Tucker, Gilbert.
Woolner, Hugh.
Ward, Miss Anna.
Williams, Richard M., Jr.
Warren, Mrs. F.
Wilson, Miss Helen A.
Williard, Miss C.
Wick, Miss Mary.
Wick, Geo.
Widener, valet of.
Widener, Mrs. George D., and
    maid.
White, Mrs. J. Stuart.
Young, Miss Marie.

LIST OF SURVIVORS—SECOND CABIN

Abesson, Mrs. Hanna.
Abbott, Mrs. R.
Argenia, Mrs., and two children.
Angel, F.
Angle, William.
Baumthorpe, Mrs. L.

Balls, Mrs. Ada E.
Buss, Miss Kate.
Becker, Mrs. A. O., and three
    children.
Beane, Edward.
Beane, Mrs. Ethel.

Bryhl, Miss D.
Beesley, Mr. L.
Brown, Mr. T. W. S.
Brown, Miss E.
Brown, Mrs.
Benthan, Lillian W.
Bystron, Karolina.
Bright, Dagmar.
Bright, Daisy.
Clarke, Mrs. Ada.
Cameron, Miss. C.
Caldwell, Albert F.
Caldwell, Mrs. Sylvan.
Caldwell, Alden, infant.
Cristy, Mr. and Mrs.
Collyer, Mrs. Charlotte.
Collyer, Miss Marjorie.
Christy, Mrs. Alice.
Collet, Stuart.
Christa, Miss Ducia.
Charles, William.
Croft, Millie Mall.
Doling, Mrs. Elsie.
Drew, Mrs. Lulu.
Davis, Mrs. Agnes.
Davis, Miss Mary.
Davis, John M.
Duvan, Florentine.
Duvan, Miss A.
Davidson, Miss Mary.
Doling, Miss Ada.
Driscoll, Mrs. B.
Deystrom, Caroline.
Emcarmacion, Mrs. Rinaldo.
Faunthorpe, Mrs. Lizzie.
Formery, Miss Ellen.
Garside, Ethel.
Gerrecai, Mrs. Marcy.
Genovese, Angere.
Hart, Mrs. Esther.
Hart, Eva.
Harris, George.
Hewlett, Mrs. Mary.
Hebber, Miss S.
Hoffman, Lola.
Hoffman, Louis.
Harper, Nina.
Hold, Stephen.
Hold, Mrs. Anna.
Hosono, Masabumi.
Hocking, Mr. and Mrs. George

Hocking, Miss Nellie.
Herman, Mrs. Jane, 2 daughters
Healy, Nora.
Hanson, Jennie.
Hamatainen, W.
Hamatainen, Anna.
Harnlin, Anna, and child.
Ilett, Bertha.
Jackson, Mrs. Amy.
Juliet, Luwche.
Jerwan, Mary.
Juhon, Podro.
Jacobson, Mrs.
Keane, Miss Nora H.
Kelly, Mrs. F.
Kantar, Mrs. S.
Leitch, Jessie.
Laroche, Mrs., and
    Miss Simmone.
Laroche, Miss Louise.
Lehman, Bertha.
Lauch, Mrs. Alex.
Laniore, Amella.
Lystrom, Mrs. C.
Mellinger, Elizabeth.
Mellinger, child.
Marshall, Mrs. Kate.
Mallett, A.
Mallett, Mrs. and child.
Mange, Paula.
Mare, Mrs. Florence.
Mellor, W. J.
McDearmont, Miss Lela.
McGowan, Anna.
Nye, Elizabeth.
Nasser, Mrs. Delia.
Nussa, Mrs. A.
Oxenham, Percy J.
Phillips, Alice.
Pallas, Emilio.
Padro, Julian.
Prinsky, Rosa.
Portaluppi, Emilio.
Parsh, Mrs. L.
Plett, B.
Quick, Mrs. Jane.
Quick, Mrs. Vera W.
Quick, Miss Phyllis.
Reinardo, Miss E.
Ridsdale, Lucy.
Renouf, Mrs. Lily.

Rugg, Miss Emily.
Richards, M.
Rogers, Miss Selina.
Richards, Mrs. Emilia, two boys,
  and Mr. Richards, Jr.
Simpson, Miss.
Sincock, Miss Maude.
Sinkkonnen, Anna.
Smith, Miss Marion.
Silven, Lylle.
Trant, Mrs J.
Toomey, Miss. E.
Troutt, Miss E.
Troutt, Miss Cecelia.
Ware, Miss H.

Watter, Miss N.
Wilhelm, Chas.
Wat, Mrs. A., and two children.
Williams, Richard M., Jr.
Weisz, Mathilde.
Webber, Miss Susie.
Wright, Miss Marion.
Watt, Miss Bessie.
Watt, Miss Bertha.
West, Mrs. E. A.
West, Miss Constance.
West, Miss Barbara.
Wells, Addie.
Wells, Master.
Wells, Miss.

A list of surviving third cabin passengers and crew is omitted owing to the impossibility of obtaining the correct names of many.

ROLL OF THE DEAD

FIRST CABIN

Allison, H. J.
Allison, Mrs., and maid.
Allison, Miss.
Andrews, Thomas.
Artagaveytia, Mr. Ramon.
Astor, Col. J. J., and servant.
Anderson, Walker.
Beattie, T.
Brandeis, E.
Bucknell, Mrs. William, maid of.
Baumann, J.
Baxter, Mr. and Mrs. Quigg.
Bjornstrom, H.
Birnbaum, Jacob.
Blackwell, S. W.
Borebank, J. J.
Bowen, Miss.
Brady, John B.
Brewe, Arthur J.
Butt, Major A.
Clark, Walter M.
Clifford, George Q.
Colley, E. P.
Cardeza, T. D. M., servant of.
Cardeza, Mrs. J. W., maid of.

Carlson, Frank.
Corran, F. M.
Corran, J. P.
Chafee, Mr. H. I.
Chisholm, Robert.
Compton, A. T.
Crafton, John B.
Crosby, Edward G.
Cummings, John Bradley.
Dulles, William C.
Douglas, W. D.
Douglas, Master R., nurse of.
Evans, Miss E.
Fortune, Mark.
Foreman, B. L.
Fortune, Charles.
Franklin, T. P.
Futrelle, J.
Gee, Arthur.
Goldenberg, E. L.
Goldschmidt, G. B.
Giglio, Victor.
Guggenheim, Benjamin.
Hays, Charles M.
Hays, Mrs. Charles, maid of.

Head, Christopher.
Hilliard, H. H.
Hipkins, W. E.
Hogenheim, Mrs. A.
Harris, Henry B.
Harp, Mr. and Mrs. Charles M.
Harp, Miss Margaret, and maid.
Holverson, A. M.
Isham, Miss A. E.
Ismay, J. Bruce, servant of.
Julian, H. F.
Jones, C. C.
Kent, Edward A.
Kenyon, Mr. and Mrs. F. R.
Klaber, Herman.
Lamberth, Williams, F. F.
Lawrence, Arthur.
Long, Milton.
Lewy, E. G.
Loring, J. H.
Lingrey, Edward.
Maguire, J. E.
McCaffry, T.
McCaffry, T., Jr.
McCarthy, T.
Middleton, J. C.
Millet, Frank D.
Minahan, Dr.
Meyer, Edgar J.
Molson, H. M.
Moore, C., servant.
Natsch, Charles.
Newall, Miss T.
Nicholson, A. S.
Ovies, S.
Ornout, Alfred T.
Parr, M. H. W.
Pears, Mr. and Mrs. Thomas.
Penasco, Mr. and Mrs. Victor.
Partner, M. A.

Payne, V.
Pond, Florence, and maid.
Porter, Walter.
Puffer, C. C.
Reuchlin, J.
Robert, Mrs. E., maid of.
Roebling, Washington A., 2d.
Rood, Hugh R.
Roes, J. Hugo.
Rothes, Countess, maid of.
Rothschild, M.
Rowe, Arthur.
Ryerson, A.
Silvey, William B.
Spedden, Mrs. F. O., maid of.
Spencer, W. A.
Stead, W. T.
Stehli, Mr. and Mrs. Max Frolicher.
Stone, Mrs. George, maid of.
Straus, Mr. and Mrs. Isidor.
Sutton, Frederick.
Smart, John M.
Smith, Clinch.
Smith, R. W.
Smith, L. P.
Taussig, Emil.
Thayer, Mrs., maid of.
Thayer, John B.
Thorne, G.
Vanderhoof, Wyckoff.
Walker, W. A.
Warren, F. M.
White, Percival A.
White, Richard F.
Widener, G. D.
Widener, Harry.
Wood, Mr. and Mrs. Frank P.
Weir, J.
Williams, Duane.
Wright, George.

SECOND CABIN

Abelson, Samson.
Andrew, Frank.
Ashby, John.
Aldworth, C.
Andrew, Edgar.
Bracken, James H.
Brown, Mrs.
Banfield, Fred.

Bright, Narl.
Braily, bandsman.
Breicoux, bandsman.
Bailey, Percy.
Bainbridge, C. R.
Byles, The Rev. Thomas.
Beauchamp, H. J.
Berg, Miss E.

Benthan, I.
Bateman, Robert J.
Butler, Reginald.
Botsford, Hull.
Boweener, Solomon.
Berriman, William.
Clarke, Charles.
Clark, bandsman.
Corey, Mrs. C. P.
Carter, The Rev. Ernest.
Carter, Mrs.
Coleridge, Reginald.
Chapman, Charles.
Cunningham, Alfred.
Campbell, William.
Collyer, Harvey.
Corbett, Mrs. Irene.
Chapman, John H.
Chapman, Mrs. E.
Colander, Eric.
Cotterill, Harry.
Deacon, Percy.
Davis, Charles.
Dibben, William.
De Brito, Jose.
Denborny, H.
Drew, James.
Drew, Master M.
David, Master J. W.
Dounton, W. J.
Del Varlo, S.
Del Varlo, Mrs.
Enander, Ingvar.
Eitemiller, G. F.
Frost, A.
Fynnery, Mr.
Faunthorpe, H.
Fillbrook, C.
Funk, Annie.
Fahlstrom, A.
Fox, Stanley W.
Greenberg, S.
Giles, Ralph.
Gaskell, Alfred.
Gillespie, William.
Gilbert, William.
Gall, S.
Gill, John.
Giles, Edgar.
Giles, Fred.
Gale, Harry.

Gale, Phadruch.
Garvey, Lawrence.
Hickman, Leonard.
Hickman, Lewis.
Hume, bandsman.
Hickman, Stanley.
Hood, Ambrose.
Hodges, Henry P.
Hart, Benjamin.
Harris, Walter.
Harper, John.
Harbeck, W. H.
Hoffman, Mr.
Herman, Mrs. S.
Howard, B.
Howard, Mrs. E. T.
Hale, Reginald.
Hiltunen, M.
Hunt, George.
Jacobson, Mr.
Jacobson, Sydney.
Jeffery, Clifford.
Jeffery, Ernest.
Jenkin, Stephen.
Jarvis, John D.
Keane, Daniel.
Kirkland, Rev. C.
Karnes, Mrs. F. G.
Keynaldo, Miss.
Krillner, J. H.
Krins, bandsman.
Karines, Mrs.
Kantar, Selna.
Knight, R.
Lengam, John.
Levy, R. J.
Lahtiman, William.
Lauch, Charles.
Leyson, R. W. N.
Laroche, Joseph.
Lamb, J. J.
McKane, Peter.
Milling, Jacob.
Mantoila, Joseph.
Malachard, Noll.
Moraweck, Dr.
Mangiovacchi, E.
McCrae, Arthur G.
McCrie, James M.
McKane, Peter D.
Mudd, Thomas.

Mack, Mrs. Mary.
Marshall, Henry.
Mayberg, Frank H.
Meyer, August.
Myles, Thomas.
Mitchell, Henry.
Matthews, W. J.
Nessen, Israel.
Nicholls, Joseph C.
Norman, Robert D.
Otter, Richard.
Phillips, Robert.
Ponesell, Martin.
Pain, Dr. Alfred.
Parkes, Frank.
Pengelly, F.
Pernot, Rene.
Peruschitz, Rev.
Parker, Clifford.
Pulbaum, Frank.
Renouf, Peter H.
Rogers, Harry.
Reeves, David.
Slemen, R. J.
Sobey, Hayden.

Slatter, Miss H. M.
Stanton, Ward.
Sword, Hans K.
Stokes, Philip J.
Sharp, Percival.
Sedgwick, Mr. F. W.
Smith, Augustus.
Sweet, George.
Sjostedt, Ernst.
Taylor, bandsman.
Turpin, William J.
Turpin, Mrs. Dorothy.
Turner, John H.
Troupiansky, M.
Tirvan, Mrs. A.
Veale, James.
Watson, E.
Woodward, bandsman.
Ware, William J.
Weisz, Leopold.
Wheadon, Edward.
Ware, John J.
West, E. Arthur.
Wheeler, Edwin.
Werman, Samuel.

The total death list was 1,635. Third cabin passengers and crew are not included in the list here given owing to the impossibility of obtaining the exact names of many.

CHAPTER XXI

Searching for the Dead

SENDING OUT THE *MACKAY-BENNETT* AND *MINIA*—BREMEN
PASSENGERS SEE BODIES—IDENTIFYING BODIES—
CONFUSION IN NAMES—RECOVERIES

A few days after the disaster the cable steamer *Mackay-Bennett* was sent out by the White Star Line to cruise in the vicinity of the disaster and search for missing bodies.

Two wireless messages addressed to J. Bruce Ismay, president of the International Mercantile Marine Company, were received on April 21st at the offices of the White Star Line from the cable ship *Mackay-Bennett*, via Cape Race, one of which reported that the steamship *Rhein* had sighted bodies near the scene of the *Titanic* wreck. The first message, which was dated April 20th, read:

> "Steamer *Rhein* reports passing wreckage and bodies 42.1 north, 49.13 west, eight miles west of three big icebergs. Now making for that position. Expect to arrive 8 o'clock to-night.
>
> (Signed) "MACKAY-BENNETT."

The second message read:

> "Received further information from *Bremen* (presumably steamship *Bremen*) and arrived on ground at 8 o'clock p.m. Start on operation to-morrow. Have been considerably delayed on passage by dense fog.
>
> (Signed) "MACKAY-BENNETT."

After receiving these messages Mr. Ismay issued the following statement:

> "The cable ship *Mackay-Bennett* has been chartered by the White Star Line and ordered to proceed to the scene of the disaster and do all she could to recover the bodies and glean all information possible.
>
> "Every effort will be made to identify bodies recovered, and any news will be sent through immediately by wireless. In addition to any such message as these, the *Mackay-Bennett* will make a report of its activities each morning by wireless, and such reports will be made public at the offices of the White Star Line.
>
> "The cable ship has orders to remain on the scene of the wreck for at least a week, but should a large number of bodies be recovered before that time she will return to Halifax with them. The search for bodies will not be abandoned until not a vestige of hope remains for any more recoveries.
>
> "The *Mackay-Bennett* will not make any soundings, as they would not serve any useful purpose, because the depth where the *Titanic* sank is more than 2,000 fathoms."

On April 22d the first list of twenty-seven names of bodies recovered was made public. It contained that of Frederick Sutton, a well-known member of the Union League of Philadelphia. It did not contain the name of any other prominent man who perished, although it was thought that the name "George W. Widen" might refer to George D. Widener, son of P. A. B. Widener, of Philadelphia. The original passenger lists of the *Titanic* did not mention "Widen," which apparently established the identity of the body as that of Mr. Widener, who, together with his son, Harry, was lost.

The wireless message, after listing the names, concluded, "All preserved," presumably referring to the condition of the bodies.

A number of the names in the list did not check up with the *Titanic*'s passenger list, which led to the belief that a number of the bodies recovered were members of the *Titanic*'s crew.

MINIA SENT TO ASSIST

At noon, April 23d, there was posted on the bulletin in the White Star office this message from the *Mackay-Bennett* dated Sunday, April 21st:

> "Latitude, 41.58; longitude, 49.21. Heavy southwest swell has interfered with operations. Seventy-seven bodies recovered. All not embalmed will be buried at sea at 8 o'clock to-night with divine service. Can bring only embalmed bodies to port."

To Captain Lardner, master of the *Mackay-Bennett*, P. A. S. Franklin, vice-president of the White Star Line, sent an urgent message asking that the company be advised at once of all particulars concerning the bodies identified, and also given any information that might lead to the identification of others. He said it was very important that every effort be made to bring all of the bodies possible to port.

Mr. Franklin then directed A. G. Jones, the Halifax agent of the White Star Line, to charter the *Minia* and send her to the assistance of the *Mackay-Bennett*. Mr. Jones answered this telegram, and said that the *Minia* was ready to proceed to sea, but that a southeast gale, which generally brings fog, might delay her departure. She left for Halifax.

NAMES BADLY GARBLED

On April 24th no wireless message was received from the *Mackay-Bennett*, but the White Star Line officials and telegraphers familiar with the wireless alphabet were busy trying to reconcile some of the names received with those of persons who went down on the *Titanic*. That the body of William T. Stead, the English journalist and author, had been recovered by the *Mackay-Bennett*, but through a freakish error in wireless transmission the name of another was reported instead, was one of the theories advanced by persons familiar with the Morse code.

BREMEN SIGHTED MORE THAN A HUNDRED BODIES

When the German liner *Bremen* reached New York the account of its having sighted bodies of the *Titanic* victims was obtained.

From the bridge, officers of the ship saw more than a hundred bodies floating on the sea, a boat upside down, together with a number of small pieces of wood, steamer chairs and other wreckage. As the cable ship *Mackay-Bennett* was in sight, and having word that her mission was to look for bodies, no attempt was made by the *Bremen*'s crew to pick up the corpses.

In the vicinity was seen an iceberg which answered the description of the one the *Titanic* struck. Smaller bergs were sighted the same day, but at some distance from where the *Titanic* sank.

The officers of the *Bremen* did not care to talk about the tragic spectacle, but among the passengers several were found who gave accounts of the dismal panorama through which their ship steamed.

Mrs. Johanna Stunke, a first-cabin passenger, described the scene from the liner's rail.

"It was between 4 and 5 o'clock, Saturday, April 20th," she said, "when our ship sighted an iceberg off the bow to the starboard. As we drew nearer, and could make out small dots floating around in the sea, a feeling of awe and sadness crept over everyone on the ship.

"We passed within a hundred feet of the southernmost drift of the wreckage, and looking down over the rail we distinctly saw a number of bodies so clearly that we could make out what they were wearing and whether they were men or women.

"We saw one woman in her night dress, with a baby clasped closely to her breast. Several women passengers screamed and left the rail in a fainting condition. There was another woman, fully dressed, with her arms tight around the body of a shaggy dog.

"The bodies of three men in a group, all clinging to one steamship chair, floated near by, and just beyond them were a dozen bodies of men, all of them encased in life-preservers, clinging together as though in a last desperate struggle for life. We couldn't see, but imagined that under them was some bit of wreckage to which they all clung when the ship went down, and which didn't have buoyancy enough to support them.

"Those were the only bodies we passed near enough to distinguish, but we could see the white life-preservers of many more dotting the sea, all the way to the iceberg. The officers told us that was probably the berg hit by the *Titanic*, and that the bodies and ice had drifted along together."

Mrs. Stunke said a number of the passengers demanded that the *Bremen* stop and pick up the bodies, but the officers assured them that they had just received a wireless message saying the cable ship *Mackay-Bennett* was only two hours away from the spot, and was coming for that express purpose.

Other passengers corroborated Mrs. Stunke.

THE IDENTIFED DEAD

On April 25th the White Star Line officials issued a corrected list of the identified dead. While the corrected list cleared up two or more of the wireless confusions that caused so much speculation in the original list, there still remained a few names that so far as the record of the *Titanic* showed were not on board that ship when she foundered.

The new list, however, established the fact that the body of George D. Widener, of Philadelphia, was among those on the *Mackay-Bennett,* and two of the bodies were identified as those of men named Butt.

THE *MACKAY-BENNETT* RETURNS TO PORT

After completing her search the *Mackay-Bennett* steamed for Halifax, reaching that port on Tuesday, April 30th. With her flag at half mast, the death ship docked slowly. Her crew manned the rails with bared heads, and on the aft deck were stacked the caskets with the dead. The vessel carried on board 190 bodies, and announcement was made that 113 other bodies had been buried at sea.

Everybody picked up had been in a life-belt and there were no bullet holes in any. Among those brought to port were the bodies of two women.

THE *MINIA* GIVES UP THE SEARCH

When at last the *Minia* turned her bow toward shore only thirteen additional bodies had been recovered, making a total of 316 bodies found by the two ships.

Further search seemed futile. Not only had the two vessels gone thoroughly over as wide a field as might likely prove fruitful, but, in addition, the time elapsed made it improbable that other bodies, if found, could be brought to shore. Thus did the waves completely enforce the payment of their terrible toll.

LIST OF IDENTIFIED DEAD

Following is a list of those whose identity was wholly or partially established:

Astor, John Jacob.	Anderson, W. Y.
Adonts, J.	Allison, H. J.
Ale, William.	Butt, W. (seaman).
Artagaveytia, Ramon.	Butt, W. (may be Major Butt).
Ashe, H. W.	Butterworth, Abelj.
Adahl, Mauritz.	Bailey, G. F.
Anderson, Thomas.	Barker, E. T.
Adams, J.	Butler, Reginald.
Aspalande, Carl.	Birnbaum, Jacob.
Allen, H.	Bristow, R. C.

Buckley, Katherine.
Chapman, John H.
Chapman, Charles.
Connors, P.
Clong, Milton.
Cox, Denton.
Cavendish, Tyrrell W.
Carbines, W.
Dutton, F.
Dashwood, William.
Dulles, W. C.
Douglas, W. D.
Drazenoui, Yosip (referring
    probably to Joseph Draznovic).
Donati, Italo (waiter).
Engineer, A. H. F.
Elliott, Edward.
Farrell, James.
Faunthorpe, H.
Gill, J. H.
Greenberg, H.
Gilinski, Leslie.
Graham, George.
Giles, Ralph.
Givard, Hans C.
Hansen, Henry D.
Haytor, A.
Hays, Chales M.
Hodges, H. P.
Hell, J. C.
Hewitt, T.
Harrison, H. H.
Hale, Reg.
Hendekeric, Toznai.
Hinton, W.
Harbeck, W. H.
Holverdon, A. O. (probably A. M.
    Halverson of Troy).
Hoffman, Louis M.
Hinckley, G.
Hospital Attendant, no name given.
Johansen, Malcolm.
Johansen, Eric.
Johansson, Gustaf J.
Johansen, A. F.
Jones, C. C.
Kelly, James.
Laurence, A.
Louch, Charles.
Long, Milton C.
Lilly, A.
Linhart, Wenzell.

Marriortt, W. H. (no such name
    appears on the list of passengers
    or crew).
Mangin, Mary.
McNamee, Mrs. N. (probably Miss
    Elleen McNamee.)
Mack, Mrs.
Monros, Jean.
McCaffry, Thomas.
Morgan, Thomas.
Moen, Segurd H.
Newell, T. H.
Nasser, Nicolas.
Norman, Robert D.
Petty, Edwin H.
Partner, Austin.
Penny, Olsen F.
Poggi,—.
Ragozzi, A. Boothby.
Rice, J. R.
Robins, A.
Robinson, J. M.
Rosenshine, George.
Stone, J.
Steward, 76.
Stokes, Philip J.
Stanton, W.
Straus, Isidor.
Sage, William.
Shea,—.
Sutton, Frederick.
Sother, Simon.
Schedid, Nihil.
Swane, George.
Sebastiano, Del Carlo.
Stanbrocke, A.
Tomlin, Etnest P.
Talbot, G.
Villner, Hendrick K.
Vassilios, Catalevas (thought to be
    a confusion of two surnames).
Vear, W. (may be W. J. Ware or
    W. T. Stead).
Widener, George W.
Williams, Leslie.
Wirz, Albert.
Wiklund, Jacob A.
Wailens, Achille.
White, F. F.
Woody, O. S.
Wersz, Leopold.
Zacarian, Mauri Der.

1912–2012
A Survivor and the Centennial

Lawrence Beesley,
New York Times,
APRIL 29, 1912

I have been asked by the editor of *The Times* to review the whole circumstances of the sinking of the *Titanic* from the point of view of a survivor as well as from that of the ordinary reader who has followed the evidence given before the Senate Committee. The only reason that makes me think I am fitted to accede to the request is that I have absolutely no bias in the matter. I was alone on board and have lost no friends by the disaster; the few belongings I had were of no value beyond their immediate utility, with the exception of money locked in the purser's safe, and this, by the way, the White Star Line has mostly refunded on my bare statement as to the amount. I knew no officer on board the *Titanic*, and the only official of the line I spoke to was Second Officer Lightoller on the *Carpathia*, and under the following circumstances:

While on board the *Carpathia* I had written a letter to *The London Times*, urging the taking of immediate steps to insure safety of passengers and pointing out as dispassionately as possible the reasons for the disaster, without seeking to apportion the blame for it. This letter appeared in *The London Times* on Saturday last, and I understand they were glad to have it as the opinion of a survivor. It became known on the *Carpathia* that such a letter was in preparation, and Lightoller came to me with

Mr. Ismay's compliments to ask if he could take the letter to Mr. Ismay. I have never seen Mr. Ismay.

I hesitated, knowing that while it did not seek to affix blame, the deduction would be that there was blame attachable somewhere—where I did not know and I did not wish Mr. Ismay to think we were planning to criticize either his officers or his company. However, I knew every statement in the letter was absolutely justifiable and likely to help forward the question of passenger safety, and so I sent the letter to Mr. Ismay. He returned it without raising the slightest objection to it. I asked Lightoller to read it. He did so, and said it was calculated to help all concerned—the officers and crew no less than the passengers.

I mention these details only to make it quite clear that my connection with officials of the line is limited to a few moments' conversation, and that I know no motive that induces me to either criticize or defend their actions.

Now, the facts of the disaster are briefly these: The *Titanic*, with a lifeboat provision for saving less than one in three of its passengers, proceeded at full speed through an iceberg region, in which, moreover, it was definitely known that icebergs had been seen and might be expected. An awful indictment! An unbelievable accusation, were it not that we know every detail is attested to by scores of responsible witnesses.

But let us analyze the whole circumstances in a just manner. Let us not form hasty judgments or make rash statements. The power of correct analysis is unfortunately sadly lacking in the average man and woman, and most people are prone to rush to rapid conclusions on totally insufficient evidence. Now, I take it what the editor of *The Times* wishes me to do is analyze as closely as possible the reasons, motives, and aims of those concerned in the disaster, and as far as in me lies I will do so.

I take it there are two main questions to be considered: (1) At whose door should the blame for this overwhelming disaster be placed, and, (2) What are the precautions to be adopted in the future against the repetition of such a disaster?

Now, I think the first of these questions is not by any means the more important; in fact, it should be considered only as a means to aid the efficiency of the methods suggested in the second question. Our motive in fixing responsibility should not be that some person or corporation shall be pilloried and punished; that helps neither them nor the public safety. No one dreams that the ship was lost with deliberate intent. If it be proved that any one has been guilty of criminal negligence, let it be brought home to him or to them and let punishment be meted out if it is thought well; but criminal negligence will be found a difficult thing to prove, and the traveling public that denounces the officials concerned may find the charge a possible boomerang that returns to wound themselves.

It will, therefore, be better to take the second question first and consider what are the precautions to be adopted in the future against the repetition of such a disaster. The general public cannot attempt to discuss such technical questions as bulkhead compartments and double bottoms: they are for the expert in ship construction: but is not the main question after all one of ordinary common sense which the general public is quite as capable of using as the trained official? Perhaps by his very ignorance of technical construction details the average man is not so apt to lose sight of the simpler precautions. The following points will, I think, occur to everyone as being eminently sane and rational. The fact that they have not been attended to in the past seems unbelievable, but several factors, some of which I hope to discuss shortly, have tended to eliminate these safeguards from the policy of sailing mail passenger vessels.

The route fixed by agreement among the steamship lines is normally a safe one, but apparently we are faced this year with an exceptionally large icefield, extending much further south than is usual. It is normally safe, however, only with due precautions: it can never be safe at full speed in the dark when icebergs are a possibility.

But if safety is assured by fixing the steamship lane further south, even much further south, so that an extra day is taken for the passage, let it be done. Only the speed maniac will grumble, and public opinion will soon rise up and tell such a man he is a public offense and a danger to all who travel, whether by sea or by land. We must not forget the effect, largely unconscious, no doubt, which this demand for saving an extra day or hour has on the policy of those engaged in catering to the traveling public.

The protection of a searchlight is two-fold—the ability to sweep the sea for many hundreds of yards ahead and discern anything afloat and the utility of searchlight flashes as signals to other ships. The vessel that was only five miles away when the *Titanic* struck could not fail to have returned when a powerful searchlight lighted her up and so made known the *Titanic*'s distressed condition.

I do not say, however, that an iceberg is an easy thing to detect, even with a searchlight, but it would seem quite possible to see a berg quite far ahead to avoid it. I suppose no one has any doubt that the *Titanic* would be safe now had there been a searchlight fitted on her. The conditions for its use were ideal that night.

The provision of sufficient boats to enable each passenger to claim a seat is an elementary precaution. It should be compulsory on the steamship companies to assign a numbered place in a particular boat to each passenger. Passenger drills with the crew assigned to each boat should also be compulsory. There would be no necessity for the enforcement of the unwritten law of "women and children first," for all would have a place. The forcing apart of wife from husband, the painful scenes of parting such as the *Titanic* witnessed, would not be possible.

But the provision of lifeboats is not alone a remedy. In some conditions it would be the poorest of safeguards. Remember that when we embarked from the *Titanic* the climatic conditions were such as are found only in many years, perhaps—an absolutely calm sea. No wind, an unclouded sky—ideal conditions for transferring closely packed boatloads of people from one vessel to another. Given a rough sea, combined with the lack of knowledge of seamanship evident in the crew of most of the boats that were afloat, and the number who handed in their names on board the *Carpathia* would have to be halved or divided by even a larger figure than two.

Is the increase in the size of a ship in itself any precaution against sinking? I venture to think not, except in a sinister way—that in the event of collision with a smaller ship the larger one is more likely to come off the better. On the other hand, I think it may be a positive danger. Every student of mechanics knows that the striking impact of a moving body is determined by its momentum, and the formula $M = m \times v$ is a statement of the principle that the momentum of a body is equal to the product of the mass into the velocity. Now the larger "m" is, the greater the momentum, even if "v" remains the same, or even if "v" is sensibly reduced and "m" is large the momentum may still be enormous.

It is related that in the early days of the Peninsular wars English soldiers would see spent cannon balls rolling comparatively slowly toward them, and, stopping down to stop them, would find themselves deprived of their hands. What they could do with a cricket ball could not be done with a cannon ball rolling at perhaps a much less speed.

When the *Titanic* struck "m" was the highest yet attained in any age, and "v" was very high, although not the highest known; but, undoubtedly, m multiplied by v for the *Titanic* at the moment of striking, was the greatest possible for any of them afloat on the sea. Could any form of construction provide against such a force of impact? Could any plates be made strong enough to resist that terrific shock? I think not.

We are told that it would have been better had we headed straight for the berg and collided head on instead of having the side cut open. Probably it would, but even then would anything stand the shattering destruction behind that mass of 60,000 tons moving at 25 miles an hour? I do not know, but I think not. Certainly not unless passengers' boats are to be built as ironclads are, with protective armor.

Would it be possible to have a cruising lightship in iceberg regions, fitted with every possible signal apparatus—Marconi system, searchlight and flashlight, submarine signaling, to give warning to every ship approaching such regions of the position of icebergs, their probable direction and amount of daily drift. It might at least be worth considering, at the iceberg season and be paid for internationally.

But each of these precautions is useless if our other precaution be avoided—that of reducing speed in dangerous conditions. Look at the formula again—when "v" is zero, M = m × o, which is M = o; the striking impact is nil; "m × o" is the only real safeguard there is: the other things are good, but they are not even necessary in dangerous conditions. M × v = o for every ship afloat. You cannot eliminate "m" from the formula—that is constant—but you can make "v" anything you like from the highest speed your boilers are capable of down of zero. I wonder how it would be to display on the bridge of every ship the following notice: "M = m × v. Where 'v' is 25 knots the force of impact of this vessel is ___ thousands foot-tons. Where 'v' is zero, the force of impact is nil." Not that every officer does not know this, but the reminder might be useful.

Having considered the precautions that may be adopted for the future, let us now consider the conditions in which the *Titanic* and her passengers and crew were found from the moment of collision until they were picked up by the *Carpathia* or perished in the icy, cold water of the mid-Atlantic. If there is any responsibility to be fixed, let us see if we can discover where. It will help every Captain and officer and passenger in the future to know who or what is to blame for the *Titanic* sinking on her maiden voyage.

Now in analyzing the facts as presented to us, it must, of necessity, be that some questions to which we would like a reply cannot at this time be answered. Some of those who could answer are, alas, no longer here, and some are silent because officialdom sets a seal on their lips. But I do not think there are many such questions. The facts are too well known and public opinion is too much aroused to permit retention of much information that will be for the common good.

Let us take the officials one by one—the order of taking them is purely for convenience, and see what circumstances, if any, point to the fixing of responsibility for the disaster.

First Officer Murdoch.—He was on duty on the bridge at the time of collision and had been for some time previously. He was not responsible either for the speed of the ship nor for the course that it was taking. The lookout says he warned him of icebergs some time before the collision but got no reply; if so, this was negligence, but he is not here to give evidence on his own behalf.

Is the lookout an unbiased witness? I think not. Is it conceivable that any officer who was not mad or intoxicated (and this is ample evidence that the chief officer was active in getting away lifeboats subsequently—I saw him doing so—and he was neither of these) would disregard such a warning? Suppose the chief officer were here and said "I never had the slightest warning from the crow's nest of any iceberg until just before the collision."

His statement would be at least as reliable as that of the lookout. It is said: "No wonder he shot himself." But did he? And if he did, was it because he had deliberately neglected a precaution that would endanger his own life and that of thousands of others. I cannot think it possible.

It is said, too, that when he did see the berg he should have headed for her; that the glancing blow cut her open in the most vulnerable place. But what a choice to have to make! How many men would have the courage to head for the berg when every instinct told them to turn the ship away—even supposing it was not the best thing to turn her away! I cannot see how he is to blame.

As commander the Captain is responsible directly for the course and the speed. Whoever else is on board and however much other officers might tender their advice to him, he alone is responsible for the conditions under which the ship is running, and at first sight it seems difficult to see how he can escape responsibility for the disaster. But here we must be cautious.

Did he do anything which was in defiance of all custom in running his ship at full speed through the iceberg region? Did he do anything that has not been done by many Captains for years past? (I do not say every Captain, but many Captains of fast mail-passenger steamers.) Did he defy and outrage all precedent in not slowing down? I think the answer to all these is "No."

I suppose it is difficult for a landsman to estimate the probabilities of collision with an iceberg in mid-ocean. He is apt to magnify them far too much. The sea is wide, the ship is small in comparison, and the chances of collision with anything but the largest iceberg (which ours was probably not) are very small. I do not wish to seem to take away any responsibility that should be laid on Captain Smith, but as he is not here to defend himself, let us all see that no undeserved censure be meted out to him. He took the risk which many other Captains have taken. What the chances were in taking the risk no man can say, but in his case the awful thing happened that should never have happened. In the case of all other Captains who have taken a similar risk it did not happen. If he is to be blamed it seems they are all equally blamable for the disaster, for he took the same risk as they did— no more or no less. Remember how the fastest boats are timed to run: "Leave New York Wednesday, dine in London the following Monday," and it is done.

Now there must be times when fog and icebergs are dangerous factors, but do the vessels slow down much? My information is that they do not, but if I am wrong, then it will be very easy to give particulars that such and such a boat on a certain date was so many hours or days late because of reduced speed through fog and icebergs. Extracts from ships' logs can be cited, &c. The following was told me by an experienced traveler:

> We left Southampton by a boat timed to do the journey to New York in seven days. From the moment of leaving Queenstown to docking at New York there was fog except for the brief space of half an hour, and they did the journey in some hours over the seven days.

If such experiences are uncommon, and if the best boats do not take risks, then let us hear that it is so, and the public will rejoice to know. It will not be so in the future, I am convinced, but for the sake of Captain Smith it seems important to know what the custom has been, for if he has taken a risk many take, the responsibility for such loss of life is fixed on a common system, to which many owners and Captains have agreed, perhaps unconsciously. If he took an uncommon and extraordinary risk, then it seems he is largely to blame.

From another point of view, do not let us magnify the seeming enormity of running full speed in iceberg regions. I am informed by a very experienced officer that the movements of icebergs are most unaccountable. A ship will hear that bergs are ahead in a certain latitude and longitude, and on reaching the position no trace of them can be seen. Perhaps a warm current has swept around them and melted them. Again, news will be heard of a ship ahead with no mention of icebergs, and presently in the same position the ship following will sight numbers of them. I am told there is no question concerning navigation so uncertain as the diagnosis of the presence of icebergs. Cold air is a factor, but cold winds blow across from Labrador, and, on the other hand, a single berg large enough to sink a ship does not necessarily create a cold atmosphere.

Low temperature is another factor, but here again an uncertain one. Look at the map and see how the cold current running down from Labrador meets the warm Gulf Stream; as they meet they do not mingle, nor do the run necessarily side by side; it is a common thing for them to interlace and run in streaks. Interlace the fingers of the hands, and it gives an elementary idea of how the temperature of the water may vary. The thermometer may read something like this as the vessel runs across these streaks: Thirty-five degrees, 60 degrees, 34 degrees, 59 degrees, and so on, all within a few miles.

From what has been said in some sections of the press, it would seem as if the boat was deliberately run through a locality in which it was certain an iceberg was floating in a particular position and no precautions were taken to avoid such a position—in fact, that the utmost criminal negligence was observed; but to say so is to become hysterical. What seems likely is that the risk was taken which it is a frequent custom to take, and the unusually southern position of the field and bergs as well as the large number of the latter, united to increase enormously the probabilities of collision.

So that if you blame Captain Smith you must blame a large number of other people. Shall you blame Captain Rostron of the *Carpathia*, who "knew icebergs were there but went ahead at full speed, stopped at 4:10 because of iceberg ahead," and when the day dawned icebergs were around his ship and on every part of the horizon? He must have been near them many times in the night. He took the risk in a splendid cause, and no one is more grateful to him than I am that he did so, and never did a day dawn with greater rejoicing for me than when I climbed aboard his ship. But he did take the risk. I admit there is no comparison between the reasons why he took the risk and why Captain Smith took his, but after all Captain Rostron had his own ship and passengers to consider, and he could not take too great a risk; the fact that he took it at all means it was not considered to be such a danger as we, who have known only the abnormal and not the normal result of taking the risk, might suppose.

I do not think anyone can say Capt. Smith can be held solely responsible.

Not many men have had to undergo such a castigation at the hands of the press as Mr. Ismay. He has been called an arrant coward for leaving at all. He should have sunk with the boat in company with the Captain and Chief Officer. He was responsible for the speed, the course, the whole accident, in fact—and then in a moment of danger he ran away. The equipment was faulty and the White Star Line is responsible for criminal negligence and damages can be recovered from it. The Captain was apparently completely under Mr. Ismay's thumb and had to do as Mr. Ismay told him.

All this and more has been leveled at Mr. Ismay. It may be true in part, but is not very likely to be true *in toto*; it may not be true at all. He says he left in a boat when there were no other women passengers near. This is corroborated by witnesses and is extremely probable. The dimensions of the ship were huge. The number on the first-class deck at any time would be small compared with the deck space, and it is exceedingly probable it was as he said. The evidence of Mr. Lightoller is that the Chief Officer bundled Mr. Ismay into a boat. It seems a very natural act for an officer of the line to perform toward the head of the line. The officer would have a natural anxiety to save his chief, the one who directed mainly the policy of the line.

I left in boat 13, when a call for ladies had been made three times and not answered and no ladies were visible, and was then invited to enter the boat. Mr. Ismay left under very similar circumstances. It is said that as managing director he should have remained and gone down, but I think it is quite a debatable point. If he had interfered in the navigation, control and conduct of the ship. Yes. If he had insisted on certain conditions of speed. Yes. If he had insisted on any other rights than those of any other passenger. Yes. But did he do all these things? He says he did not, and I do not know that any strong evidence has been brought forward to disprove his statement.

After all, what are the probabilities? He says he had the information which the Captain and all other officers had about the icebergs, and adds he would not dream of suggesting to an officer of Captain Smith's experience what should be done. That sounds reasonable. He was not a navigator, and he could not suggest. He might express a wish to go fast and Captain Smith in the relation of an official to a managing director might desire to comply with such a wish, and might be unconsciously—or even consciously—swayed to take a greater risk than he would have done if Ismay were not there. But here we are on the delicate ground of surmise as to what passed in Captain Smith's mind—and that we shall never know.

In weighing Mr. Ismay's responsibility, the difficult question has to be considered as to how far a managing director who knew nothing of navigation could influence a Captain of the line whose duty it was to know everything about navigation and thereby to control absolutely the lives of the thousands of people committed to his care without a suggestion of advice from anyone not a navigator. It does not seem likely Capt. Smith would be so influenced, but I admit the possibility and there it must be left. It is no more than a possibility, and should there be no evidence to the contrary, we ought to assume that the course and speed were controlled by Capt. Smith. There is Mrs. Ryerson's testimony, but this Mr. Ismay denies absolutely.

Let us remember Mr. Ismay as being questioned not by marine experts, but by men who know nothing of the sea—and less than nothing, when he is asked whether the watertight compartments were a refuge for passengers. One rather gets the impression that

Mr. Ismay was prejudged before he went to the inquiry. If so, he has not been fairly treated and we must give him absolute justice.

The *Cedric* messages again have been read as showing an attempt on the part of Mr. Ismay to escape inquiry, but this can be dismissed on two grounds—first, that Mr. Lightoller now accepts responsibility for sending them and would not have dreamed of sending them had he known there was to be an inquiry in America; and, secondly, Mr. Ismay knew it was quite impossible to avoid an inquiry. He knew perfectly well that he would have to stand up before marine and other experts in London and be subject to the most rigid cross-examination, and he knows today that he will still have to do it.

The White Star Line has been criticized for not planning the boat equipment properly or for sending her to sea before her full equipment was on board.

As regards the boat accommodation it was entirely insufficient to accommodate the people on board, but let us bear in mind that the White Star Line set out to build an absolutely unsinkable boat, and in their opinion they had done so. They knew, they said, that the *Titanic* could not be sunk, and from the evidence before them they were quite justified in that knowledge. So that lifeboats were a superfluity from one point of view, but they carried them because they had to do so by Board of Trade regulations; and, again, the ship might always be called upon to rescue lives of other people at sea. But if the theory of the unsinkable boat deluded them into not providing lifeboat accommodation for all on board it helped in another way. When the *Titanic* struck everyone said:

"Well, we are all right; this boat cannot sink. We shall have to wait here until another ship comes along to take us off."

This, I have little doubt, stopped panic and prevented those rushes for boats which might have taken place had the theory not been so widely and firmly held.

But here, again, if you blame the White Star, you must blame other lines similarly. The *Titanic* was at any rate better equipped than other boats, i. e. on the unsinkable theory plus sixteen lifeboats and four rafts.

Naturally, I do not wish to criticize the Cunard Line and their ship the *Carpathia*; but because I noticed her equipment posted up on the public screen, I noted it mentally and think the figures are as follows: Highest possible total of crew and passengers, 2,864; boat equipment, 20 boats with accommodation for 800 passengers—(I think this is perhaps higher than the accommodation, but I have put it as high as possible)—and no rafts or collapsible boats. This would be a lower accommodation per head than the *Titanic*, and I don't think the *Carpathia* was built as an unsinkable boat. Now, the Cunard's record is that of not having lost a life, and a record that they are justly proud of; but judged from this question of boat accommodation alone, the *Titanic* was better equipped than the *Carpathia*.

Again, the Board of Trade had subjected the *Titanic* to a rigid inspection and had passed her. The White Star had complied to the full with the law of the land. The system again, and not this one particular steamship line! "They ought to have foreseen the danger." Well, so ought the Board of Trade: they employ the best experts, presumably. And then the French government and the American government have the right of veto on the entry of any ship into their ports.

If the White Star had been so negligent, why did not these Governments stop their entry? The French, and particularly the American experts must share the responsibility with the Board of Trade and the White Star Line. The American particularly, because the traffic is greater with America, and the Government had only to say the word and lifeboats would have been on board the next day. The responsibility is with the system to which three Governments have agreed.

Again. Let anyone read the standing instructions of the White Star Line to its Captains. They are to "run no risks": "the safety of lives of passengers is the ruling principle" to insure "a reputation for safety." This is a clear and definite statement of policy, and if the instructions are disobeyed the company's rules are broken, and it cannot be held responsible.

On the other hand, custom establishes many unwritten laws, and may override printed instructions. It seems it did in this case.

Did the White Star know its printed instructions were regularly disobeyed, or did it think the risks taken were negligible? I think the question should be answered.

I would like to give here a personal experience of the Marconi apparatus on board the *Titanic*. It would seem to show the apparatus was not the best obtainable.

I coded a message (which I still have) on the day before the collision, to my friends in London, and took it to the purser for transmission. To my surprise he said:

"We cannot accept this, because our apparatus has only a range of 200 miles. We shall be in touch with Cape Race tomorrow, and can send it then, but I will ring up the operating room."

He did so, and was told there was no one in communication with us, and so the message was returned with the remark again that we reached only 200 miles. He may have been wrong in his estimate of the distance, but in any case it had not apparently a very long range.

The glasses for the lookout seem to have been an omission, but whether they would have helped to avert the disaster is problematical. The ship was nearly a sixth of a mile long, and at the speed she was traveling it is doubtful whether she could be turned away from an object half a mile away without some part of her touching, and with the peculiarly dark atmosphere of the night, I don't suppose the lookout could have seen icebergs half a mile away. He says he could have seen them in time to avert the disaster, but perhaps he has not considered the tremendous length of the ship, and the room required to take her out of her course.

The number of practical seamen seems to have been too small. I heard of several boats without one. Ours had none, and a stoker took command. This same stoker told me there were only 30 seamen among a crew of 800, but I have no means of checking his statement. If true it seems far too small.

In many boats there was no food, water or lights, either colored or white. This was the case in mine, and yet No. 13 was not launched until over an hour after the collision. There should have been time to put these bare necessities in.

I hope I am not criticizing unduly here. Perhaps the organization was not developed, or perhaps it broke down under the strain. But in a boat these things are essentials and should always be available. The drills would have insured their proper provision.

The method of embarking passengers seems to be open to some criticism. The boats I saw were loaded to standing room— 65 in mine—and then lowered some 70 feet into the water. Neither tackle nor boats are meant to stand such a strain. They did stand it, fortunately. Again, is not the risk of upsetting such a boatload very great? These are the reasons why the officers thought it better that the first boats should be only partially filled and sent away. They might have stood by and taken more aboard from rope ladders, &c., had the crew been organized. I suppose the correct way is to lower the boat and then embark passengers, but was the *Titanic* arranged for that? I am told it was not possible in the way she was built.

There is one more person whose responsibility should be considered, and I have purposely left him to the last, because he is the most important. He is the average man who travels. Columbus took ninety days in a forty-ton ship. A friend of mine crossed fifty years ago in a paddle steamer that took six weeks. And now we cross in something over four days. And all the time "m" and "v" in the formula are increasing and their product "M" is raised day by day until one shudders at the craze for speed and luxury, for in ships size spells luxury. The public demand it and the lines supply it, and that is why the Titanic sank.

You cannot have both "m" and "v" high in the formula, and until we sacrifice one or both to some extent the danger will always be the same. No bulkheads or double bottoms or extra lifeboats or searchlights are of lasting value while "m" and "v" leap upward!

I think no responsibility will ever be fixed on an individual or on individuals for this disaster. All those who have cried for speed—you and I and our neighbor—have to share it among ourselves in so far as we have expressed a wish to travel faster and in greater comfort, for the expression of such a desire and the discontent with what we call slow travel (a very relative consideration when we remember Columbus!) are the seed sown in the minds of men which presently bear fruit in an insistence on greater speed and size. You and I may not have done it directly, but we may have talked about it and thought about it and after all, no action begins without thought.

I said at the commencement that accusations sometimes come back to wound the accuser; let every man who has ever grumbled to a ship's officer about the slow speed, take it to heart. He had, perhaps, something to do with the sinking of the *Titanic*.

And now to consider one or two other matters arising out of the disaster. I should like to ask readers of *The New York Times* a question that has occurred to me in studying the lists of the rescued. It is this: What is the relative value of the lives of a first-class passenger and a steerage passenger? I have worked out the percentage of the saved of the four classes, and find it as follows: First-class, 63.6 percent; second-class, 39 per cent; steerage, 26.7 per cent; officers and crew, 22.3 per cent. They are instructive, those figures. The payment of about £15 excess of first over third, gives you more than twice the chance of your life being saved! Who can say that a first-class passenger's life is of more value to the community than that of a steerage passenger? It may be that it is so actually, at this present time, but perhaps not potentially so. But the possession of a few more pieces of a particular metal determines the value of a life and not the relative merits of such a life.

John Ericsson, from Sweden, may come in the steerage to America with infinitely greater means of blessings to the community in himself and his family than the millionaire in the first saloon, but the percentages of those saved show that he is not allowed the same opportunity of expressing such blessing.

Again, Major Butt and Col. Astor and Mr. Straus died as brave men died, but did not John Brown and Wilhelm Klein and Karl Johanssen? And yet they are not chronicled, and no newspaper has columns on their self-sacrifice and personal courage. But we know these things were true, and we can bear testimony now to every brave man who perished in the steerage, even if we know not his name.

But with sufficient boat accommodation these distinctions would never have had to be drawn. Think of it! A few more boats, only a few more pieces of wood nailed together, and many brave men and women for whom this country and the whole world mourns would be here and these words would not be written.

One incident has occurred to me during the week that has elapsed since we landed in New York that may be of interest, especially to those who had friends on board. Among the passengers were the Rev. and Mrs. Carter, who were on their way to Canada. Mr. Carter was instrumental in arranging on the Sunday evening, a few hours before we struck, what he called a "hymn sing-song."

There was no evening service, and he invited to the saloon such passengers as cared to come to sing hymns. Any one was allowed to choose a hymn, and, as many were present and were thoroughly enjoying the quite informal gathering, the singing went on to quite a late hour.

Mr. Carter was apparently well acquainted with the history of many of the hymns, their authors, where they were written and in what circumstances, and he interested all present with his remarks on each hymn before it was sung. I recollect that many chose hymns dealing with safety at sea. "For Those in Peril on the Sea" was sung by all with no hint of the peril that lay but a very few miles ahead.

Mr. Carter closed with a few words of thanks to the purser for allowing him to use the saloon, made a few remarks as to the happy voyage we had had on a maiden trip and the safety there was in this vessel; and then the meeting closed with an impromptu prayer by him. This cannot have been more than two hours before the *Titanic* struck.

My motive in mentioning this is that some of those who have lost relatives may like to know that their friends must have been helped and cheered at the last by the words that they had sung but a short time before; the sound of singing voices must have been still a conscious one to many as they stood on the deck faced with the "peril on the sea."

I will finish with a few purely personal remarks. My only excuse for putting them on record is that to me they are absolutely true. I do not make them with any intention of asking a single person to believe in them or to agree with me in what I say, but, having been face to face with the possibility of death and having seen its shadow rather near, I may perhaps not be trespassing on the columns of *The Times* in saying how I consider I was saved.

I have been a Christian Scientist in England for the last six years, and was on my way to America to study the greater work in New York, Boston and the West. The moment I realized there was any danger I turned at once to the method and habit of thought which are incumbent on a Christian Scientist—the attempt to eliminate fear from the human mind. After dressing and before going on deck I read quietly, and then went upstairs with a knowledge that fear was almost entirely eliminated and that opportunity to escape from the peril that threatened was a right we ought all to be able to claim. This condition of mind enabled me to stand quietly on the deck and watch boats being lowered until the moment came when I was able to get a place in a boat without depriving any one of room. I was asked to go by one of the crew in a perfectly natural manner. There were only a few men standing near, and they all came away, leaving the deck quite clear.

I think it certain that I should have walked about seeking every available opportunity to escape had I not been taught by Christian Science to wait quietly and get rid of fear. Had I gone about seeking opportunities, I do not imagine I should now be writing these words. I need hardly add that my gratitude to Christian Science and its founder, Mrs. Eddy, is unbounded.

LAWRENCE BEESLEY

New York Times,
MAY 8, 1912

May I trespass on your space in order to correct a statement I made in an article that appeared in your issue of April 29? I said that the *Titanic* lifeboats were not supplied with bread and water, and so far as I was aware this was correct; none could be found in the lifeboat I came in, and several passengers from other lifeboats related a similar experience. I have, however, received from Second Officer Lightoller a letter in which he says:

> One statement only (in the article) is not correct, namely; that bread and water were lacking in the boats. Mr. Pitman and myself examined every boat from the *Titanic* on board the *Carpathia* and found ample supply of fresh biscuits and two casks (beakers) of water in every lifeboat.

I am sure you will allow me through your columns to make this correction. I can explain the mistake only by saying we could not find these necessities in the dark night and with a crowded boat. I know your readers will be glad to have this additional evidence of preparation on the part of the owners and officers of the *Titanic*.

LAWRENCE BEESLEY
Roxbury, Mass.
May 6, 1912

AFTERWORD

My grandfather, Lawrence Beesley, wrote his book about the *Titanic* within a few weeks after arriving in New York aboard the rescue ship *Carpathia*. Before him as he wrote, he mentions in the book, was "a small cardboard square: 'White Star Line. R.M.S. Titanic. 208." The label was the receipt for an envelope of money he had handed to the *Titanic*'s purser. "Along with other similar envelopes it may still be intact at the bottom of the sea," he wrote in 1912.

One day in May 1995, I was called by Michael Findlay, a historian who had been examining the artifacts retrieved from the *Titanic*'s wreck site eight years earlier. He had recognized a label No. 208 as the counterpart to my grandfather's receipt. It had lain for seventy-five years beneath 12,500 feet of water on the sea floor some four hundred miles off the coast of Newfoundland, preserved like many other documents in a leather bag. I don't know what became of my grandfather's receipt; its counterpart, now the property of the salvor, seems to have been better protected.

The *Titanic* keeps resurfacing to haunt our memories because its loss was a perfect monument to human folly. The great ship was being driven at high speed through an iceberg field without adequate technology to spot icebergs or enough lifeboats for all its passengers.

The loss of the ship through technology and miscalculation

foreshadowed the far greater disaster that arose from the same causes two years later in World War I.

Even now, a century later, the story of the *Titanic* continues to resonate. It was not just lives that were lost in the tragedy but a way of life. Both in England and the United States, society was then more stratified and ordered. The ships' officers believed women and children should have first access to the available lifeboats, and the men on board accepted this convention even at the cost of their own lives.

No one rushed the boats. The orchestra kept playing until the last moments. My grandfather in his book remarked at length on these scenes of social discipline. "What controlled the situation principally was the quality of obedience and respect for authority which is a dominant characteristic of the Anglo-Saxon race," he wrote. "Passengers did as they were told by the officers in charge: women went to the decks below, men remained where they were told and waited in silence for the next order."

Whether from race or culture, the social prerogatives of class and gender prevailed. Of the women passengers travelling first class, 97 percent survived. Of the men in second class, just 8 percent lived.

The sinking of the *Titanic* marked the watershed between the relatively calm seas of the Victorian era and the turbulence of the two world wars that were to follow—a warning that all the social and political certainties of the preceding age were about to be upturned.

As for my grandfather, he was just an individual caught in the tides of a historic tragedy. He had given up his career as a science teacher at Dulwich College in London to become a Christian Science practitioner. On April 10, 1912, then aged thirty-four, he boarded the *Titanic* at Southampton, intending to visit the United States for the first time and to meet with his youngest brother Arthur, who lived in Toronto. He paid £13 for a second-class ticket.

My grandfather was not a conformist, and it was to this habit of mind that he owed his escape. In the minutes after the lifeboats were being prepared for launch, a rumor went around that the men were to board them from the port side. Everyone moved to that side of the ship, but my grandfather stayed on the starboard side. He does not give a clear reason in his book for his decision not to follow the crowd, and perhaps it was one he could not explain to himself.

As he watched a lifeboat of women being lowered to the sea, a crew member called up to ask if there were any women on his deck. My grandfather said there were not, and the crew member replied, "Then you had better jump." To that chance interchange he owed his life, and his descendants theirs.

NICHOLAS WADE